What Else Works?

What Else Works?

Creative work with offenders

Edited by

**Jo Brayford, Francis Cowe,
John Deering**

WILLAN
PUBLISHING

Willan Publishing
Culmcott House
Mill Street, Uffculme
Cullompton, Devon
EX15 3AT, UK
Tel: +44(0)1884 840337
Fax: +44(0)1884 840251
e-mail: info@willanpublishing.co.uk
Website: www.willanpublishing.co.uk

Published simultaneously in the USA and Canada by

Willan Publishing
c/o ISBS, 920 NE 58th Ave, Suite 300,
Portland, Oregon 97213-3786, USA
Tel: +001(0)503 287 3093
Fax: +001(0)503 280 8832
e-mail: info@isbs.com
Website: www.isbs.com

First published 2010

ISBN 978-1-84392-766-2 paperback
     978-1-84392-767-9 hardback

British Library Cataloguing-in-Publication Data

A catalogue record for this book is available from the British Library

FSC
Mixed Sources
Product group from well-managed
forests and other controlled sources

Cert no. SGS-COC-2482
www.fsc.org
© 1996 Forest Stewardship Council

Project managed by Deer Park Productions, Tavistock, Devon
Typeset by TW Typesetting, Plymouth, Devon
Printed and bound by T J International Ltd, Trecerus Industrial Estate, Padstow, Cornwall

Contents

Figures and tables

Figures

Tables

Acknowledgements

The idea for this work arose from the Newport Centre for Criminal and Community Justice (NCCCJ) annual conference held in Newport on 18 April 2008: 'Creative Practice with Offenders and Other Socially Excluded People'. Indeed, four of the chapters in this book were a direct result of papers or workshops presented at the conference. The editors are staff of the Centre based at University of Wales, Newport, and work in collaboration with others to develop research and teaching within criminology and community justice which critically integrates theory, policy and practice. The Centre aims to promote and develop opportunities for research, practitioner collaboration and staff development within a broad range of social, criminal and community justice settings.

NCCCJ is also committed to encouraging exploration of the Welsh Criminal and Social Justice context and promoting collaboration with other centres in Wales both nationally and internationally in looking at the impact of language, culture and difference on social inclusion.

We would like to acknowledge the contribution of our colleague Eirlys Jones to the work of the Centre and her valued support to our students working in the Probation Service and the collaborative approach of our colleagues in other Welsh HEIs who have supported the development of criminology at Newport over the past ten years.

Notes on contributors

Dr Jo Brayford is a Senior Lecturer and Programme Leader for Criminology and Community Justice at the University of Wales, Newport. She also teaches on the probation programme and across the social sciences. Prior to this Jo worked as Research Officer (Effective Practice) for the National Probation Service (Gwent Area) where she produced a wealth of reports that contributed to the 'What Works' agenda and Home Office Accreditation Panels. Her research interests include applied criminology, prison (in particular female offenders) and social exclusion.

Dr Francis Cowe is Director of Academic Development at the University of Wales, Newport and founder and head of the Newport Centre for Criminal and Community Justice. His research interests are in the fields of applied criminology, residential treatment and resettlement of offenders, suicide and self-harm and applied research methodologies. He has taught extensively on probation, criminal and community justice and social sciences and has previously worked as a probation officer, senior lecturer, principal lecturer and associate dean.

Dr John Deering is Senior Lecturer in Criminology and Criminal Justice at the University of Wales, Newport, where he is programme leader for the Probation BA Degree. He teaches across the undergraduate programmes in criminology, criminal justice and youth justice. A former social worker, probation officer and probation manager, his research interests include the attitudes and values of probation practitioners and probation practice within a changing criminal justice system. He has previously published evaluations of aspects of probation practice and on the links within probation between theory and practice.

Hindpal Singh Bhui is a Team Leader in HM Inspectorate of Prisons. He leads the immigration detention team and has been the Inspectorate's policy leader on both race equality and foreign national prisoners. He is also a Visiting Senior Lecturer in Criminal Justice at the University of Hertfordshire. Formerly a probation officer, he was the editor of *Probation Journal: The Journal of Community and Criminal Justice* between 1997 and 2007. He has published a number of papers in probation, prisons and race equality journals.

Martin C. Calder established Calder Training and Consultancy in 2005 after having managed the child protection and domestic violence services in Salford. He currently focuses on the deficits of government guidance for operational staff and the development and dissemination of assessment frameworks across all areas affecting good outcomes for children and young people. He is currently an Honorary Research Fellow at the Sheffield Hallam University.

Dr Mark S. Carich is currently employed with the Illinois Department of Corrections at Big Muddy River Correctional Center, and is on the faculty of Lindenwood University in St Charles, Missouri, Counseling Department. At Big Muddy, he coordinates the sex offender programmes, including the Sexually Dangerous Persons Assessment and Treatment Program. He has been with the Illinois Department of Corrections since 1985 and has worked with the SDPs since 1989. He has been coordinating the SDP program since 1990. He has published extensively in the field of psychology, assessment and treatment of sex offenders, and he has edited three newsletters pertaining to sex offender assessment and treatment. Dr Carich has recently published with others the following: (1) co-authored the *Adult Sexual Offender Assessment Report* (2003, Safer Press); (2) co-edited the *Handbook for Sexual Abuser Assessment and Treatment* (2001, Safer Press); (3) co-authored *Contemporary Treatment of Adult Male Sex Offenders* (2003, Russell House Publishers).

Dr Peter A. Carich is a retired clinical counselling psychologist from private practice. He has previously taught in departments of psychology, sociology, education, counselling and business. He is currently teaching at Lindenwood University as an adjunct professor teaching group psychotherapy, research and statistics, among other courses in psychology. He also teaches in counselling at University of Missouri-St Louis. He is a Life Member of the American Psychological Association and member of the American Group Psychotherapy Association. Previous publications include the use of hypnotherapy in severe clinical trauma cases. He has a BSc in Psychology, Sociology and Education; MS in Counselling; PhD in Counselling, Research and Statistics; and an MBA.

Claudia Carter joined Forest Research in July 2006 as Project Leader in the Social and Economic Research Group, Environmental and Human Sciences Division. Claudia completed a Geography degree at Aberdeen

University in 1993, followed by an MSc degree in Environmental Management at Stirling University (1995). She carried out research at the geography department at Cambridge University, and a few months later joined the UK Centre for Economic and Environmental Development (UK CEED) as Research and Publications Officer (1996–98). Claudia then became Research Associate and Project Manager at the Department of Land Economy, University of Cambridge (1998–2001) and Researcher in the Socio-Economic Research Programme at the Macaulay Institute (2002–06). Her current focus is on carrying out research exploring ways and benefits for offenders and those on probation to become active in nature conservation and forestry work.

Sally Cherry is a former probation officer who moved into a career in training and training management. She has worked for NACRO and local authorities and ran her own training and consultancy business for seven years. Until March 2007 she was Assistant Director of Midlands Probation Training Consortium (MPTC) and when this amalgamated with Midlands Regional Probation Training Consortium she moved there to lead on management development. While at MPTC she worked closely with the Approved Premises Pathfinder (2002–05), developing a group work programme (LiHMO) for residents and developing and delivering training and consultancy on pro-social modelling and systematic motivational work. She is the author of *Transforming Behaviour: Pro-social Modelling in Practice* (Willan, 2nd edition, 2010).

Liz Dixon is the Hate Crime Co-ordinator for London Probation, and is currently developing best practice and interventions for those charged with terrorist-related offences. She produced the *Diversity and Prejudice Pack*, a toolkit for working with racist and hate offending, and has developed hate crime training for criminal justice staff. She has worked as a probation officer both in the community and in prisons and has also been Senior Lecturer in Criminal Justice at Brunel University and the University of Hertfordshire. She has published a number of articles, mainly on working with offenders convicted of race hate crime, and is an expert practitioner for RaceActionNet.

Mark Drakeford is Professor of Social Policy and Applied Social Sciences at Cardiff University. Since 2000 he has been the Cabinet health and social policy adviser at the Welsh Assembly Government. A former probation officer, youth justice worker and community development worker, he has written and published widely in the fields of poverty, youth justice and social policy-making in Wales.

Pauline Durrance is the Senior Researcher for London Probation. She is also a Visiting Fellow at the University of Hertfordshire and was formerly a Research Fellow in Health Psychology at University College London. She has published articles on probation and social work education, and on programmes for women and black and minority ethnic offenders.

Lee Gregory is a former community development worker and has just commenced his PhD at Cardiff University examining the role of time banking in community health initiatives. He carried out the research fieldwork which informs his chapter with Mark Drakeford.

Duncan Holtom is Senior Researcher at the People and Work Unit. He led the external evaluation of the Personal Support in Custody Pilot Projects for the Welsh Assembly Government. Much of his research and evaluation work has focused upon education and training for young people, including evaluations of Learning Pathways 14–19 and RAISE (Raising Attainment and Individual Standards of Education) and research into the impacts and benefits of the youth service in Wales. He completed his PhD at the University of Swansea and has worked as an Associate at the universities of Swansea and Queensland, Australia. Prior to his Masters degree he worked as an English teacher as Xinyang Teachers' College in China and completed his undergraduate degree at the University of Manchester.

Fergus McNeill is Professor and Deputy Head (Research) in the Glasgow School of Social Work (a joint venture of the universities of Glasgow and Strathclyde) and a Network Leader in the Scottish Centre for Crime and Justice Research (at the University of Glasgow). Prior to becoming an academic in 1998, Fergus worked for a number of years in residential drug rehabilitation and as a criminal justice social worker. His research interests and publications have addressed a range of criminal justice issues including sentencing, community penalties and youth justice. Latterly his work has focused on the policy and practice implications of research evidence about the process of desistance from offending. His book *Reducing Reoffending: Social Work and Community Justice in Scotland* (co-authored with Bill Whyte) was published by Willan in April 2007.

Mike Maguire is Professor of Criminology and Criminal Justice, now working part-time at both Cardiff and Glamorgan universities. Over a long career, he has researched and published on a wide range of topics, particularly around burglary, victimisation, accountability in criminal justice, risk, new directions in policing, and correctional politics and practice. He has undertaken many research studies, for example in the fields of parole and the resettlement of prisoners. He is a member of the Correctional Services Accreditation Panel for England and Wales, senior academic adviser to the Community Safety Research Team in the Welsh Assembly Government, and a former member of the Parole Board and of the South Wales Area Probation Board. He co-edits the *Oxford Handbook of Criminology*, currently available in its fourth edition, and is the series editor of a successful book series published by Open University Press.

Frank Porporino, PhD has a doctorate in clinical psychology and has been Senior Partner in a Canadian-based consulting company for the last 16 years, T3 Associates Inc. His earlier career in the public service spanned several decades as the Director General of Research and Statistics for the Correctional Service of Canada and as a psychologist in a number of federal correctional institutions. Frank has published extensively on issues related to What Works as well as on the effects of imprisonment and coping styles of offenders, the assessment of risk and needs levels, mental health problems, and drug and alcohol abuse patterns among offenders. He has developed a number of well-known cognitive behavioral programmes for offenders, three of which have been accredited in England and Wales, and he has provided consulting and training services worldwide to jurisdictions in over 15 countries. He is a member of the Correctional Services Accreditation Panel in England and Wales, the Research Council and International Relations Committee of the American Correctional Association, is on the Board of Directors of the International Corrections and Prisons Association, and is on the Board of Trustees for SAFE, a charitable foundation dedicated to improving the quality of educational services for offenders in African countries.

Aaron Pycroft is Senior Lecturer within the Institute of Criminal Justice Studies at the University of Portsmouth. His primary interests are in the field of substance misuse, multiple needs and the process of rehabilitation and he has developed a number of study units in this area. Prior to working at Portsmouth, he worked in the substance misuse field as a practitioner and senior manager.

Peter Raynor is Professor of Criminology and Criminal Justice at Swansea University. A former probation officer, his research over the last 35 years has included work on victims, drugs, youth justice, pre-sentence reports, through-care and resettlement of prisoners, risk and need assessment, the effectiveness of probation and programmes, and the impact of probation on minority ethnic offenders. He has published widely on criminal justice issues, including the recent books *Rehabilitation, Crime and Justice* (with Gwen Robinson) and *Race and Probation* (with Lewis, Smith and Wardak). His book *Understanding Community Penalties*, co-written with Maurice Vanstone, has recently been republished in Chinese. He has been a member of accreditation panels for offending behaviour programmes in England and Wales and in Scotland, and has served on the West Glamorgan Probation Committee and the South Wales Probation Board.

Jenny Roberts' career as a probation officer included managing an experimental community service scheme, research into prisoners' families, and 18 years as Chief Officer of the Hereford and Worcester Probation Service. She was Chair of the Association of Chief Officers of Probation from 1991–92, and its lead link with the prison service for over four years. She was a member of the Carlisle Committee which reviewed the parole system of England and Wales in 1988–89. She is Chair of Trustees of the Asha Women's Centre, Worcester (1993 to present) and was a member of the Ministry of Justice Together Women Project Board in 2006–08.

Maurice Vanstone is Emeritus Professor of Criminology and Criminal Justice in the Centre for Criminal Justice and Criminology at the University of Wales, Swansea. He has experience of practice, training and research on community sentences over a 30 year period, and has been a regular contributor to teaching and research. He is the author of *Supervising Offenders in the Community: a History of Probation Theory and Practice* (2004 and 2007) and co-editor (with Philip Priestly) of *Offenders or Citizens? Readings in Rehabilitation* (Willan forthcoming).

Beth Weaver is Lecturer in Social Work at the Glasgow School of Social Work, universities of Glasgow and Strathclyde. Her primary area of research interest is in desistance, resettlement and reintegration and the implications for criminal and community justice policy and practice generally, and for community penalties in particular. She has a particular interest in biographical and narrative methodologies. Beth previously worked as a criminal justice social worker and as a MAPPA Coordinator in South West Scotland.

Chris Wilson qualified as a social worker in 1983. He joined the probation service in 1992 and in 1995 was appointed Treatment Manager at the Thames Valley Sex Offender Project. Chris was a member of the design team for the accredited Thames Valley Sex Offender Group Work Programme and subsequently worked as a national trainer in the programmes implementation. Appointed in 2002 as Project Manager for Hampshire and Thames Valley Circles of Support and Accountability, Chris was instrumental in adapting the Canadian Circles model to a British context. The success of Circles in England and Wales has led to the creation of a government-funded organisation called Circles UK to ensure that further Circles development is rooted in best practice as developed by Hampshire and Thames Valley. Chris is now the National Development Manager for Circles UK. He has been published in both British and North American journals and co-wrote the module on Community Initiatives for the MSc Course in Assessment and Treatment of Sexual Offending Behaviour delivered by Leicester University.

Part One

Chapter 1

Introduction

Francis Cowe, Jo Brayford and John Deering

This chapter provides some discussion of the central theme of the book as well as an introduction to Part One. The central argument presented is that more recent understandings of 'what works' have been dominated by policy and practice that have originated from 'top-down' initiatives and policy proposals. The origins of these processes can be located in the increasing tendency for government to centralise control over the probation service and youth justice services; practice over recent decades has become increasingly directed by politicians and central senior management rather than practitioners and local managements. Moreover, the National Offender Management Service (NOMS) at national level is populated overwhelmingly by staff with little or no professional experience of probation practice (McKnight 2008). This desire for centralised control and direction is located in the 'logic' of the new public management and managerialism. While this is influenced in turn by a desire to implement methods of practice that are based in evidence and effective in terms of the reduction of re-offending, the authors argue that these factors have led to an over-reliance on cognitive behaviourism as a theory of intervention and group work as a system of delivery, as well as the risk factor basis of current interventions with young offenders. In turn this has led to the exclusion of other theories and forms of intervention and the downplaying of the relationship between the supervisor and the supervised, something that is being increasingly seen as fundamental to effectiveness (see for example Downden and Andrews 2004). Further factors include the emphasis from government that the task of the probation service is mainly to protect the public and manage and punish (and label) 'offenders', although retaining rehabilitation as one of its aims. Most recently, the development of NOMS and the Offender Management Model suggests that the central consistent relationship between supervisor and supervised is under threat and that practice intervention may become increasingly fragmented.

Practice has increasingly become associated with interventions design-ed for 'offenders' or people perceived as 'problems or problematic' rather than practice that had been co-created or constructed from relationships with offenders, practitioners and policy-makers. Current top-down initi-atives have the potential to exclude offender and practitioner rather than engage social agency and encourage creativity and personal responsibil-ity-taking. 'Top-down' interventionist and/or surveillance-focused prac-tice that lacks engagement with the person as a whole and ignores the wider context of people's lives may not only ignore real opportunities for change and development but may in fact work against long-term change and risk reduction.

Each of the following chapters will encourage the reader to think about past and current policy, practice and the relationships 'these people' have with practitioners. Apart from Vanstone (who outlines past 'creative practice' and discusses what he refers to as 'lost opportunities'), each of the authors explores the theme of creative and change-focused practice, or explores a particular approach to practice. Readers will be encouraged to question whether, and how, practice could be different. Thus each chapter proposes, or at least offers, different perspectives from current orthodoxy and explores the kinds of activities practitioners are currently engaged in and ways in which they may be able to work more creatively. Some will be new perspectives; others will have been forgotten or hidden by current practice. The book as a whole will argue that it may be unhelpful to continually think of probation service users (and younger offenders) as 'offenders' *per se* or of socially excluded people as 'problems' to be managed in particular ways or who can be 'treated' in certain ways. Readers are invited to consider the extent to which the authors' sugges-tions are creative alternatives that could help reduce both re-offending and the wider, but related, risk of social exclusion. None of the content of the book should be taken as a call for a return to a mythical 'golden age' when the expert practitioner intervened effectively as he or she saw fit, but rather as a debate about the complexities of working to reduce crime and the necessity of a curious and flexible approach to such a significant social problem.

A brief history of current policy and practice

Before considering the range of topics and arguments within the main body of the book, it is perhaps worthwhile to consider some of the ways in which we have arrived at the point described above. While much of what follows discusses the evolution of probation practice, parallels may also be drawn with how successive governments and policy-makers have treated those considered to be outside some or many of the supposed norms of society, the socially excluded.

For most of its history, the probation service (including in its work with younger offenders) can be seen as an agency of modernity *par excellence*, in that it operated broadly within the positivist paradigm of expert diagnosis and assessment of the causes of individual offending, then seeking to reduce the likelihood of re-offending *via* a range of interventions. From roughly the 1920s and 1930s the casework approach was pre-eminent, based in psychological approaches. Casework was seen as representing professionalism and was regarded as effective, despite the absence of effectiveness research (Raynor and Vanstone 2002: 41). The main vehicle for this, the probation order, was not a sentence of the court before the Criminal Justice Act 1991; previously it had been an alternative and an opportunity to reform.

These assumptions became undermined with the 'nothing works' paradigm of Martinson (see Lipton *et al.* 1975) and the work of Brody (1976) and Folkard *et al.* (1976) in the 1970s. These studies purported to show that no transformative intervention had been shown to be effective in reducing re-offending. At the same time, the psychological approach was seen as being theoretically slack, ignorant of wider social context and possibly coercive, rather than humanitarian (Wootton 1959, cited in Raynor and Vanstone 2002: 42; American Friends Service Committee 1971). Although 'nothing works' was criticised and then recanted (see for example McGuire 2001) it nevertheless had a considerable impact on official policy. The government came to see the probation order as an ineffective 'treatment for crime' and turned its attention elsewhere (Raynor and Vanstone 2002: 58). Home Office funding for research into rehabilitation virtually ceased and it became more interested in criminal justice systems and the probation service as a cheaper alternative to custody. Managerialist concepts of efficiency and effectiveness became increasingly important, and outputs rather than outcomes were to become the main indicators of success *via* the 1984 Statement of National Objectives and Priorities (SNOP) (Newburn 2003: 138).

However, it is far from clear how much impact the 'nothing works' debate had on the majority of practitioners, many of whom probably continued to see their role as rehabilitative (Vanstone 2004). In his chapter Vanstone covers the recent history of 'creative work', pointing out that there had been a strong strain of innovation in practice throughout the service's 100-year history. This was in the main 'idiosyncratic and individualised', but it revealed a continuing curiosity and search for improved and more effective methods of supervision. While most of this period saw practice concerned with the personal, there were some signs of engagement with the social, something that has perhaps been lost in the recent moves to managerialist control.

Overall, the 'received wisdom' is that in the period since the SNOP (Home Office 1984) the service has become a 'law enforcement agency' concerned with the management and punishment of offenders and the protection of the public (Home Office 2000; Garland 2001; Rose 2000). However, there is some evidence that the reality of this situation is more complex, with some practitioners at least continuing to work towards behavioural change in individual offenders *via* a more individualised manner approach based on offender needs and responsiveness and their own use of professional judgement and discretion (see Lynch 1998; Kemshall and Maguire 2002; Robinson 2002; Deering 2008). Overall, in the latter part of the twentieth century and into the twenty-first, probation practice may be seen as characterised by some continuity in terms of individualised interventions despite major organisational and policy changes (Vanstone 2004).

Of course, the government and management of the service have not moved to a purely managerial, law enforcement position, and a commitment to 'rehabilitation' (usually seen as synonymous with 'reducing re-offending') has been retained. However, this commitment is in the main rooted in the use of cognitive behaviourist approaches to personal change, along with more practical access to support services in areas such as accommodation, drug and alcohol misuse and training. Furthermore, this commitment is seen as ultimately subsumed by a managerialist agenda (Lewis 2005) and an underlying belief in government that crime is committed deliberately and rationally by 'bad people' (Faulkner 2008). The 'what works?' (it originally had a question mark) movement had begun to emerge from Canada in the late 1980s and early 1990s. Based in cognitive behaviourism, claims were increasingly made that something could indeed 'work' (see McGuire 2001). 'What works' aimed to rehabilitate persistent offenders and saw itself as far more than an alternative to custody. In the early part of the 1990s, however, its use was limited to a small number of probation services with chief probation officers who had a personal interest, until it came to be seen as central to a New Labour approach (Newburn 2003: 152–4). According to Raynor and Vanstone (2002: 94), one major influence on the change of status of 'what works' from a minority interest to one of central importance was the support of the probation inspectorate, which helped persuade the New Labour government to set up 'pathfinder' projects of certain cognitive behavioural programmes, with the intention of evaluating their effectiveness in reducing re-offending. In due course, the Home Office embraced 'what works' *via* the Effective Practice Initiative (Home Office 1998). These developments met some hostility (Gorman 2001; Mair 2004; Merrington and Stanley 2000) on the basis that the programmes had a thin evidence base, employed a pathological model, and that not all individuals were suited to a 'one-size-fits-all' approach. They have also been called into question by adherents of the 'desistance' approach to offending, who question the treatment model's effectiveness as essentially missing the point about why and how offenders *decide themselves* to give up offending (see Farrall 2002; and in this book the chapters by Porporino and Weaver and McNeill).

However, these objections had little influence and the accredited programmes initiative represented a huge investment in transformative work and the probation service itself. While this might at first be seen as an endorsement of the probation officer 'relationship role', what has been called the 'new rehabilitation' (Vanstone 2004) was not based on unconditional assistance, but on cognitive behavioural programmes backed up by rigid enforcement. Furthermore, the emphasis on enforcement, breach and toughness is seen as a political and value-laden one, rather than having any evidence base; the link between tough enforcement, compliance and subsequent re-offending is both under-researched and highly contested (Bottoms 2001; Mair 2004; Hedderman and Hough 2004; May and Wadwell 2001; Merrington and Stanley 2007). Of course, this description is one that takes a macro, or at least mezzo, level look at practice: that is, one outlined by government and senior management. The extent to which practitioners subscribed to the 'new' part of the 'new rehabilitation' is far less clear and practice may have had more continuity in terms of providing broad notions of 'help' than has been assumed (Deering 2008).

With the election of the Labour government in 1997, there could be discerned differences in policy and attitude towards the service, but also some continuity. Rhetoric from government throughout this period continued about the need for the criminal justice system to become even tougher and to be 're-balanced in favour of the victim' (and against the offender) (NAPO 2006a, 2006b; Travis 2006). At the same time and in an example of the government's acknowledgement of the wider social context of crime (and not just of the 'need to punish') it published the *Reducing Re-offending: National Action Plan*, followed in Wales by *Joining Together in Wales*, which involved the Welsh Assembly Government (Home Office 2004b; NOMS 2006a).

However, Newburn (2003) regards New Labour as ultimately desiring to centralise and control the probation service as well as other agencies within the wider public sector, partly due to a mistrust of professional groups which it saw as conservative and anti-modernisation (Flynn 2002: 344–5) and thus likely to try and oppose its wider plans for the service. The creation of the NPS in April 2001 can be seen to be employing certain aspects of modernisation and managerialism such as the control of professional groups and the setting of financial controls and targets (see below). However, it is also seen to illustrate a contradiction within New Labour policy in that the creation of a centralised service within the Home Office was set against the establishment of local probation area boards with responsibility for certain aspects of policy and practice. However, overall the continuing tendency was to centralise, something identified by Martin Wargent of the Probation Boards' Association, who noted, a year after the creation of the NPS, that it was moving 'backwards into an over-centralised system' (Nash and Ryan 2003: 163). At the time of writing (summer 2009) the future remains uncertain, with the possible increase in probation trusts revealing something of a reversal of central control over governance, but perhaps less so over practice.

Despite the NPS being only some two years old, in 2003 the government commissioned a report to look into the overall function and management of the post-sentence elements of the criminal justice system. The Carter Report – *Managing Offenders, Reducing Crime – The Correctional Services Review* (Carter 2003) – was published in December 2003 and the government's response was made within barely a month, in January 2004. *Reducing Crime – Changing Lives* (Home Office 2004a) announced that NOMS would be set up in June 2004, with the objectives of punishing offenders and reducing re-offending. It also outlined the government's commitment to 'contestability', whereby NOMS would procure intervention services with offenders from a wide range of bodies, including from the private and voluntary sectors, through a 'planned programme of market testing' (2004a: 34). Between 2004 and 2007 the emerging NOMS went through a number of different operational models, as did the prospects for the governance of the probation service. In July 2007, the Offender Management Act was finally passed, creating NOMS as a legal entity.

Both the NPS and NOMS have continued the process of establishing practice that employs theories of change based in cognitive behaviourism, but that also recognise the role of socio-economic and other factors, at least to some extent. To date at least, the cognitive behaviourist element has continued, in the main to be delivered by accredited programmes, while provision put in place to address issues such as homelessness, drug and alcohol misuse and education or training have been carried out increasingly by partner agencies (Crow 2003). As a result, the current snapshot of practice is one that is directed from above and based in group work, with more personalised 'help' being provided outside the probation service. This model, encapsulated in the NOMS Offender Management Model (NOMS 2006b), has moved the probation practitioner (both probation officer and probation service officer) to a position of offender 'manager' charged with assessing and managing risk and sequencing interventions.

Although this book in the main deals with interventions with adult offenders, the recent history of youth justice can be seen to have similar elements. Soon after their election in 1997 the New Labour government created under the 1998 Crime and Disorder Act, multi-agency youth offending teams whose prime purpose (and that of the youth justice system) has been the 'prevention of youth crime'. This is broadly based on earlier 'preventive' interventions underpinned by the so-called 'risk factor paradigm' promoted by, among others, the work of Farrington (Youth Justice Board 2001). Alongside this, interventions based in cognitive behaviourism and the stressing of the responsibility of young offenders and their families for the former's behaviour have been imposed in a top-down approach driven by government through the Youth Justice Board.

Some reasons for current policy and practice?

Theories of late modernity seek to explain the broad social influences that underlie government approaches to crime and justice in general and that these have in turn encapsulated the movement described above towards a top-down and narrow model for probation practice. Along with the 'rise of risk', the 'new penality' (Kemshall 2003; Feeley and Simon 1992), 'modernisation' (Senior et al. 2007) and 'populist punitiveness' (Bottoms 1995), late modern theories provide a backdrop to these developments. While discussing these macro-theories, it needs to be stressed that they are not regarded as determinist, 'controlling' government behaviour; such developments in the end are the result of real politicians making real decisions based on belief, ideology and perceptions of political expediency.

Since around the 1970s many commentators have been describing the onset of the late modern or postmodern world, which has seen a (at least partial) collapse of faith in 'progress' and ideas of liberal plurality, tolerance and inclusion towards socially marginalised groups, including and perhaps especially, offenders (Garland 2001; Loader and Sparks 2002; Pratt 2002). The root causes of these changes are seen to be the development of the consumer society *via* the growth of global capitalism from the 1950s, which brought unprecedented personal wealth. Subsequent attitudes made the acquisition of more widely available material goods seem increasingly important while other social forces, such as changing social and economic mobility, the consequent breakdown of old social relations such as church and local community structures, an increase in divorce and single people living independently and a decrease in levels of deference, contributed to a rapidly changing social world. This increasingly cosmopolitan world can be seen to open up new social, economic and political relations, but also challenges and causes the dislocation of traditional institutions such as family, community, and the church. This is seen as liberating for some, but as a source of insecurity, confusion and fear for others (Pratt 2002: 183). It is this social dislocation that is seen as the 'cause' of the significant increase in crime that occurred from the 1950s to around the end of the 1980s and early 1990s. At the same time, this period saw the rise of the popular media, with its sensationalist emphasis on crime that added to feelings of the prevalence of crime and risk within everyday life. For Pratt, this changed society from one of post-war certainty and stability to the very opposite (2002: 183). As a result, he sees cultural values evolving over this period from tolerance and forbearance to animosity and hostility to anyone seen as threatening the decreased levels of personal security.

Alongside these feelings of insecurity and dislocation, the new penality is seen as resulting from the rise of the idea that it is possible to predict, assess and manage risk presented by offenders, as well as putting forward the greater use of custody as a penal aim in itself. Its basis is the emergence of actuarial assessment techniques being applied to offenders. Feeley and Simon (1992) originally developed this thesis, regarding actuarial classification as becoming one of the defining characteristics of the criminal justice system in western nations. This is seen as coinciding with (and complementary to) the rise of the political new right and neo-liberal ideas of crime being committed mainly *via* rational choice and the subsequent need to punish more severely to deter and exact more proportionate retribution. Neo-liberal ideas played down the socio-economic influences on crime, extolling the idea of 'responsibilisation' – the notion that humans are rational and free actors *completely* in control of and responsible for their behaviour. Feeley and Simon's thesis is that this approach has resulted in crime policy being seen as the management and more severe punishment of aggregate groups rather than the transform-ation of individuals, and that evidence of this is talk of 'high risk' groups, 'persistent offenders', the necessity of assessing and managing risk and the increased use of custody. This has been accompanied by an increase in the use of community sentences for offences that would previously have received fines or discharges: in other words, by a general 'up-tariffing' of sentencing. In probation terms, risk began to emerge after the CJA 1991, and after 1997 the New Labour government enshrined risk assessment into the work of the service with the creation of the NPS and its list of five aims, the first of which was the 'protection of the public'. This had a prerequisite of the identification and management of offenders according to their perceived level of risk (Home Office 2001). Kemshall sees the risk agenda becoming increasingly integrated in the work of the service, it being embraced in a 'pragmatic adaptation to the new penality of the New Right' (2003: 92).

The conversion of the Labour Party to 'talking tough' about crime is a further factor. In January 1993 Tony Blair, then Shadow Home Secretary, declared that a future Labour government would be 'tough on crime, tough on the causes of crime'. For Roberts *et al.*, 'penal parsimony now looked ... to be an electoral liability' (2003: 47). This change in Labour policy, and the claim by the Conservative Home Secretary Michael Howard in October 1993 that 'prison works', led to what might be called a auction of tough talking and formed what Bottoms refers to as 'populist punitiveness'. In brief, populist punitiveness can be described as govern-ments (and sentencers) becoming more punitive in their rhetoric, policy and practices because they believe this will be in line with 'public opinion' and thus electorally popular. Politicians are seen as not necessarily believing that such changes are required to address the problem of crime, but rather simply to curry public favour (Bottoms 1995). Of course, such policy developments could also have occurred due to successive governments believing tougher policies to be 'right'.

The final elements affecting government policy for the probation service in this period were modernisation and managerialism. Managerialism has had a significant impact upon the governance of the public sector since the late 1970s and early 1980s. It has also been termed the 'new public management' (NPM) and its development began roughly with the Conservative governments from 1979 and has continued without significant changes with the New Labour governments since 1997. Indeed, it has been described as a 'permanent revolution' that has redefined the relationship between the state and the public and is seen as a vehicle for a 'modern' Britain. Managerialism and the NPM that emerged in the 1980s are seen as having the following characteristics (Osborne and Gaebler 1992; Clarke *et al.* 2000; Flynn 2002):

- The 'steering of the ship' from the centre, rather than the rowing.

- The decentralisation of authority.

- Budgets decentralised and managers given increased 'authority to manage'.

- Organisations viewed as 'chains of low-trust relationships' linked by contracts and formal relationships.

- Attention paid to outputs and performance, not inputs.

- Services to be provided *via* a 'purchaser–provider' split, with competition, not monopoly.

- Resources to be earned, not just spent.

- Prevention to be invested in, as well as cures.

Senior *et al.* (2007) discuss the idea of modernisation as based in and similar to managerialism and the NPM but differing from it in certain important facets. Modernisation is seen as part of Giddens' 'Third Way' (1999, cited Senior *et al.* 2007: 16) which promoted the updating and modernisation of public services and was seen as very much one of the 'big ideas' of the incoming prime minister in 1997, Tony Blair (Raine 2002). It is said to contain the following elements of managerialism: the 'three E's' of economy, effectiveness and efficiency; the creation of quasi-markets; contracting out of services; and a reduction in workforce numbers employed by the public sector. However, for Senior *et al.*, modernisation mediated these concepts by a commitment to social values such as equality of opportunity, social solidarity and some commitment to public consultation and democratisation (2007: 17), and a less antagonistic approach to the public sector. However, a significant divergence from the NPM is the increase in central control over policy inherent in modernisation, rather than its decentralisation.

At central government level, the trend is for 'horizontal' communication and collaboration between departments to deliver policies based on 'joined-up thinking'. Such policies are then driven downwards and enforced by a combination of 'censure, compliance and commitment' (Senior *et al.* 2007: 30). Censure involves denunciation of opposition, while compliance is achieved by league tables and performance targets for agencies that are subject to inspection, 'failing' organisations then being threatened with the arrival of government 'hit squads' to take over local management to 'improve standards'. Senior *et al.* see compliance as not only directing practice but also forming part of the hegemony of modernisation through changes to discourse and language. Complementing this hegemony and perhaps an example of it is the existence of commitment, shown by a new breed of professionals believing in and extolling the virtues of modernising policies. For Raine, modernisation produced benefits for the probation service, such as improved level of knowledge about weaknesses in existing systems and greater focus, but the resulting performance targets have tended to skew practice and become an end in themselves, rather than a means to improved practice overall (Raine 2002: 338). In this way, modernisation is also seen as an ideology and one with a social force of its own. Such an ideology is useful in defining 'us' and 'them', enabling opponents of particular policies to be dismissed as anti-modernisation. However, Senior *et al.* argue against imbuing such a social construct with causal power, stressing the importance of agency in mediating and changing its impact at various levels.

These broad, macro level theories, together with their impact at policy and operational level, are seen as providing the conditions for the narrow approach to practice that, it is argued, is the current state of probation and youth justice practice. Government, policy-makers and senior managers are seen as wishing to control probation practice minutely and this can only be achieved by practice that is suitable for audit: that is, measurable. In turn this has inevitably led to prescribed programmes, as the 'messy' world of more creative, individualised needs-based practice could not be so monitored. This and the evidence of effectiveness (McGuire 2001) that underpins the emergence of group-based cognitive behaviourism (however disputed) has proved a seductive approach to 'offender management'. However, as mentioned, there are some indications that practice itself has not entirely conformed to these changes and the basis of a more creative approach may remain within the modern-day service. As early as the 1990s an alternative view about the role of the practitioner was being presented in the limited number of studies about individual supervision, stressing the need for a professional relationship between practitioners and their supervisees and that such an approach can be effective in terms of both compliance and re-offending (Brown 1998; Rex 1999; Trotter 1999).

In a similar vein, Robinson studied the role of risk in case allocation within the probation service and asserts that the notion that offenders were becoming managed as aggregates of risk as somewhat simplistic (Robinson 2002: 8–14), with assessments modified on the basis of practitioner judgement. She found a tension arising from a level of acceptance of the need to manage risk and a degree of optimism about the possibilities of rehabilitation, emanating from 'what works'. However, the rehabilitation in question was not the 'old' type of unconditional assistance, but rather one of rehabilitation with an aim of reducing re-offending and hence protecting the public, all defined within a risk management agenda. In a study around practitioner behaviour concerning high risk of harm cases, Kemshall and Maguire (2002) found examples of practitioners making individual assessments of cases, and that these determined practice responses rather than some prescribed process influenced by 'new penality thinking'. More recently, a few empirical studies have revealed samples of probation practitioners and trainees indicating attitudes and practices receptive to a more person-based, individualised practice, one that is premised on the ability of the individual to change and the important role of probation supervision in potentially facilitating such change (Annison et al. 2008; Deering 2008).

Furthermore, it is argued by Burnett and McNeill (2005) that some aspects of a culture and practice linked to rehabilitation may have begun to re-emerge within government itself in the early part of the twenty-first century. They cite high-ranking officials within NOMS talking about the need for a 'personal relationship approach' and of the importance of 'relating to the offender' (2005: 225, citing Mann 2004 and Grapes 2004). A further example of what is perhaps a slow re-emergence of the official recognition of the importance of a skilled and flexible interpersonal approach with offenders was the work of McNeill et al. (2005) in completing a literature review for the Scottish Executive around effective supervision. Finally, having conducted a meta-analysis of studies that had evaluated the effective elements in offender supervision, Downden and Andrews (2004) concluded that these could be encapsulated in the 'core correctional practices': the effective use of authority, pro-social modelling and a genuine and effective working relationship, rather than a rigid attachment to any 'one size fits all' approach.

The chapters in Part One

It is into this picture of an apparently monolithic model of practice that the arguments in the following chapters appear. The authors variously argue that some existing practice has creative and flexible elements in it;

others put the case for such approaches to be considered as potentially being more humanistic and effective. The probation service under NOMS is facing perhaps the greatest challenge of its 100-year history; is it to remain a vehicle for constructive attempts at 'help' for offenders to change, or will it move further towards being a law enforcement, management agency, doing little more than assessing risk and sequencing interventions? Will youth offending services increasingly stress preventive intervention based on a determinist risk factor paradigm and personal responsibility?

Part One of the book sets the scene by looking at the history of probation practice, the emergence over the past decade or so of 'desistance' theories, which seek to explain desistance from crime in terms of the individual redefining himself or herself as a non-offender rather than as a result of cognitive 'retraining', and finally a reconsideration of how best emerging evidence about effectiveness could be integrated into new forms of group-based interventions. Vanstone describes practice that was more flexible and innovative, based in a desire to develop better and more effective ways of supervision. He sees this attitude and approach being squeezed out of the service by government's tendency to centralise and control the work of the service; this necessitated a change to practice that was prescribed and hence measurable. A return to a more flexible approach is seen as preferable, not because it was inherently more effective (there is no evidence that it was) but because it was curious. With more recent developments in evaluation and research, Vanstone argues for a more creative, flexible approach but one that is self-critical, enquiring and based upon rigorous evaluation and preparedness to change. Vanstone warns against harping back to a golden age, arguing both that this has never existed and also that there are positive elements to the current cognitive behaviourist backbone of practice.

Following on from this, Weaver and McNeill provide a comprehensive and very clear *précis* of desistance theories and report upon the limited number of empirical studies into why some individuals come to give up an offending lifestyle that has, on occasions, persisted over many years. Although the various studies they analyse come to some differing conclusions about why people give up offending, the overall message of desistance is one that challenges the current top-down model of what works, in that (among many other things) it asserts that individuals must decide themselves to desist and that statutory supervision must support this process collaboratively, rather than impose some type of 'treatment' upon them. What this means for supervision practice is as yet far from clear, but they note that: 'the desistance process seems to have common elements for all or at least most people – developing maturity, the emergence of new social ties that hold particular subjective significance for the individuals concerned and, sometimes, a renegotiation of personal identity' (Weaver and McNeill, p. 55 below).

Finally in this section, Porporino (one of the principal theoreticians and practitioners behind 'what works' and co-author of the Reasoning and Rehabilitation Programme – T3 Associates 2000) argues that evaluation of any form of intervention needs to move away from the 'blind empiricism' of outcomes research to fully consider *why* and *how* certain individuals desist from offending. He argues for a more integrated interventionist approach that seeks to combine elements of the risk management, desistance and motivational paradigms, all of which he sees as potentially making a positive contribution. Calling for continued and enhanced evidence of effectiveness, he describes how 'sense and sensitivity' needs to be incorporated: sense in how a broad range of evidence can be incorporated into the design of services for offenders, and sensitivity in how offenders are assisted and encouraged to change gradually (and at their pace) rather than forcing it *via* time-limited interventions. He concludes by offering some suggestions as to how interventions based in programmes might look in this new, integrated approach.

Following these three opening chapters, Part Two provides a broad discussion of how a more creative practice does and/or could exist and provide a more dynamic and constructive attempt at the rehabilitation and/or resettlement of offenders, thus making a positive contribution towards crime reduction rather than just crime reduction as an end. The argument presented is that current approaches not only miss opportunities to reduce crime but risk not seeing individuals as ends in themselves in need of social justice and social inclusion.

References

American Friends Service Committee (1971) *The Struggle for Justice*. New York: Hill and Wang.

Annison, J., Eadie, T. and Knight, C. (2008) 'People First: Probation Officer Perspectives on Probation Work', *Probation Journal*, 55 (3): 259–72.

Bottoms, A. (1995) 'The Philosophy and Politics of Punishment and Sentencing', in C. Clarkson and R. Morgan (eds) *The Politics of Sentencing Reform*. Oxford: Clarendon Press.

Bottoms, A. (2001) 'Compliance and Community Penalties', in A. Bottoms, L. Gelsthorpe and S. Rex (eds) *Community Penalties: Changes and Challenges*. Cullompton: Willan Publishing.

Brody, S. (1976) *The Effectiveness of Sentencing*. London: HMSO.

Brown, I. (1998) 'Successful Probation Practice', in A. Gibbs (ed.) *Proceedings of the Probation Studies Unit Second Colloquium*. Oxford: Oxford Centre for Criminological Research.

Burnett, R. and McNeill, F. (2005) 'The Place of the Officer–Offender Relationship in Assisting Offenders to Desist from Crime', *Probation Journal*, 52 (3): 221–42.

Carter, P. (2003) *Managing Offenders, Reducing Crime – The Correctional Services Review*. London: Home Office Strategy Unit.

Clarke, J., Gewirtz, S. and McLaughlin, E. (2000) 'Reinventing the Welfare State', in J. Clarke, S. Gewirtz and E. McLaughlin (eds) *New Managerialism, New Welfare?* London: Sage.

Crow, I. (2003) *The Treatment and Rehabilitation of Offenders.* London: Sage.

Deering, J. (2008) 'Attitudes, Values, Beliefs and Practices in Probation: Continuity or Change?' PhD thesis, Cardiff University.

Downden, C. and Andrews, D. (2004) 'The Importance of Staff Practice in Delivering Effective Correctional Treatment: A Meta Analysis', *International Journal of Offender Therapy and Comparative Criminology*, 48: 203–14.

Farrall, S. (2002) *Rethinking What Works with Offenders.* Cullompton: Willan Publishing.

Faulkner, D. (2008) 'The New Shape of Probation in England and Wales: Values and Opportunities in a Changing Context', *Probation Journal*, 55 (1): 71–83.

Feeley, M. and Simon, J. (1992) 'The New Penology: Notes on the Emerging Strategy for Corrections', *Criminology*, 30 (4): 449–75.

Flynn, N. (2002) *Public Sector Management*, 4th edn. Harlow: Pearson.

Folkard, M., Smith, D. and Smith, D. (1976) *IMPACT: Intensive Matched Probation and After-Care Treatment.* London: HMSO.

Garland, D. (2001) *The Culture of Control.* Oxford: Oxford University Press.

Gorman, K. (2001) 'Cognitive Behaviourism and the Holy Grail', *Probation Journal*, 48 (1): 3–9.

Grapes, T. (2004) 'Offender Management Definitions: NOMS Draft Policy Paper', unpublished.

Hedderman, C. and Hough, M. (2004) 'Getting Tough or Being Effective: What Matters?', in G. Mair (ed.) *What Matters in Probation.* Cullompton: Willan Publishing.

Home Office (1984) *Statement of National Objectives and Priorities.* London: Home Office.

Home Office (1998) *Effective Practice Initiative*, Probation Circular 35/98. London: Home Office.

Home Office (2000) *National Standards for the Supervision of Offenders in the Community.* London: Home Office.

Home Office (2001) *A New Choreography: An Integrated Strategy for the National Probation Service for England and Wales.* London: Home Office.

Home Office (2004a) *Reducing Crime – Changing Lives.* London: Home Office.

Home Office (2004b) *Reducing Re-offending: National Action Plan.* London: Home Office.

Kemshall, H. (2003) *Understanding Risk in Criminal Justice.* Maidenhead: Open University Press.

Kemshall, H. and Maguire, M. (2002) 'Public Protection, Partnership and Risk Penality: The Multi-Agency Risk Management of Sexual and Violent Offenders', in N. Gray, J. Laing and L. Noaks (eds) *Criminal Justice, Mental Health and the Politics of Risk.* London: Cavendish.

Lewis, S. (2005) 'Rehabilitation: Headline or Footnote in the New Penal Policy?', *Probation Journal*, 52 (2): 119–35.

Lipton, D., Martinson, R. and Wilks, J. (1975) *The Effectiveness of Correctional Treatment.* New York: Praeger.

Loader, I. and Sparks, R. (2002) 'Contemporary Landscapes of Crime, Order and Control: Governance, Risk and Globalisation', in M. Maguire, R. Morgan and R.

Reiner (eds) *Oxford Handbook of Criminology*, 3rd edn. Oxford: Oxford University Press.

Lynch, M. (1998) 'Waste Managers? The New Penology, Crime Fighting and Parole Agent Identity', *Law and Society Review*, 32 (4): 839–69.

Mair, G. (2004) 'Introduction: What Works and What Matters', in G. Mair (ed.) *What Matters in Probation*. Cullompton: Willan Publishing.

Mann, S. (2004) 'Effective Implementation', in *Management of Evidence-Based Practice in Probation*, proceedings of a Conference held by Conférence Permanente Européenne de la Probation and the National Probation Service for England and Wales, Oxford, 3–5 March 2004.

May, C. and Wadwell, J. (2001) *Enforcing Community Penalties: The Relationship Between Enforcement and Reconviction*, Home Office Findings 155. London: Home Office.

McGuire, J. (2001) 'What Works in Correctional Intervention? Evidence and Practical Implications', in G. Bernfeld, D. Farrington and A. Leschied (eds) *Offender Rehabilitation in Practice: Implementing and Evaluating Effective Programs*. Chichester: Wiley.

McKnight, J. (2008) *Has Probation been Taken Over by the Prison Service?* NAPO. Available at: www.napo2.org.uk/napolog/archives/2008/05/has_probation_b.html (accessed 2 June 2008).

McNeill, F., Batchelor, S., Burnett, R. and Knox, J. (2005) *21st Century Social Work. Reducing Re-Offending: Key Practice Skills*. Edinburgh: Scottish Executive.

Merrington, S. and Stanley, S. (2000) 'Doubts About the What Works Initiative', *Probation Journal*, 47 (4): 272–5.

Merrington, S. and Stanley, S. (2007) 'Effectiveness: Who Counts What?', in L. Gelsthorpe and R. Morgan (eds) *Handbook of Probation*. Cullompton: Willan Publishing.

NAPO (2006a) 'NOMS Legislation Pulled!', *NAPO News* (176). London: NAPO.

NAPO (2006b) *Restructuring Probation – What Works? NAPO's Response to the Home Office Consultation Paper 'Restructuring Probation to Reduce Re-offending'*. London: NAPO.

Nash, M. and Ryan, M. (2003) 'Modernising and Joining-up Government: The Case of the Prison and Probation Services', *Contemporary Politics*, 9 (2): 157–69.

NOMS (2006a) *Joining Together in Wales*. London: Home Office.

NOMS (2006b) *The NOMS Offender Management Model*, 2nd edn. London: NOMS.

Newburn, T. (2003) *Crime and Criminal Justice Policy*, 2nd edn. Harlow: Longman.

Osborne, D. and Gaebler, T. (1992) *Reinventing Government: How the Entrepreneurial Spirit is Transforming the Public Sector*. Reading: Addison-Wesley.

Pratt, J. (2002) *Punishment and Civilisation*. London: Sage.

Raine, J. (2002) 'Modernisation and Criminal Justice', in D. Ward, J. Scott and M. Lacey (eds) *Probation: Working for Justice*, 2nd edn. Oxford: Oxford University Press.

Raynor, P. and Vanstone, M. (2002) *Understanding Community Penalties: Probation, Policy and Social Change*. Buckingham: Open University Press.

Rex, S. (1999) 'Desistence from Offending: Experiences of Probation', *Howard Journal of Criminal Justice*, 38 (4): 366–83.

Roberts, J., Stalans, L., Indermaur, D. and Hough, M. (2003) *Penal Populism and Public Opinion*. Oxford: Oxford University Press.

Robinson, G. (2002) 'Exploring Risk Management in Probation Practice: Contemporary Developments in England and Wales', *Punishment and Society*, 4 (1): 5–25.

Rose, N. (2000) 'Government and Control', *British Journal of Criminology*, 36 (4): 321–39.

Senior, P., Crowther-Dowey, C. and Long, M. (2007) *Understanding Modernisation in Criminal Justice*. Buckingham: Open University Press.

T3 Associates (2000) *Reasoning and Rehabilitation Revised: A Handbook for Teaching Cognitive Skills*. Ottawa: T3 Associates.

Travis, A. (2006) 'Reid plans mixed economy in criminal justice system, *The Guardian*, 28 September.

Trotter, C. (1999) *Working with Involuntary Clients*. London: Sage.

Vanstone, M. (2004) *Supervising Offenders in the Community: A History of Probation Theory and Practice*. Aldershot: Ashgate.

Youth Justice Board (2001) *Risk and Protective Factors Associated with Youth Crime and Effective Interventions to Prevent it*. London: YJB.

Chapter 2

Creative work: an historical perspective

Maurice Vanstone

The very creation of probation was an innovation, and its early practitioners were pioneers assisted not by manuals and good practice guides but by a rough template bequeathed by evangelical, soul-saving police court missionaries. It was inevitable, then, that practice should be shaped more by individual creativity than by organisational norms and expectations: how to save a soul might have had a spiritual and biblical context, but its process was very much left in the hands of the particular practitioner when face to face with the particular, wayward citizen. It should not surprise us, therefore, that people working in the probation service have never lacked imagination or the enthusiasm for innovatory ways of endeavouring to achieve their goals. Indeed, in some ways the history of probation practice can be seen as a continual quest for effective ways of resolving people's problems and helping them to lead crime-free lives; however, that quest has invariably been idiosyncratic, uncharted, often unsustainable and impermanent – albeit simple at its core. With echoes of McWilliams (1987), Statham and Whitehead (1992) have argued that successive layers of complexity have been superimposed on this simplicity – first, religious fervour, second, scientific treatment, and third, management with its accompanying manipulation – and although theirs is a broadly accurate analysis it perhaps oversimplifies the final layer. As this chapter attempts to demonstrate, there was a phase in the early stages of development of what McWilliams terms the 'rise of policy', when some managers took advantage of what was by then an admittedly fragile tradition of autonomy in the probation service to further their vision of management and leadership, before it was eclipsed by the spreading shadow of the managerialist school. It is relatively late in the history of the service that the quest for effectiveness has been organised and managed in ways that have become increasingly conservative and myopic and lacking in the innovation and vision of individuals and teams of practitioners. It will be a central argument of this chapter that those developments, which might be generalised under the epithet What Works, have constituted a great missed opportunity – the opportunity to foster an evidence-based approach that accommodates leaps of often eccentric imaginations as opposed to rigidly formulaic prescriptions, to encourage the social scientist-practitioner and not the dutiful plodder, and to foster and encourage leaders instead of policy apparatchiks.

As well as exploring the anatomy of that opportunity and the reasons it was missed (and this includes the impact of the politicisation of crime), this chapter asks what can be learned from history; what can be learned from innovations in practice such as, for example, early group work, detached community work, and specific work with female and ethnic minority offenders; and how work intended to change the offending trajectory of people's lives might still capitalise on the ideas of practitioners and visionary leaders.

A creative history

A study of the first half-century of the probation service's history provides solid grounds for believing that early probation officers were anxious to extend their repertoire of techniques, widen their knowledge, and broaden their horizons.[1] Interested academics and officers visited America and Europe seeking to gather information. Cecil Leeson, the former probationer who wrote what was effectively the first probation textbook (Leeson 1914), spent two years in America examining their ways of working; Warner (1929) drew on her experience in America to argue for a new scientific approach that incorporated the best traditions of the instinctive and common-sense approach prevalent in the United Kingdom; and another officer, Chinn (1930, 1931), promulgated his knowledge of American casework theory and methods. Some practitioners identified the limitations of working with isolated individuals. Croker-King (1915) used her own home as a prototype reporting centre for boys under her supervision; Mrs Cary (1915) held twice-weekly evening sessions in a hired church hall for girls on probation; other officers used volunteers (Leeson 1914) and experimented with notions of self-governance in Boys' Clubs; and some services exploited specialist expertise in areas such as employment (Page 1992). By the 1940s and 1950s psychology had taken its place alongside the common-sense homilies of the average probation officer, and some officers carried the early idea of bringing groups of probationers together into the new scientific era (Rimmer 1995). Others experimented on barges, training ships and campsites (Page 1992; Pearce 1951; Pratt and Ratcliffe 1954; Walker and Morley 1954), and once the treatment model became entrenched in practice theory officers extended their activities into therapeutic hospital experiments (Parker and Bilston 1959), treatment groups of one kind or another (Ashley 1962; Freeguard 1964; McCullough 1963) and advanced casework (Golding 1959; Parkinson 1965, 1966).

The next 30 years or so were no less inventive. Confident in the belief that a combination of mutual support, encouragement and less formal relationships between helpers and the helped increased responsibility and self-control, officers continued to exploit the great outdoors on the water (Harding 1971; Durbin 1982), on farms (Bunning 1975), in adventure centres (Voelcker 1969); and the great indoors in existing youth clubs (Carpenter and Gibbens 1973), converted waiting rooms (Dobson 1975), and on film projects (Adams and Howlett 1972). The point about these now familiar aspects of the ideological and practice history of probation is that they were almost entirely the result of individual rather than organisational effort, they were based on an untested belief in the ability to change people, they were wholly unevaluated (in any sense that a modern probation officer might understand), they pre-dated any evaluative criticism (though not the scepticism of the likes of C. S. Lewis and Barbara Wootten),[2] and they were largely free of accountability. They can be judged as a positive aspect of that history, but they were not part of a golden age of probation practice: they were no doubt deficient and semi-professional but they demonstrated that some practitioners were not satisfied with traditional methods and left to their own devices could experiment and alter the cultural and organisational space within which they worked. What is also interesting about this period is that it contains examples of probation interest in the broader context of probationers' lives, the particular needs of marginalised people, and curiosity about the effectiveness of practice some time before the emergence of What Works, and concern about the best way to organise the provision of services before the government developed its particular vision of what probation service it wanted (Holdaway and Mantle 1992).

A broader context

In an acknowledgement of the limitations of social work intervention, Jordan (1979) and Walker and Beaumont (1981) argued that empathic relationships are no compensation to people enduring problems of poverty and deprivation; in doing so they were not suggesting that agencies such as probation (and the practitioners within them) were impervious to the wider social problems of people, but simply that their focus was on individuals and that their approach towards practice was cautious. No doubt many shared the idea of service-users as fellow citizens and genuine participants in the development of their communities, but in a convincing analysis Jordan (1990: 138–9) suggests that most interpreted it in a very cautious way. Moreover, Jordan asserts that in 'the probation service, this caution and categorization has been even more marked', and the dearth of initiatives focused on the social rather than the personal is testament to that. Nevertheless, prior to the Effective Practice Initiative of the late 1990s some Services, either through policy or encouragement, focused on the social and economic aspects of people's lives. Thus, at the beginning of the 1970s, while some officers were thinking about the potential of community involvement (Mason 1972), some Services were experimenting with the idea. In an area office in Sheffield contacts were made with various individuals such as doctors, health visitors, councillors, schools, tenants' associations, and health and social security offices to tap 'reservoirs of help' on the housing estate, and that work was aided by a community officer who enlisted volunteers, ex-offenders and various community leaders to tackle local problems (Goff 1972). North Yorkshire and Northumbria Services introduced debts and benefits specialists (Ward 1979; Northumbria Probation Service 1994); Inner London Service set out specifically to enhance the awareness of its staff about social issues (Broadbent 1989); and the South Glamorgan Service encouraged and supported the creation of a Housing Society to ameliorate the accommodation problems of young people (Drakeford and Vanstone 1996).[3]

Helping the marginalised

During this period there was a growing recognition of deficiencies in the response of probation services to the particular needs of ethnic minority groups and women. In 1976 a Home Office meeting held between the Race Relations Adviser at the Home Office and representatives from five probation areas and two regional staff development offices determined to set up two four-day seminars on this aspect of the probation service's work (Taylor 1981). They concluded that the probation service needed to professionalise its response to the needs of ethnic minority groups, widen its understanding of cultural difference, develop training and staff development, increase its knowledge of relevant legislation, and improve liaison with local ethnic minority groups. West Midlands Probation and After Care Service responded by creating the role of Ethnic Liaison Officer at senior management level and undertaking a survey of the views of its staff, which revealed a depth of concern about the problems of those people from ethnic minority groups with whom the service had dealings, and identified areas related to equality of justice in need of further investigation. The survey also detailed four projects serving the particular needs of ethnic minority groups. They were the Handsworth Alternate Scheme, staffed entirely by young black workers and funded by a Home

Office grant administered by the National Association for the Care and Resettlement of Offenders (NACRO), which focused on developing new facilities of accommodation, employment, education, recreation, and social support for between 17 and 25 young black probationers; the Handsworth Project, which involved dance and drama, electronics, and mother and baby groups, as well as an educational visit to Jamaica and training for staff and magistrates; an Activity Centre concentrating on employment and skills development; and the Donkey Driving Group involving borstal boys and disabled people. (The latter is a very good example of a project resulting from the imagination, drive and motivation of one female officer, who had set it up when working as a liaison officer for Hewell Grange Borstal.)

It is not my intention to single out this particular service as an exemplar, but its efforts are particularly well documented. There were others, already described in detail (Vanstone 2007), worthy of summary. Jones and her colleagues (1993) and Mistry (1993), in response to what they perceived as predominantly male-focused supervision structures in a patriarchal society, established groups for women, run by women and premised on the notion of self-empowerment; and the Nottinghamshire and West Yorkshire Services redesigned resources specifically to meet the needs of women (Hirst 1996; Hay and Stirling 1998). The North Thames Resource Unit set up a programme expressly for black probationers and delivered by black staff (Jenkins and Lawrence 1992); and officers in the St Pauls area of Bristol responded to the voices of ethnic minority groups, expressed as they were in the 1981 uprising, literally by taking to the streets (Lawson 1984).

Displays of curiosity

It is broadly true, as I have suggested above, that the bulk of innovative activity during this period went unevaluated, but it would be wrong to assume from this that the service was devoid of curiosity. There is good evidence of a commitment to evaluation that not only pre-dates What Works but was sustained by both individual practitioners and management, and sometimes with the involvement of academics. Shaw and Crook (1977) not only pre-empted recent attention to motivation (Fabiano and Porporino 2002) but introduced an albeit rare use of control groups for their 18-month follow-up evaluation of reconvictions; and Weaver and Fox (1984) sustained their group for sex offenders for a ten-year period and evaluated it over a seven-year period using reconviction data, psychological analysis and a postal questionnaire. Also in the early 1980s, McGuire and Priestley (1981) facilitated a project that created the opportunity for probation officers to run social skills programmes in the community and in prison. Twenty-nine officers participated in a five-day

23

residential course in which they formulated social skills programmes, the aims of which included improving confidence, job skills, self-awareness, and examining offending; moreover, evaluation was built into the programme designs. Between October 1980 and February 1981 17 programmes were run, and in addition to the feedback from participants being positive the overall evaluation concluded that social skills methods could be used by probation officers in interesting and innovative ways. At the end of that decade, two probation officers, inspired by McGuire and Priestley's (1985) rediscovery of the offence as a direct focus of probation work, established an offending behaviour programme based on a pilot study that also built evaluation into its design (Linscott and Crossland 1989).

Clearly, the point about these examples is that they demonstrate a grass-roots interest in whether or not practice was effective, but that interest was not confined to practitioners. Significantly, a number of Services not only took the initiative by supporting, re-sourcing and encouraging experimentation but also invited the scrutiny and accountability that comes with evaluation. Quite properly, the following examples have been cited as part of What Works history in the United Kingdom, but they are included here also because they illustrate the potential – extant in a service still relatively unencumbered by government dictat – for internally generated innovation subject to the rigours of evaluation.

Building on what had been learned from the Young Offender Project set up in 1984, the Hereford and Worcester Probation Service established the Programme for Achievement, Challenge and Training (PACT), which extended the provision to people who might be at risk of a custodial sentence (Hereford and Worcester Probation Service 1989). Not only was it focused on criminogenic needs such as offending behaviour, relationships, addictions, employment, violence and leisure, it involved use of the ground-breaking Geese Theatre Group, which had been improvising with drama and theatre techniques in prisons and day centres; and it was subject to 'regular monitoring' and independent evaluation. In South Wales, the Afan Alternative, which from 1980 had been experimenting with the use of psycho-drama with people who otherwise would have been in prison, was evaluated by Raynor (1988). Similarly, the evaluation of offending behaviour groups that had been run in the West Midlands between 1986 and 1990 (Davies and Lister 1992) involved analysis of re-offending, the views of the people who had gone through the programmes, and in-depth analysis of the offending patterns of a sub-sample.

Each of these initiatives emanated from a curiosity at local level about whether innovation was having the desired effect. Obviously, the context of that curiosity was not just local; after all, a few years earlier the government had published its vision of the service's future (Home Office 1984), and as Davies and Lister (1992: 2) point out in their explanation of the need for the research, 'the Home Office has expressed a wish for the Probation Service to move centre-stage in the fight against crime'. The point is, however, that the 'landscape of provision produced by the long years of Conservative administration ... and the thorough-going privileging of the private over the public' inherited by the New Labour administration of 1997 (Drakeford and Vanstone 2000: 370) had not at this stage fully impacted on the probation service: to a significant extent, governance of policy and practice remained local and the services still held remnants of power. The government had 'expressed a wish', which no doubt influenced the motivation of managers to display accountability, but the desire to prove the service's worth to the community was, as these exemplars of locally grown (and evaluated) innovations make clear, already embedded in the culture of the service.

Alternative organisation

Such innovation was not confined to practice. During this period some services supported experimentation in the way in that practice was organised and managed. As Sutton (no date) describes, in the mid-1970s the central Bristol team forged a new team-based approach motivated by awareness of the limitations of traditional 'one-size-fits-all supervision' in reducing offending (limitations that the team viewed as the probation service's rather than those of the probationer), and encompassing short-term work, contracts, differential treatment, and diversion from custody. Following an assessment at the Social Enquiry Report stage of suitability for placement in a group, people placed on probation were allocated to an induction group.[4] This entailed seven sessions in which the reasons for offending were explored, an assessment of need agreed, and a contract made. Depending on the detail of the contract the probationer would be allocated to one or more of the programmes on offer – one-to-one, low priority contact, the social skills group (practical day-to-day living), the Thursday club (an evening day centre), the heavy drinkers group (focused on motivation to change), the informal Friday coffee morning, a group to look at human emotions (run by probation officer and university lecturer), the day centre, a course for chronically unemployed, family therapy, and voluntary community service. Thus the team was able to offer up to 33 hours of contact and deal with more heavily convicted probationers.[5] Similar developments occurred in Preston (Butterworth 1980), Cheltenham (Stanley 1982), and Leicester (Hardiker 1977). As Hardiker put it, these initiatives were significant, among other reasons, because the probation service historically had not formulated objectives and management had 'had a servicing function' (1077: 55), whereas now services and teams were putting objectives into operation thus rationalising processes of administration and contributing to a more efficient service to the courts.

A reading of the descriptions of these projects is interesting, of course, but particularly because of what they have to say about the role of managers. In Preston, for example, the 'Bureaucratic model of a Senior allocating work to officers carrying out work in isolation was to be buried, and the Senior was to carry out a vital co-ordinating and enabling function, was to be responsible for structure of the team's method of working, review specialisms and officer development [sic], and liaise with management and outside Agencies' (Butterworth 1980: 23); and in clarifying his senior officer role, Stanley (1982: 488) explained that the 'responsibility for allocation remained with me, but within the meeting it became a shared process [and the] views of those participating were taken into account'. What these descriptions show is that prior to the onset of the managerialism described by McWilliams (1987), the shoots of an organic (yet accountable) model of management in line with that expounded by McWilliams (1980) later in this chapter were clearly visible, shoots that were about to be uprooted by an intensification in government interest in probation and an inexorable increase in governance over the service (Robinson 2001).

Discovering the probation service

It was, perhaps, ominous that in the same year as the Thatcher government took office a Home Office reconviction study revealed less than encouraging information about probation's effectiveness. Phillpotts and Lancucki's (1979) sample of 5,000 people returned probation reconviction rates of 89 per cent for people of five or more convictions compared to 88 per cent for custody, and provided a rather inauspicious introduction of the service to a government recently elected on an explicitly 'get tough' on crime ticket. The Conservative government had not lost faith with the probation service, but in the next few years it was to bring an old acquaintance into a close, controlling relationship that would demand accountability. With the Statement of National Objectives and Priorities (Home Office 1984) the government set off a train of policy developments that would culminate in a service unrecognisable to the practitioners and managers involved in the creative projects referred to above. The story has been told many times and will not be repeated here other than to say that it hinged on changes in language, the introduction of the concept of punishment in the community (Home Office 1988), and the development of management systems designed to monitor and focus on targets and cost control (Audit Commission 1989). What is more pertinent to this chapter is how and why it happened, and with what effect. Answering those questions leads us into the worlds of accounting and journalism.

Humphrey and Pease (1993) explored the impact of the process of new accountability (the contours of which they outlined as national and local objectives, financial management systems, the examination by the Audit Commission and the National Audit Office, and the efficiency scrutiny of the probation inspectorate) by listening to the views of probation staff (in four probation areas) on changes in the provision and management of probation work. The researchers were certainly not Luddites and supported a rational approach to funding, so their exposure of the superficiality and unintended consequences of this particular 'rationality' assumes a greater gravitas. Tellingly, they highlight tensions between the agendas of people on probation and bureaucracy, a loss of trust in probation work, an increased faith in remote managerial functions, a growing dominance of court interests, and the de-skilling of increasingly stressed staff. Indeed, in one piercingly insightful observation they suggest that the process is in danger of 'displacing activity from the important but unmeasurable, to the less important but measurable' (1993: 109): thus, the core of probation work – the influential relationship – is pushed to the margins. Finally, with an irony I suspect they were very conscious of, they argue that accounting systems are being readily taken on board because of belief that they have required controlling qualities, but add that 'whether the desired "new world" of a "structured", "focused", "accountable" and efficient organization will be achieved and be fitting of such desire' (1993: 67–8) is more an act of faith than anything else.

This 'new world' organisation also needed a new language: a punitive culture needed tough words (Rumgay 1989). Nowhere was this clearer than in the Green Paper *Punishment, Custody and the Community* (Home Office 1988), and in a trenchant analysis Garland (1989) exposes an ambivalence in the paper that he attributes to the government's wish to appear tough without incurring the costs that would inevitably follow such an aspiration. So, the government attempted to achieve the duality of promoting 'a get-tough measure but also a progressive reform' (1989: 4), diverting people from custody (liberal) and making community sanctions appear more punitive in the public's mind (reactionary). However, as Garland explains, 'the language of penal policy is also a social and political rhetoric which helps shape human relations and cultural sensibilities' (1989: 16), and with hindsight it was inevitable that an organisation like probation, whose history was based on the notion of providing a constructive form of criminal justice rather than a punitive one, should end up as a value-compromised, rudderless NOMS forced to fit into a punitive culture. Garland suggests that the government behaved as if that punitive mentality was 'a given fact of the world to which governments (and penal practitioners) must somehow adapt' (1989: 14). Now, political ideology might offer an explanation for this, but the fact that successive governments of the left and right have continued to pursue such policies suggests that it is only a partial explanation: the full explanation requires some reflection on the rise of populist punitiveness and the politicisation of crime (Bottoms 1995; Downes and Morgan 1997).

The politicisation of crime

This rise involved the breakdown of the post-war liberal consensus and its replacement with social authoritarianism (Scraton 1987), the emergence of a new political order predicated on separation and exclusion as opposed to integration and inclusion (Brownlee 1998; Young 1999), the extension of state control (Cohen 1985; Mathiesen 1983), and a media obsession with crime. Much weight has been put on the latter phenomenon as the main explanation for the new punitive consensus: in essence, distorted and unrepresentative media coverage of crime heightens public fears, which when expressed increases the political vulnerability of politicians who appear *soft* on crime. In offering an alternative theory, Beckett (1997) argues that in America politicians use their power and sympathetic media to reconstruct interpretations of crime, its causes and required responses in ways that are conducive to the achievement of their particular and preferred political agendas and in order to stage-manage public opinion. (Her research demonstrated that political interest and media coverage were closely correlated to public concerns about crime but actual rates of crime were not.) Recently, and nearer to home, Ryan (2006), in his examination of what he terms the 'punitive paradox' – an increase in punitive appetites at a time when the public should feel more secure about crime – has added an interesting interpretation that throws new light on the traditional explanations for the rise of the punitive political culture. He partly accepts the political media conspiracy theory, but is critical of its limitations. In his view, 'changes in our political culture and the arrival of new media technologies make the public voice a far more powerful player in the policy-making process than was once the case' (2006: 32), and therefore simply and exclusively blaming the 'usual suspects' is not viable as an argument. Growing public independence has been enhanced by mass education and 'the growth of the information and communication society' (2006: 39), and so the old deference to authority and superiors has been replaced by active citizenship. The result of this 'repositioning of the public voice' is that 'governments now need to engage with the public in a way that was not envisaged in the decades immediately after 1945' (2006: 42). There are soft spots in his argument (for example, the question of how current voter apathy fits with the rise of the public voice); nevertheless, it adds a useful dimension to thinking about populist punitiveness, and raises questions about how far probation has been a powerless victim in the associated political processes and how far it has missed opportunities to manage and project itself differently.

A lost opportunity

There are two inextricably linked dimensions to this lost opportunity, namely the failure to inculcate a more organic style of management into the culture of the service (McWilliams 1980), and the failure to capitalise on the service's innate curiosity about effectiveness. Reflecting back, the beginning of the 1980s seems to have been a pivotal moment in the shaping of probation's style and structure of management. In unpublished notes, McWilliams (1980) makes the critical point that decisions about management structures are second order decisions and decisions about models are first order, and that if models are not thought through properly or are vague or not understood, this may lead to inappropriate structures. In the same year a report on management structure concluded that further bureaucratisation was unavoidable, but a minority report expressed opposition to this and argued for more emphasis on greater autonomy for the competent officer (Clarke and McNeil 1980). Even seven years later the Association of Chief Officers of Probation (1987: 3) argued for developments to 'build upon the established strengths of the probation service, utilise the skills of its professional and other fieldwork staff and work with the grain of the service' and warned that any other kind of approach risks 'disorientation, dislocation and inefficiency' rather than involvement in community initiatives and environmental crime prevention improvements. In questioning the appropriateness of further bureaucratisation, McWilliams argues that the service had moved from being an organic or adaptable organisation (characterised by personal involvement, achievement orientation, continual adjustment, shared group tasks, lateral and vertical communications, and consultation) to a mechanistic or bureaucratic one (characterised by 'impersonality, ascribed roles and rules, rational efficiency, rigid hierarchical structure, mainly vertical communications, specialism of tasks and expectations' (1980:4), and that during this period it was divided by supporters of the two approaches: on the one hand, formal control of organisation, staff and activities and a further extension of bureaucratic structure, and on the other hand, a more organic, flexible style. In order to counter the drift towards the former, he asserts that the service needed to promote a culture founded on healthy criticism of all ideas, policies and practices; self-determination within a critical culture; substantive rather than merely formal accountability; continuous adjustment and re-defining of individual tasks; lateral as well as vertical communication; and consultation more than direction:

> ... within the critical culture persons would be expected and encouraged to reflect critically on the organisational and professional norms, rules and customs of the institution in which they operate. Above all, people would be expected to reflect critically on their own views as much as those of others and actively seek criticism for themselves. (McWilliams 1980: 12, underlining in the original)

The new model, therefore, would be critically competent with 'a routine deference to criticism', would be made up of potentially self-determining and self-controlling people within a critical culture, would encourage substantive accountability as opposed to formal accountability (real, collective), and would have a 'head' which 'is both close to and understands the heart' (1980: 14). Sadly, however, bureaucracy has prevailed.

Conclusion

It has not been the purpose of this chapter to claim that a healthy, effective probation service has been undermined by policies totally inimical to traditional probation work: the probation service has not always been healthy or effective. Nor does it claim that the current dominant practice paradigm, cognitive behaviouralism, has been entirely a bad thing. It has had some justifiable criticism (Worrall 2000; Gorman 2001), but it has also made some positive contributions to probation practice and policy direction. The point is that increased governance from the centre combined with an acquiescent bureaucratic management structure has resulted in the stifling of innovation and the imposition of too narrow a practice agenda, and it need not have been like this. The organic style of management proposed so long ago by McWilliams might have ensured a recognition that practitioners 'do need guidance about effective structures and skills, but they also need to exercise their professional discretion and have a degree of freedom to innovate and to adapt prescribed structures to meet unexpected needs as well as those officially recognised' (Dixon 2000: 21), thus making the probation service less susceptible to the pathologising of people and more involved in contributing to social justice (McNeill 2000). This is not an unrealistic argument for a return to a golden unaccountable age: a concern with realistic and effective practice is vital. However, the opportunity to exploit that concern and keep evaluation organic too rather than bureaucratised was, and maybe still is, there. Even though Underdown (1998) identified only four programme exemplars, he noted several others that were promising, and perhaps this should not be surprising because, as Raynor (1997) reminded us, most innovative research in the 20 years that preceded his observations had been undertaken outside of the remit of the Home Office. Therefore, he goes on to say, there is a need for central research strategy 'to have a broad and non-parochial agenda, informed by a wide range of ideas and sources, and sufficient resources to be genuinely helpful' (1997: 66); and the kind of comprehensive and eminently practical guide to evaluating a wide range of groups that probation services need to assist in this (actually commissioned by Home Office, HMIP, ACOP and NPRIE) exists (Merrington and Hine 2001).[6] Moreover, as Lorraine Gelsthorpe has recently argued, developments in the provision of services to women – the Women's Offending Reduction Programme (WORP) (Home Office 2004), the Corston Report (2007), projects such as the Asha centre in Worcester, and the *Offender Management Guide to Working with Women* (Ministry of Justice 2008) – suggest political attitudes and commitments that might open the door to a new welfarism bolstered by traditional probation values.[7] It may be too late – and the truth is that currently no one knows what values will prevail and what shape a future NOMS or equivalent might take – but it is probably true to say that the probation service could continue to make a genuine, non-punitive, effective and constructive contribution to social and criminal justice if it was given sufficient freedom to rediscover its confidence and promote that contribution directly and unashamedly to the communities that it is intended to serve.

Notes

1 For a full description of practice during this period see Vanstone (2003, 2004, 2007).
2 See Wootton (1959) and Lewis (1949).
3 An interesting aspect of this development is that it grew from a discussion that three probationers had in a café in Weymouth and the subsequent actions they took.
4 For a full description of this phenomenon see Brown and Seymour (1984).
5 A survey of 628 cases revealed that the general service caseload consisted of 43 per cent first offenders and 14 per cent over six, in contrast to the team caseload which consisted of 17 per cent first and 38 per cent over six.
6 Sadly, though, it lies gathering dust on some office shelf.
7 Loraine Gelsthorpe, 'Women, Penal Reform and the Probation Service', Twelfth Annual Bill McWilliams Memorial Lecture, Institute of Criminology, Cambridge, 24 June 2009.

References

ACOP (1987) *Probation – the Next Five years. A Joint Statement by the Association of Chief Officers of Probation, Central Council of Probation Committees, and National Association of Probation Officers*. Wakefield: Association of Chief Officers of Probation.

Adams, C. and Howlett, J. (1972) 'Working with Clients in the Group Setting or Diversionary Therapy', *Probation Journal*, 18 (2): 54–6.

Ashley, P. D. (1962) 'Group Work in the Probation Setting', *Probation*, 10 (1): 6–8.

Audit Commission (1989) *The Probation Service: Promoting Value for Money*. London: HMSO.

Beckett, K. (1997) *Making Crime Pay. Law and Order in Contemporary American Politics*. New York: Oxford University Press.

Bottoms, A. E. (1995) 'The Philosophy and Politics of Punishment and Sentencing', in C. M. V. Clarkson and R. Morgan (eds) *The Politics of Sentencing*. Oxford: Clarendon Press.

Broadbent, A. (1989) 'Poor Clients: What Can I do?', *Probation Journal*, 36: 151–4.

Brown, A. and Seymour, B. (eds) (1984) *Intake Groups for Clients: A Probation Innovation*. University of Bristol.

Brownlee, I. (1998) *Community Punishment: A Critical Introduction*. Harlow: Longman.

Bunning, M. R. (1975) 'The Summit Club', *Probation*, 22 (1): 22–5.

Butterworth, R. (1980) *Preston West: One Probation Team's Method of Working*. Preston: Lancashire Probation and After-Care Service.

Carpenter, M. and Gibbens, F. (1973) 'Combined Operations (Intermediate Treatment)', *Probation*, 20 (3): 84–7.

Cary, Mrs (1915) 'Social Clubs for Probationers; their Needs and Objects', *The National Association of Probation Officers*, 6: 102–3.

Chinn, H. (1930) 'A Comparative Study of Probation in America', *Probation*, 1 (4): 56–9.

Chinn, H. (1931) 'Home Visiting', *Probation*, 1 (6): 84–5.

Clarke, H. and McNeil, D. H. (1980) *Report of the Working Party on Management Structure in the Probation and After-Care Service*. London: Home Office.

Cohen, S. (1985) *Visions of Social Control*. Cambridge: Polity Press.

Corston, J. (2007) *The Corston Report: A Review of Women with Particular Vulnerability in the Criminal Justice System*. London: Home Office.

Croker-King, E. (1915) 'Juvenile Probation', *The National Association of Probation Officers*, 5: 66–7.

Davies, H. and Lister, M. (1992) *Evaluation of Offending Behaviour Groups*. Birmingham: West Midlands Probation Service.

Dixon, L. (2000) 'Punishment and the Question of Ownership: Groupwork in the Criminal Justice System', *Groupwork*, 12 (1): 6–25.

Dobson, G. (1975) 'Team Work Before Groupwork', *Probation Journal*, 22 (1): 17–22.

Downes, D. and Morgan, R. (1997) 'Dumping the "Hostages to Fortune"? The Politics of Law and Order in Post-War Britain', in M. Maguire, R. Morgan and R. Reiner (eds) *The Oxford Handbook of Criminology*, 2nd edn. Oxford: Clarendon Press.

Drakeford, M. and Vanstone, M. (eds) (1996) *Beyond Offending Behaviour*. Aldershot: Arena.

Drakeford, M. and Vanstone, M. (2000) 'Social Exclusion and the Politics of Criminal Justice: A Tale of Two Administrations', *Howard Journal*, 39 (4): 369–81.

Durbin, R. J. (1982) 'A Barge Experiment', *Probation Journal*, 29 (2): 51–3.

Fabiano, E. and Porporino, F. (2002) *Focus on Resettlement – A Change*. Canada: T3 Associates.

Freeguard, M. (1964) 'Five Girls against Authority', *New Society*, 18–20.

Garland, D. (1989) 'Critical Reflections on "Punishment, Custody and the Community"', in H. Rees and E. Hall Williams (eds) *Punishment, Custody and the Community: Reflections and Comments on the Green Paper*. Papers presented at the Second International Criminal Justice Seminar, April 1989, London School of Economics. London: London School of Economics.

Goff, D. (1972) 'An Approach to Community Involvement', *Probation Journal*, 18 (3): 68–72.

Golding, R. R. W. (1959) 'A Probation Technique', *Probation*, 11 (1): 9–11.

Gorman, K. (2001) 'Cognitive Behaviourism and the Holy Grail', *Probation Journal*, 48 (1): 3–9.

Hardiker, P. (1977) *A Probation Intake Team in Action.* Leicester: Leicestershire Probation Service and University of Leicester.

Harding, J. (1971) 'Barge Cruising: An Experiment in Group Work', *Probation,* 17 (3): 45–7.

Hay, A. and Stirling, A. (1998) 'Women Need Women', *Probation Journal,* 45 (1): 36–8.

Hereford and Worcester Probation Service (1989) *Programme for Achievement and Challenge.* Worcester: Hereford and Worcester Probation Service.

Hirst, G. (1996) 'Moving Forward: How Do We Do That?', *Probation Journal,* 43 (2): 58–63.

Holdaway, S. and Mantle, G. (1992) 'Governing the Probation Service: Probation Committees and Policy Making', *Howard Journal,* 31 (2): 120–32.

Home Office (1984) *Probation Service in England and Wales: Statement of National Objectives and Priorities.* London: Home Office.

Home Office (1988) *Punishment, Custody and the Community.* London: HMSO.

Home Office (2004) *Women's Offending Reduction Plan.* London: Home Office.

Humphrey, C. and Pease, K. (1992) 'Effectiveness Measurement in the Probation Service: A View from the Troops', *Howard Journal,* 31: 31–52.

Jenkins, J. and Lawrence, D. (1992) 'Black Groups Initiative Review', unpublished paper, Inner London Probation Service.

Jones, M., Mordecai, M., Rutter, F. and Thomas, L. (1993) 'A Miskin Model of Groupwork with Women Offenders', in A. Brown and B. Caddick (eds) *Groupwork with Offenders.* London: Whiting and Birch.

Jordan, B. (1979) *Helping in Social Work.* London: Routledge and Kegan Paul.

Jordan, B. (1990) *Social Work in an Unjust Society.* Hemel Hempstead: Harvester Wheatsheaf.

Lawson, J. (1984) 'Probation in St Pauls: Teamwork in a Multi-racial, Inner City Area', *Probation Journal,* 31 (3): 93–5.

Leeson, C. (1914) *The Probation System.* London: P. S. King and Son.

Lewis, C. S. (1949) 'The Humanitarian Theory of Punishment', *20th Century: An Australian Quarterly Review,* 3 (3): 5–12.

Linscott, C. J. and Crossland, R. S. (1989) *Offending Behaviour Group Programme.* Devon Probation Service.

Mason, J. H. (1972) 'Community Involvement – Casework or Politics', *Probation Journal,* 18 (2): 44–7.

Mathiesen, T. (1983) 'The Future of Control Systems: The Case of Norway', in D. Garland and P. Young (eds) *The Power to Punish: Contemporary Penality and Social Analysis.* London: Heinemann.

McCullough, M. K. (1963) 'Groupwork in Probation', *New Society,* 21: 9–11.

McGuire, J. and Priestley, P. (1981) *A Social Skills Project.* Bristol: South West Regional Committee for Staff Development.

McGuire, J. and Priestley, P. (1985) *Offending Behaviour: Skills and Stratagems for Going Straight.* London: Batsford.

McNeill, F. (2000) 'Making Criminology Work: Theory and Practice in Local Context', *Probation Journal,* 47 (2): 108–18.

McWilliams, W. (1980) 'Management Models and the Bases of Management Structures', unpublished paper.

McWilliams, W. (1987) 'Probation, Pragmatism and Policy', *Howard Journal,* 26: 97–121.

Merrington, S. and Hine, J. (2001) *A Handbook for Evaluating Probation Work with Offenders*. Birmingham: West Midlands Probation Service.

Ministry of Justice (2008) *Offender Management Guide to Working with Women*. London: Home Office.

Mistry, T. (1993) 'Establishing a Feminist Model of Groupwork in the Probation Service', in A. Brown and B. Caddick (eds) *Groupwork with Offenders*. London: Whiting and Birch.

Northumbria Probation Service (1994) *Survey of Probation Practice on Poverty Issues*. Northumbria Probation Service.

Page, M. (1992) *Crime Fighters of London: A History of the Origins and Development of the London Probation Service 1876–1965*. London: Inner London Probation Service Development Trust.

Parker, K. and Bilston, W. G. (1959) 'Belmont: A Therapeutic Opportunity', *Probation*, 9 (3): 36–7.

Parkinson, G. (1965) 'Casework and the Persistent offender', *Probation*, 11 (1): 11–17.

Parkinson, G. (1966) 'Passivity and Delinquency', *Probation*, 12 (2): 59–65.

Pearce, W. H. (1951) 'Probationers in Camp', *Probation*, 6 (2): 15–16.

Phillpotts, G. J. O. and Lancucki, L. B. (1979) *Previous Convictions, Sentence and Reconviction: A Statistical Study of a Sample of 5000 Offenders Convicted in January 1971*, Home Office Research Study 53. London: HMSO.

Pratt, E. G. and Ratcliffe, S. (1954) 'Arethusa Camp: Notes and Criticisms', *British Journal of Delinquency*, VI (1): 53–61.

Raynor, P. (1988) *Probation as an Alternative to Custody*. Aldershot, Avebury.

Raynor, P. (1997) 'Crumbs of Comfort: A Comment on Andrew Underdown's Paper', in R. Burnett (ed.) *The Probation Service: Responding to Change*, Proceedings of the Probation Studies Unit First Annual Colloquium, 16–17 December 1996, Kellog College, Oxford. Probation Studies Unit Report No. 3. University of Oxford Centre for Criminological Research.

Rimmer, J. (1995) 'How Social Workers and Probation Officers in England conceived their Roles and Responsibilities in the 1930s and 1940s', in J. Schwieson and P. Pettit (eds) *Aspects of the History of British Social Work*. Reading: University of Reading.

Robinson, G. (2001) 'Power, Knowledge and "What Works" in Probation', *Howard Journal* 40 (3): 235–54.

Rumgay, J. (1989) 'Talking Tough: Empty Threats in Probation Practice', *Howard Journal*, 28 (3): 177–86.

Ryan, M. (2006) 'Red Tops, Populists and the Irresistible Rise of the Public Voice(s)', in M. Mason (ed.) *Captured by the Media: Prison Discourse in Popular Culture*. Cullompton: Willan Publishing.

Scraton, P. (ed.) (1987) *Law, Order and the Authoritarian State*. Milton Keynes: Open University Press.

Shaw, R. and Crook, H. (1977) 'Group Techniques', *Probation*, 24 (2): 61–5.

Stanley, A. R. (1982) 'A New Structure for Intake and Allocation in a Field Probation Unit', *British Journal of Social Work*, 12 (5): 487–506.

Statham, R. and Whitehead, P. (1992) *Managing the Probation Service: Issues for the 1990s*. London: Longman.

Sutton, D. (no date) 'A New Approach to Probation Supervision', Unpublished paper.

Taylor, W. (1981) *Probation and After-Care in a Multi-Racial Society*. London: Commission for Racial Equality and the West Midlands County Probation and After-Care Service.

Underdown, A. (1998) *Strategies for Effective Offender Supervision: Report of the HMIP What Works Project*. London: Home Office.

Vanstone, M. (2003) 'A History of the Use of Groups in Probation Work: Part One – From "Clubbing the Unclubbables" to Therapeutic Intervention', *Howard Journal*, 42 (1): 69–86.

Vanstone, M. (2004) 'A History of the Use of Groups in Probation Work: Part Two – From Negotiated Treatment to Evidenced-based Practice in an Accountable Service', *Howard Journal*, 43 (2): 180–202.

Vanstone, M. (2007) *Supervising Offenders in the Community: A History of Probation Practice*. Aldershot: Ashgate.

Voelcker, M. (1969) 'Hafod Meurig: An Experiment in "Intermediate Treatment"', *Probation*, 15 (1): 8–12.

Walker, M. and Beaumont, B. (1981) *Probation Work: Critical Theory and Practice*. Oxford: Blackwell.

Walker, P. and Morley, R. E. (1954) 'A Barge Experiment', *Probation*, 7 (6): 63–4.

Ward, K. (1979) 'Fuel debts and the probation service', *Probation Journal*, 26 (4): 110–14.

Warner, Miss (1929) 'The Technique of Probation', *Probation*, 1 (1): 10–11.

Weaver, C. and Fox, C. (1984) 'Berkeley Sex Offenders Group: A Seven Year Evaluation', *Probation Journal*, 31 (1): 43–6.

Wootton, B. (1959) *Social Science and Pathology*. London: George Allen & Unwin Ltd.

Worrall, A. (2000) 'What Works at One Arm Point? A Study in the Transportation of a Penal Concept', *Probation Journal*, 47 (3): 243–9.

Young, J. (1999) *The Exclusive Society*. London: Sage.

Chapter 3

Travelling hopefully: desistance theory and probation practice

Beth Weaver and Fergus McNeill

Introduction

This chapter aims to explore the impact of desistance theory and research on probation practice to date and to examine underdeveloped aspects of this important interface. We aim first to review the few empirical studies that have specifically focused on the role that probation may play in supporting desistance and also wider debates about the implications of desistance research for probation and social work practice. By seeking to explore and understand the processes through which people come to cease offending – with or without intervention by criminal justice agencies – desistance research potentially provides a wealth of knowledge for policy and practice, and directs those involved in criminal justice practice towards a series of issues that have been, until recently, somewhat neglected in the pursuit of 'evidence-based' practice. These issues include the significance of officer–offender relationships in the process of rehabilitation (Burnett and McNeill 2005), and the significance of the social contexts of offending and desistance (Farrall 2002; McCulloch 2005; McNeill and Whyte 2007). Though these are important issues, this chapter seeks to move beyond them by exploring other crucial but underdeveloped dialogues between desistance research and probation practice around questions of identity and diversity.

Desistance theories

While there is no agreed theoretical or operational definition of desistance, most criminologists have associated desistance with *both* ceasing *and* refraining from offending. Rather than being a linear progression to the state of non-offending, however, the process of desistance has been likened to a zigzag path (Glaser 1964) and to a drifting in and out of offending (Matza 1964). Maruna and Farrall (2004) have suggested a key distinction, which we discuss in some detail below: primary and secondary desistance. Primary desistance refers to any lull or crime-free gap in the course of a criminal career. Secondary desistance is defined as the movement from the behaviour of non-offending to the assumption of a role or identity of a non-offender or 'changed person' (Maruna and Farrall 2004). Though the usefulness of this analogy has been contested (Bottoms *et al.* 2004), it does seem likely that where policies and practices are concerned with re-offenders who have acquired criminal or criminalised identities the concept of secondary desistance may be particularly useful (McNeill 2006).

In reviewing explanations of desistance, Maruna (2000) identifies three broad theoretical perspectives in the desistance literature, relating to age and maturational reform, life transitions and the social bonds associated with them, and narrative changes in personal and social identity. Increasingly, desistance theorists tend to try to draw these three strands together. For example, Farrall and Bowling (1999) draw on life course criminology (particularly Sampson and Laub 1993) and structuration theory (Giddens 1984; Bottoms and Wiles 1992) to propose a developmental theory of desistance. They argue that the process of desistance is 'one that is produced through an *interplay* between individual choices, and a range of wider social forces, institutional and societal practices which are beyond the control of the individual' (Farrall and Bowling 1992: 261, emphasis in original).

Some desistance theorists have increasingly focused on which changes at the level of personal cognition (Giordano *et al.* 2002) or self-identity and self-concept (Burnett 1992; Graham and Bowling 1995; Maruna 1997; Shover 1996) might precede or coincide with changes in social bonds (LeBel *et al.* 2008). Using the data set from the Oxford Recidivism Study (Burnett 1992), followed up after a decade, LeBel *et al.* (2008) attempted to disentangle the interaction between such 'subjective/agency' factors and 'social/environmental' factors. They found that subjective states measured before release had a direct effect on recidivism as well as indirect effects through their impact on social circumstances experienced post release.

Similarly, drawing on a symbolic interactionist perspective, Uggen *et al.* (2004) emphasised both the role of age-graded social bonds and the social-psychological processes underpinning these related role transitions.

In addition to changes linked to employment and family, they stress the significance of 'civic reintegration'. Building on Maruna's (2001: 7) contention that desistance requires that ex-offenders 'develop a coherent pro-social identity for themselves', and his recognition of the salience of involvement in 'generative activities' as critical to this process, they specify the varieties of civic participation that contribute to such an identity and their associated subjective meanings for desisters. They show how role transitions across socio-economic, familial and civic domains relate to identity shifts over the life course. However, Uggen *et al.* (2004: 260) also emphasise the reduced citizenship status and the enduring stigma experienced by offenders, resulting in 'the reduced *rights* and *capacities* of ex-offenders to attain full citizenship' (emphasis in original). These status deficits undermine commitment to conformity and create new obstacles to desistance and the assumption of pro-social roles. Even where ex-offenders articulate a desire to assume such pro-social roles, they 'often lack the resources and social relationships necessary to establish role commitments and solidify new identities' (Uggen *et al.* 2006: 284–5). These obstacles represent a major problem because of the important role of societal reaction in supporting (or undermining) new self-conceptions and the reinforcement of pro-social identities (Maruna and Farrall 2004); Meisen-helder (1977: 329) described this as the 'certification' stage of desistance.

Supporting desistance

The role that probation or social work may play in supporting desistance has been examined in very few empirical studies. One of the first such studies was located in New Zealand and based on extensive interviews with a randomly selected sample of 48 people who had been placed on probation in 1987 and had not been reconvicted by 1990 (Leibrich 1993). Few people spontaneously cited probation as a factor in their desistance and only half of the sample considered probation to have been useful in this regard. A revision of personal values, reassessing what is important, responding to new family commitments, desire for a better future and the development of self-respect were cited as reasons for wishing to desist, as well as fear of consequences and shame. Desistance was accomplished by tackling personal problems using interpersonal resources, accompanied by a sense of life management; this last finding might be linked to the discovery of agency to which later authors allude (see Maruna 2001; McNeill 2006).

In Leibrich's study, the quality of the supervisory relationship was cited as pivotal in supporting the process of desistance. The desisters and their probation officers shared similar views about the characteristics they deemed crucial to such relationships: having someone that they could get on with and respect, who treated them as individuals, was genuinely caring, was clear about what was expected of them and trusted them when the occasion called for it (Leibrich 1993, 1994). Negative appraisals of the supervisory relationship were attributed to a sense of being merely 'processed'; the probation officer having been late or missing appointments; and where the officer gave the impression of being curious rather than genuinely concerned. The desisters, like the probation officers, emphasised the need to identify and address causes of offending and emphasised the individuals' own motivation as an essential component of the change process (see also Farrall 2002; Maruna *et al.* 2004a).

In a study of 'assisted desistance' in England, Rex (1999) explored the experiences of 60 probationers. Most of the probationers considered probation to have assisted the process of their desistance from offending. Rex found that those who attributed changes in their behaviour to supervision described it as active and participatory. Their commitments to desist appeared to be generated by the personal and professional commitment shown by their probation officers, whose reasonableness, fairness and encouragement seemed to engender a sense of personal loyalty and accountability. Probationers interpreted advice about their behaviours and underlying problems as evidence of concern for them as people, and 'were motivated by what they saw as a display of interest in their well-being' (Rex 1999: 375). Such evidence resonates not just with Leibrich's earlier findings, but with other arguments about the pivotal role that relationships play in effective interventions (see for example, Barry 2000; Burnett 2004; Burnett and McNeill 2005; Holt 2000; Hopkinson and Rex 2003; McNeill *et al.* 2005; McNeill 2006).

Farrall (2002) explored the progress, or lack of progress, towards desistance achieved by a group of 199 probationers in England. Though over half of the sample evidenced progress towards desistance, Farrall found that desistance could be attributed to specific interventions by the probation officer in only a few cases, although assistance in identifying employment opportunities and mending damaged family relationships appeared particularly important. Paradoxically, it was in these very areas that practitioners were found to be wary of intervening. The findings indicate that in terms of the identification and resolution of 'obstacles to desistance' only a minority of probationers and practitioners worked in partnership; there was limited evidence of agreement between probationers and their supervisors about the obstacles to desistance and how best to overcome them. Overcoming obstacles was perceived by both probationers and practitioners to be contingent on a range of factors often beyond the control of either practitioner or probationer; unsurprisingly therefore, no specific method of probation intervention could be credited with successfully overcoming obstacles. Rather, desistance seemed to relate more clearly to the probationers' motivations and to the social and personal contexts in which various obstacles to desistance were addressed. Farrall (2002) goes on to argue that interventions must pay greater heed to the community, social and personal contexts in which they are situated. Necessarily, this requires that interventions be focused not solely on the individual person and his or her perceived 'deficits'. Vitally, it is social capital (see below) that is necessary to encourage desistance. It is not enough to build capacities for change where change depends on opportunities to exercise capacities.

Building on these insights, McCulloch's (2005) study, based on 12 semi-structured interviews with probationers and their probation officers in Scotland, drew on probationer and practitioner perspectives to explore the attention given to probationers' social contexts in supporting desistance from crime. Somewhat in contrast to Farrall (2002), McCulloch found that probationers and practitioners had little difficulty in reconciling the apparently polarised objectives of welfare support and offence-focused interventions; although, akin to Farrall (2002), she found that direct work in the area of employment was limited and that 'talking methods' were the most frequently cited approach to addressing social problems (see also Rex 1999). Where obstacles to desistance were successfully resolved, participants attributed this both to probation intervention and the wider normative processes that occurred in the probationer's life. McCulloch forwards a convincing argument for an increased level of probation involvement in families and local communities, and a greater focus on integration (see also Farrall 2002; Rex 1999, 2001).

Looking beyond these empirical studies of probation and desistance, other authors have analysed the implications for practice emerging from the broader desistance research. Maruna et al. (2006), reflecting on the findings of the Liverpool Desistance Study, emphasise the significance of the use of language in professional discourses and interactions with offenders. They suggest that discourses should be future-oriented, and that a focus on risks and needs should be balanced with an emphasis on the individual's strengths. Such a 'strengths-based' (Maruna and LeBel 2003), prospective focus for practice would perhaps point towards the use of 'solution-focused' approaches, which capitalise on strengths, resilience and protective factors (see McNeill et al. 2005). Furthermore, broader changes in narrative identities might be facilitated by 'narrative approaches', which aim to support the process of identity reconstruction (Parton and O'Byrne 2000; Gorman et al. 2006). Maruna et al. (2004a) suggest that the promotion of participation in generative activities, which serve to bolster and assist in sustaining desistance through a process of pro-social socialisation and identity change, might be assisted through increasing opportunities for participation in voluntary service or other opportunities to make a positive contribution to local communities. However, as McNeill and Maruna (2007: 236) observe, generativity is a two-way process and ex-offenders' efforts to contribute should be reciprocated by communities and society through recognition of those efforts and reinforcement of them. This would suggest the need, therefore, to build communities that are desistance supportive, acting 'as partners in the process of sponsoring, supporting and sustaining rehabilitation' (McNeill and Maruna 2007: 237).

Debates about generativity are linked to those around 'social capital', a term that essentially refers to the resources that reside in social networks and relationships (Field 2008). Bonding social capital denotes ties between similar people in similar situations, such as immediate family, close friends and neighbours. Though this type of social capital can tend towards reinforcing exclusive identities within relatively homogeneous groups (including criminal groups), the significance of probation officers engaging with families to assist in the strengthening, regeneration or development of new family ties has been repeatedly stated throughout the desistance literature (see Farrall 2002; McNeill and Whyte 2007; Rex 1999). Bridging social capital, on the other hand, refers to more distant ties with similarly situated persons: for example, ties that typify loose friendships with work colleagues. Bridging social capital could be developed through participation in generative activities and employment, which provide opportunities to form new relationships. This type of social capital is more inclusive and tends to generate broader identities and wider reciprocities rather than reinforcing a narrowly defined group; as such it is essential to social mobility and self-progression. Building ex-offenders' bridging social capital, as McNeill and Whyte (2007) explain, requires engaging with and reassuring community groups, communities and employers, supporting them in working with ex-offenders. As such, it might suggest a case for re-examining the salience of community learning and development practice for probation work.

New possibilities for creative practice

So far, the contents of this chapter may have been familiar, at least to those who have followed the emergence of debates about desistance theory and probation practice. In the remainder of the chapter, however, we want to engage with this book's aspirations around encouraging 'creative practice', by examining what some of the more recent developments in desistance theory and research might contribute to such practice. Our specific focus will be on issues of identity and diversity, how they impact on the experience of desistance and how creative practice might constructively engage with the opportunities and challenges they raise.

Identity, desistance and creative practice

The role and significance of identity change in desistance is contested. Bottoms *et al.* (2004), outlining the initial theoretical reflections underpinning their Sheffield Pathways Out of Crime Study (SPooCS), challenged Maruna and Farrall's (2004) emphasis on the notion of secondary desistance, questioning the extent to which identity change or cognitive transformation is a *necessary* part of explanations of desistance. They argue that to 'adopt this approach seems to suggest that if someone has experienced no strong role or identity change, but just stops offending for a significant period, he or she is not a "true" desister' (Bottoms *et al.* 2004: 371). Bottoms *et al.* later suggest that for desistance to occur in a given person's life a reduction of criminal opportunities might be the product of deliberate choice, but it might also be the accidental by-product of, for example, new employment, or a meaningful relationship. While the authors acknowledge that the process of desistance is probably the result of an interaction between social context and subjectivities or agentic factors, they question the extent to which the agent is necessarily conscious of this change as it occurs. By contrast, in Maruna and Farrall's formulation, desisters *are* aware that they are changing and indeed positively wish to change: 'Secondary desistance involves . . . a measurable, reflective and more *self-conscious* break with patterns of offending' (Maruna and Farrall 2004: 8, emphasis in original). Bottoms *et al.* (2004) query whether, although people clearly realise that they have changed when they *have* desisted, they are actually consciously aware of this change *as it occurs*.

Differences around the role of agency in these narratives may depend in part on whether they are elicited prospectively or retrospectively. Retrospective accounts of desistance may be susceptible to cognitive rationalisations that place undue or unrealistic emphasis on the role of agency (see also Farrall and Bowling 1999; Sampson *et al.* 2006). Bottoms *et al.* (2004) suggest the possibility of 'a gradual injection of greater self-responsibilisation . . . allowing oneself to stop and think about what one is doing, particularly within a social context where supportive others are indicating that this is a desirable development' (Bottoms *et al.* 2004: 376). This 'gradual injection' could also be conceived as a feature of the *transition* from primary desistance to secondary desistance or of the process of movement along the continuum from primary to secondary desistance. Indeed, findings from the SPooCS study,[1] a prospective longitudinal desistance study of 113 persistent young male adult offenders in their early twenties, emphasise both the precariousness of and the sense of struggle involved in desistance; findings resonant with Burnett's (1992) observation that, when studied prospectively, desistance appears faltering, uncertain and punctuated by relapse. Most of the sample did not completely desist from offending although there was definite evidence that the average frequency of offending had significantly reduced. Interestingly, the qualitative data from this study stressed the significance of the onset of adulthood and the realisation that the advent of new roles might require a change of lifestyle.

Table 3.1 Three models of desistance processes

Giordano et al. (2002)	Vaughan (2007)	SPooCS (ongoing)
1 General cognitive openness to change	1 Discernment: review of possible lifestyle choices	1 Current offending is influenced by a triggering event
2 Exposure to 'hooks for change'	2 Deliberation: review of pros and cons of various options (a comparison of possible selves)	2 The decision to try to change
3 Availability of an appealing conventional self		3 The offender thinks differently about himself
4 Reassessment of attitudes to deviant behaviour	3 Dedication: commitment to a new non-criminal identity	4 The offender to take action towards desistance
		5 Maintenance: the offender looks for reinforcers but may encounter obstacles

Others have tried to delineate or model processes of desistance (see Table 3.1). In conceptualising the first stages of desistance, Giordano *et al.* (2002) discuss the significance of 'openness to change', while Vaughan (2007: 393) posits an initial stage of 'discernment' where one 'reviews possible choices and puts them beside our multiple, persisting concerns around which one has hitherto structured a life dominated by crime'. Here Vaughan suggests that 'a pre-requisite for change, then, is that the agent is at least willing to consider different options' (2007: 394). Probation staff might more readily identify this as the 'contemplation' stage of Prochaska and DiClemente's 'cycle of change' (Prochaska *et al.* 1992).

The SPooCS authors suggest a five-stage model of the desistance process: current offending is influenced by a triggering event; which leads to the decision to try to change; which leads the offender to think differently about himself; which leads the offender to take action towards desistance; which requires maintenance – the offender looks for reinforcers but may encounter obstacles. Findings from SPooCS confirmed that new and strengthening social bonds appeared to be linked to successful desistance, but with the desire to change being critical and central to this. Indeed, this would appear to mirror Giordano *et al.*'s (2002) suggested second stage in their theory of cognitive transformation, which the authors view as central to the process of desistance, namely 'exposure to a particular hook or set of hooks for change' (2002: 1000) and 'one's attitude toward [it]' (2002: 1001). Additionally, the SPooCS team discovered that empathy seemed to increase over time, manifesting in the need to take into account others' feelings, a sensitivity that the authors consider as an emerging feature in moving towards desistance. Again, this process is reflected in what Vaughan (2007) terms 'the second stage of *deliberation*'. 'What gets accomplished here is a review of the pros and cons of potential courses of action and a comparison with sticking in a well worn groove of custom. What ultimately emerges is a comparison of selves – who one is and who one wishes to be' (Vaughan 2007: 394); or, as Giordano *et al.* (2002: 1001) put it, the envisioning of 'an appealing and conventional replacement self'. Vaughan (2007) emphasises that there is an influential emotional component to this comparative process which involves thinking about the reactions and feelings of others and envisaging how one's current self or identity is perceived by others.

In similar vein, Maruna and Farrall (2004: 27–8) explain that:

> a lull can turn into secondary desistance when two things happen. First, the person finds a source of agency and communion in non-criminal activities. They find some sort of 'calling' – be it parenthood, painting, coaching, chess or what Sennett (2003) calls 'craft-love'[2] – through which they find meaning and purpose outside of crime ... The second part of our desistance formula, like that of Lemert's deviance theory, involves societal reaction. The desisting person's change in behavior is sometimes recognised by others and reflected back to him in a 'delabeling process'. (Trice and Roman 1970)

The authors of the SPooCS study, in discussing their five-stage model, suggest that failure to maintain desistance in the face of obstacles may lead to relapse and a return to the beginning of the cycle (as similarly implied by Burnett 1992).[3] Healy and O'Donnell (2008), citing Vaughan (2007), propose that:

> even when offenders have nominally dedicated themselves to a new non-criminal identity, they may still experience setbacks as they negotiate their way from a criminal lifestyle with its associated benefits and demands to a completely new way of being. In the chaotic, uncertain times of primary desistance, their long-term goals may become temporarily sidelined. (Healy and O'Donnell 2008: 35)

In secondary desistance, however, crime not only stops, but 'existing roles become disrupted' and a 'reorganisation based upon a new role or roles will occur' (Lemert 1951: 76); 'desistance does involve identifiable and measurable changes at the level of personal identity or the "me" of the individual' (Maruna *et al.* 2004b: 274). The SPooCS authors themselves ultimately concede that successful maintenance and reinforcement in the face of obstacles may result in the adoption of a crime-free identity as a non-offender. It is in this secondary desistance phase that Vaughan's (2007) tertiary and final stage of 'dedication' might be positioned. He argues that to establish desistance, agents must regard their commitment to their new identity as incompatible with ongoing criminality and regard criminality as 'morally incompatible with whom they wish to be' (Vaughan 2007: 394). Indeed, the individual experiences at this juncture the fourth stage in Giordano *et al.*'s (2002: 1002) four-part theory of cognitive transformation: 'a transformation in the way the actor views the deviant behaviour or lifestyle itself'.

Healy and O'Donnell's (2008) Irish study lends further weight to the foregoing arguments. The authors studied Irish male probationers who were in an early stage of the change process and who were comparable in age with the SPooCS sample. They found that while their narratives contained a high level of motivation and modest goal aspirations in relation to the acquisition of employment or in reference to relationships, they contained little evidence of agency or generative concerns consistent with notions of secondary desistance. Healy and O'Donnell propose that their findings therefore support the view that, at least in the early stages of change, while ex-offenders do not necessarily possess a strong sense of agency, the development of social bonds may be intermediate goals that indirectly lead to desistance. The authors suggest these goals in turn forge new commitments, which then perhaps invoke a sense of an agentic self, result in a new identity and a focus on a different and possibly more altruistic set of goals.

Developing our understanding of this highly nuanced process of change is critical to both the appropriate targeting and the focus of probation (and wider criminal justice) interventions. As research contributes more to our grasp of the complexities of the sequencing of desistance processes, so probation interventions need to become rooted in much more careful assessments of where people are in the process, and what specific measures of support and encouragement may be appropriate at this moment in the unfolding but fragile process. To borrow a navigational analogy, unless and until we can locate our position on a map, we cannot plan our route. Similarly interventions that fail to locate the offender properly in the desistance process will be at best misconceived and at worst damaging. The challenge for creative practitioners, therefore, is to find new ways and means of engaging offenders and of working with them to identify where they are in relation to the desistance journey, as well as how to move forward.

But, extending the analogy, it is not enough to locate the offender in the change process; it is also necessary to locate the process in its social and cultural context. To fail to do so is to try to guide or support the journey with no awareness of the terrain through which it travels. Yet, to date, much of the literature on desistance has focused on the dynamics of desistance in relation to white men. Indeed the relationship between class, culture, ethnicity, gender, religion, spirituality and desistance has received notably limited attention. We turn now to examine the extant literature addressing some of these areas and to considering the implications.

Gender, desistance and creative practice

Despite its focus on white men, desistance research has paid surprisingly little attention to questions of masculinities. Gadd and Farrall (2004: 128) argue:

> For critical gender theorists, men's symbolic and material dependence on the nuclear family is heavily implicated in the self-same social relationships and structures that routinely reproduce patterns of male delinquency and sexual inequalities more generally (Connell 1995: ch. 5). However, this point has largely escaped the attentions of those exploring desistance from crime.

They observe that the literature, while underlining the significance of work and family life, neglects to consider 'the gendered nature of men's places within these spheres, and is hence often devoid of an analysis of power, wider social consequences and the complexity of meaning that social and personal relationships have for the people in question' (Gadd and Farrall 2004: 131). Gadd and Farrall illustrate how the structure of meanings on which men draw are embedded in a wider network of social discourses that are themselves structured by gender, race and class; in this context, individuals invest in those discursive positions that assist them to make sense of their experience. They suggest that to understand men's involvement in crime and desistance, attention needs to be paid to how men's anxieties and fears are shaped by social discourses and by contradictory and conflicting social expectations about what it is to be a 'man'. This would suggest a need for creative practice with men to attempt to explore men's specific subjective experiences of their masculinities; to explore social discourses and expectations about what it is to be a man and how these manifest in relations between men, and in relations between men and women; and to put forward alternative ways of accomplishing masculinity and identity (Gelsthorpe and McIvor 2007).

The significance of gendered social expectations emerged in a Scottish study of youthful offending (McIvor et al. 2000) which explored desistance among three groups of young people aged 14–15, 18–19 and 22–25 (see also Jamieson et al. 1999). They conducted interviews with a total of 75 'desisters' (43 male and 32 female) and 109 young people (59 male and 50 female) who were still offending or had done so recently. In the youngest group, desistance for both boys and girls was associated with the real or potential consequences of offending and with the growing recognition that offending was pointless or wrong. Young people in the middle age group similarly related their changing behaviour to increasing maturity, often linked to the transition to adulthood and related events like securing a job or place at college or university, or entering into a relationship with a partner or leaving home. For the oldest group, 'desistance was encouraged the assumption of family responsibilities, especially among young women, or by a conscious lifestyle change' (McIvor *et al.* 2000: 9). In general, the young women tended to attribute their decisions to desist to the assumption of parental responsibilities, whereas the young men focused on personal choice and agency. Among persisters, girls and young women were more often keen to be seen as desisters, perhaps reflecting societal disapproval of female offending. McIvor *et al.* (2000: 9) speculate that:

> Assigning the offending to the past rather than acknowledging it as a current or future reality may enable young women to better cope with the tensions that may arise when, on the one hand, society encourages gender equality and, on the other, continues to double condemn young women who step beyond their traditional gender roles.

Graham and Bowling's (1995) earlier study of young people aged 14–25 found similar gender differences. They noted a clear association between the transition from adolescence to adulthood and desistance from offending among young women. Young men, in contrast, were less likely to achieve independence and those that did leave home, formed partnerships and had children were no more likely to desist than those that did not. Graham and Bowling (1995: 65) speculate that life transitions 'only provide opportunities for change to occur; its realisation is mediated by individual contingencies. Males may be less inclined to grasp, or be able to take advantage of such opportunities, as females.' More recent studies have revised this conclusion to some extent, suggesting that similar processes of change do indeed occur for (some) males but that they seem to take longer to 'kick-in'; positive effects of the assumption of responsibilities in and through intimate relationships and employment are more notable in men aged 25 and over (Flood-Page *et al.* 2000; Farrall and Bowling 1999; Uggen and Kruttschnitt 1988). Thus, it seems that young men take longer to grasp the opportunities for change that these life transitions provide.

Interestingly, Giordano *et al.* (2002: 1052) suggest that despite the commonalities between males and females in their accounts of their change processes, women were more likely than men to cite 'religious conversions' and parenthood as catalysts for change. This is broadly compatible with Rumgay's (2004) theorisation of women's processes of desistance as rooted in the recognition of an opportunity to claim an alternative, desired and socially approved personal identity. Certain common identities, she suggests, such as that of a mother, may provide a 'script' by which to enact a conventional pro-social role, serving to enhance the individual's confidence in their ability to enact it successfully. This success in turn positively affects the woman's sense of self-efficacy and, alongside the deployment of other skills and strategies, assists in perpetuating the newly acquired identity (see also Maruna and Roy 2007; Giordano *et al.* 2007).

Essentially, there would appear to be some consensus that women's desistance is related to what may be broadly construed as investment in relational commitments, manifesting in generative concerns and the assumption of responsibility (Barry 2007). These include marriage, familial and parental responsibilities, awareness of peer, familial and societal disapproval, commitment to religious beliefs, concerns surrounding the consequences of continued offending and threat of consequent punishment and desistance from substance abuse (see Jamieson *et al.* 1999; McIvor 2007; Barry 2007).

Taken together, this evidence would appear to suggest the need for creative practice that supports women's efforts to change through the provision of services which take account of the realities of their lives, of what is important to them and of the social demands placed upon them (see Gelsthorpe and McIvor 2007; McIvor 2007); practices that provide practical and emotional support to them in meeting those responsibilities and commitments that are significant to them. This might include addressing, for example, housing and financial problems, assistance with childcare, access to meaningful education and employment opportunities, and support to strengthen social and familial support networks. Creative practice would be focused on empowering women to take control of their lives by being able to access opportunities not only to increase their capacity to accumulate (social) capital, but to expend capital. Barry (2007) identified this as critical to the desistance process for women, in terms of generative concerns (such as ensuring their children's welfare, making restitution to their local community) and the assumption of responsibility (such as employment or familial responsibilities). But equally creative practice must avoid inappropriately universalised or stereotypical assumptions about women's relational commitments, generative concerns or socially valorised desires to assume caring responsibilities. Other pathways to desistance need to be opened up and supported for women who chose other ways to realise their femininities.

Ethnicity, desistance and creative practice

While gender has been a neglected area, research on the relationships between ethnicity, 'race' and desistance has been even more limited to date. Some relevant studies have been conducted in the United States (Elliot 1994; Rand 1987; Hughes 1997, 1998). Elliot (1994), for example, studied offenders between ages 24 and 30 and found that white offenders desisted earlier than black offenders. Elliot speculated that contextual differences, for example in a person's workplace or living environments, might explain this phenomenon. Pager's (2003) research, conducted in Milwaukee, found that people from minority ethnic communities may face additional barriers to desistance from offending. Pager found that ex-offenders were only one-half to one-third as likely as non-offenders to be considered for employment, confirming that a criminal record presented a major barrier to obtaining employment. Furthermore, and of particular significance, Pager found that African-American ex-offenders were less than half as likely to be considered by employers than their white counterparts, and that African-American *non-offenders* fell behind even white ex-offenders. Thus, additional obstacles faced by minority ethnic offenders as a result of racism seem likely to hinder and frustrate their processes of desistance.

Bracken *et al.* (2009) examined the interplay between structural constraints and individual choice in the desistance pathways of male Canadian aboriginal gang members, with particular consideration given to their economic and social marginalisation, over-representation in the criminal justice system, and to issues of culture, history and identity. Their study underlines the significance both of increasing social capital as a mechanism for overcoming structural constraints and of reacquisition of and reconnection to a culture that can be seen as a mediating force between structure and agency. They conclude that for these young males successful desistance involves more than a decision to cease engagement in criminality and access to education or employment opportunities. It requires supporting individuals to comprehend and internally reconcile their experiences of social injustice and trauma and to assist them to reconnect with their aboriginal identities, traditions and culture.

In the UK, there is evidence that black and minority ethnic people (and particularly those of African or Caribbean origin) are over-represented in British prison populations, and indeed in the criminal justice system more broadly, compounding the disadvantage that they encounter economically, educationally and in terms of employment (Calverley *et al.* 2004, 2006; Sharp *et al.* 2006). Calverley's (2009) important exploratory qualitative investigation examined the various dynamics underpinning the process of desistance for 33 male offenders of Indian, Bangladeshi, and black and dual heritage ethnic origin resident in London. Calverley identified distinct variations in the pathways to desistance between the three groups, particularly at the level of family and community. For the Indian participants, desistance was influenced by their families' 'aspirational values' and greater access to economic, employment and educational resources, while the Bangladeshi participants' families showed a willingness to offer acceptance and forgiveness connected to strongly held religious values. Returning to religious roots and building an identity through renewed religiosity represented a viable strategy for these men. Calverley argues that for men in both of these ethnic groups, desistance was typically a more collective experience involving their families *actively* intervening, constructively and supportively, in their lives; in turn their desistance involved an expectation that they would follow particular norms of behaviour and adopt the same beliefs and values system as their families. In contrast, black and dual heritage participants experienced a much more individualised and isolated process of change. For them desistance seemed to necessitate their disengagement from previous social relationships, developing a structured lifestyle and independently initiating steps towards 'self-improvement'. This suggests the existence of what Calverley, citing Deane *et al.* (2007), refers to as different 'cultures of desistance' among different ethnic groups (Calverley 2009: 302). While desistance for all three groups seemed to require the adoption of different lifestyles, he found that the social context inhabited by black and dual heritage desisters was more problematic and more likely to hamper desistance, compared with experiences of Indian and Bangladeshi participants.

In general terms, Calverley found that the factors correlated with desistance reflected those identified elsewhere in the desistance literature: access to social capital, engagement in social institutions, the significance of social bonds to family and employment. These factors were identified as impacting the desistance process across all three groups. While he found that ethnicity in itself neither caused nor impeded desistance, his findings emphasise that ethnicity indexes significant structural differences which have implications for the operation of processes of desistance in terms of 'the availability of resources, opportunities and pathways out of crime, which in turn affect the expectations and actions of desisters themselves' (Calverley 2009: 308). Thus, while the three ethnic groups 'shared the same fundamental mechanisms responsible for promoting desistance, the socio-structural and socio-cultural differences between them affected how, when and where these mechanisms operated' (Calverley 2009: 219). Again, this underlines the significance of attending to both the socio-structural location and the cultural contexts within which desistance takes places.

Calverley's study evidences how desistance from crime is not solely a within-and-between individual phenomenon, but is also dependent on interactions between the individual and their immediate environment, community and social structure. This reinforces the need for creative practices that attend and adapt to the social and cultural contexts that offenders and their families inhabit and work to maximise the potential contribution of individual and community resources to supporting desistance and reintegration. Clearly, though, within the inevitable constraints of these social structures, it remains necessary to respect and support the individual's right to determine both how they define their ethnic and cultural identity and to what extent they wish to engage with family and community in their process of change. Practice approaches need to remain sensitive to the heterogeneity both across and within ethnicities, cultures and ethnic and cultural identities.

Religion, spirituality and creative practice

Sharp *et al.*'s analysis (2006) of the resettlement needs of black and minority ethnic offenders identified gaps in the types of support that they were more inclined to seek and to which they were more inclined to respond. They also reported that a number of service providers highlighted the significance of religion for many black and minority ethnic offenders, both in the emphasis on religion evident in their upbringing and as a feature of their familial and cultural traditions. Within prisons some black and minority offenders identified that certain needs were not being met due to security constraints or resource restrictions. Often this related to dietary requirements and accessing time and space to attend to religious practices.

Marranci[4] spent four years investigating the impact of imprisonment on Muslim identity and the effect of imprisonment on prisoners' experiences of Islam, from a sample of approximately 175 Muslim former and current prisoners across Scotland, England and Wales (Marranci 2009 forthcoming; also 2007). Marranci demonstrated that Muslim ex-prisoners encountered particular issues distinct from the non-Muslim population, yet there was little evidence of considered strategic approaches to addressing their particular resettlement needs. Muslim ex-prisoners received less support than non-Muslims in terms of accommodation and less assistance reintegrating into the community. For many current and former Muslim prisoners, in particular for those involved in alcohol or drug use,[5] their ostracism from their community and sometimes their own families served to increase the isolation they experienced (Marranci 2008); ex-prisoners often found themselves rejected from mosques due to fears surrounding allegations of extremism (Marranci 2007). Given the significance of social bonds and social ties to desistance, such experiences may present additional obstacles to desistance. Where familial support was available, Marranci explained that prison visits presented further difficulties. Muslim women were discouraged from attending prisons due not least to different cultural forms of attire and the desire to avoid drawing unwarranted attention to themselves, which had implications for the maintenance of significant relationships during periods of incarceration (Marranci 2008).

Marranci's study also illustrates how, for a number of interrelated reasons, Muslims often rediscover Islam within prison (Marranci 2007).

Among those reasons is the desire to repent and to make good, presenting (in Giordano *et al.*'s (2002) term), a 'hook for change' as they 'reconsider their life and link their experience of prison not to human punishment but to an opportunity granted by Allah to change their life' (Marranci 2007: 8). Marranci (2006) elucidates a theory of identity as encompassing two functions – it allows human beings to make sense of their autobiographical self and it allows them to express that self through symbols that communicate feelings that could not otherwise be externally communicated (see also Marranci 2007). Marranci (2007: 8) proceeds to differentiate between Islam as 'an act of identity' and Islam 'as an act of faith'. He argues that Muslims in prison often see Islam more as an act of identity than of faith:

> The act of identity is used to re-establish equilibrium within the autobiographical self and the surrounding environment. Prisoners in general, because of the prison environment and the small community in which they live, develop a strong viewpoint . . . some of them tend to develop an essentialist view of Islam based on radical dualism: Islamic versus non-Islamic. (Marranci 2007: 8)

This is heightened where Muslim prisoners suffer greater security surveillance than other inmates; he found that such intrusions were particularly directed at those who adopted religious symbols or cultural objects or exhibited a strong commitment to religious rituals and practices, at least where this was interpreted by prison authorities as evidence of radicalisation (Marranci 2007). He explains that security policies within prisons, including restricting praying in a communal space (see also Sharp *et al.* 2006) or reading the Qur'an during work breaks, effectively exacerbate rather than suppress radicalisation insofar as such attitudes, underpinned by a misrepresentative conflation of Islam with terrorism in the mass media, serves to increase the isolation and feelings of persecution experienced by Muslim prisoners. The combined effects of their experiences of incarceration, criminal justice processes and associated ostracism can lead towards disenfranchisement and anger towards a state that they perceive as oppressive and discriminatory. This experience can leave Muslim ex-prisoners vulnerable to recidivism and, for a minority, radicalisation.

Nonetheless, drawing on the findings of Bracken *et al.* (2009) and Calverley (2009), we might infer that the rediscovery of Islam has the potential to assist Muslim offenders to reconnect with their religious identities, traditions and culture so as to support their efforts to change. As Marranci (2007) suggests, this depends to an extent on the willingness of mosques, Islamic institutes and the wider Muslim community to offer support to former offenders. Of course, Islamophobic attitudes in the wider community also need to be challenged. Services need to recognise and engage with the multiplicity of communities in society, to pursue meaningful and sustained engagement with those communities and to recognise the important role of religious institutions as a resource within communities.

Maruna et al.'s analysis (2006) of the life story interviews of 75 male prisoners provides an insight into the dynamics of conversion to Christianity within prison that resonates with some aspects of Marranci's study. The authors argue that the prison environment, within which one is removed from all that is familiar and typically stripped of one's identity, is precisely the type of environment in which self-identity is likely to be called into question. As such, prisoners are 'particularly open to new ways of perceiving themselves and organising their lives' (Maruna et al. 2006: 163). Maruna et al. (2006: 161) suggest that conversion enables the prisoner to create:

> a new social identity to replace the label of criminal, [it] imbues the experience of imprisonment with purpose and meaning, [it] empowers the largely powerless prisoner by turning him into an agent of God, [it] provides the prisoner with a language and a framework for forgiveness and allows a sense of control over an unknown future.

For Maruna et al.'s respondents, their experiences of prison led them to consider:

> fundamental questions about life, death, meaning and the individual's place in the world. Not only did they seek a framework through which to interpret and attribute meaning to events they had experienced, they also sought one that would provide answers to their questions and give them ways to move forward and construct a new, positive life and self-identity. (Maruna et al. 2006: 173)

Thus, like Marranci, Maruna et al. (2006) conceptualise conversion as a process of reinterpretation of one's autobiographical self, in some respects a change process analogous to the identity transformations underpinning the process of desistance more generally. However, perhaps the unique contribution that the commitment to a form of religion may offer is a 'cognitive blueprint for how one is to proceed as a changed individual' (Giordano et al. 2007: 4); a blueprint found in the prescriptions and teachings associated with that faith, upon which the individual can draw as they embark on the process of desistance and encounter new situations and experiences. To return to the navigational analogy, religion provides a sort of map to identity transformation.

Giordano et al.'s longitudinal study (2007) allowed the authors to identify variations in ex-offenders' life circumstances that assisted them to specify the particular conditions under which commitment to religion was positively associated with desistance or otherwise. Their analysis high-lighted the importance of differentiating between respondents who describe a generally positive orientation towards religion and those who make a specific cognitive connection such that they regard their attachment to religion as incompatible with involvement in criminality, resonant of Giordano *et al.*'s fourth stage in their theory of cognitive transformation (2002, discussed above). As we have outlined previously, and as the authors demonstrate, the presence of a pro-social bond in and of itself does not appear to be sufficient to trigger or sustain desistance; rather it is the strength, quality and meaning that the social bond has for the individual (Giordano *et al.* 2007). Thus a deep and intense connection to religion may be essential if it is to exert sufficient influence to sustain the individual through the difficult process of change and if it is to facilitate identity or cognitive self-transformation associated with secondary desistance.

Indeed, in their analysis of the narratives of respondents who exhibited such a deep personal connection to Christianity, Giordano *et al.* (2007) observed a shared emphasis on the role of positive emotional changes that their attachment to Christianity heralded. Christianity was considered to inject life with meaning, to provide a source of emotional capital and thus a key resource upon which to draw in the face of stressful circumstances. Respondents not only referred to important inner personal changes in their feelings towards themselves but also to changes in their stance, attitudes or feelings towards the external world. For some respondents, their new-found commitment to religion enabled the development of different forms of social capital in terms of the consolidation or reparation of existing relationships, particularly where such relationships reinforced or affirmed their religious commitments, and the development of new relationships and social networks through affiliation to religious institutions or faith groups (see also Chu 2007 in terms of desistance from drug use).

However, Giordano *et al.* (2007) highlight that while some people may be favourably disposed towards religion, unless the associated ideologies, ideas and practices resonate with the individual, it is unlikely to act as a catalyst for change. In addition, even where a strong attachment to religion pertains, ex-offenders are often disadvantaged on multiple levels, and have social networks that are similarly disadvantaged, and they may encounter an array of what they experience as insurmountable obstacles that may overwhelm the individual and overshadow the positive effects that commitment to religion may provide, perhaps hastening a return to more familiar coping strategies, which may include substance use or a return to criminality.

Just as creative practice requires practitioners to engage with how individuals construct their identities, masculinities, femininities and ethnicities, so it requires practitioners to open up lines of enquiry and resources for desistance that may reside in religiosity and/or spirituality. The evidence above suggests that this is about both identity transformations and the development of social networks that may support them. Just as with the other aspects of identity discussed above, this is not merely a matter of the individual's subjective experience of these aspects of identity; it is as much about the social, structural and cultural conditions that conspire to make these aspects of our identities assets or liabilities in the desistance process.

Conclusion

We noted at the outset of this chapter that desistance research has already had a significant impact on debates about probation policy and practice, and that two of the key messages arising from this developing dialogue related to the reassertion of the significance of relationships (both personal and working relationships) in the change process, and the reassertion of the significance of the social context of that process. The research findings that we have reviewed in this chapter serve to strengthen these arguments, but they add new dimensions of complexity to debates about how to integrate the insights of desistance research into approaches to offender rehabilitation. None of the research that we have reviewed overturns the central and general messages of desistance research; the desistance process seems to have common elements for all or at least most people – developing maturity, the emergence of new social ties that hold particular subjective significance for the individuals concerned and, sometimes, a renegotiation of personal identity.

However, when we look more closely at the evidence around gender differences, ethnic differences and the significance of religion, we find clear evidence that the common elements of the process can be very differently experienced and constituted, depending on the socio-structural, cultural and spiritual positions that people occupy and move through as they negotiate their personal and social lives. The central practical implication of this insight – which may be obvious but which we think needed to be evidenced – is that no rehabilitative intervention that aims to support desistance can expect to succeed if it lacks sufficient sensitivity to these diversity issues. To revisit again the navigational analogy that we used in thinking about where a person might be situated in the temporal process of desistance, you simply can't help someone get to where they want to go if you don't understand where they are now. Understanding where they started, how far and how fast they have come, grasping the significance of the terrain through which they have travelled and on which they now stand, as well as the nature of the terrain and the likely pleasures and pains of the journey ahead – all of these are essential aspects of being an effective guide.

But to extend the analogy still further, if creative practice is to be critical practice, it needs to include but also extend beyond supporting the individual's journey through a seemingly determined and fixed terrain. Creative practice needs to be about more than navigating the way over, under, around or through obstacles – sometimes it needs to be about confronting and removing them. Thus, while it involves a constructivist approach that respects and engages positively and respectfully with the development of personal narratives, it also requires a commitment to challenge forms of oppression that devalue certain identities while overvaluing others. To focus solely on overcoming these obstacles at the individual level runs the risk of accepting the world as it is, thus colluding with the social structures and attitudes that diminish the resources for desistance available to marginalised groups. It is here that for practice to be truly creative it must be destructive.

We are acutely aware that this chapter has said much more about theory and research than it has about practice, and that those few suggestions we have made about creative practice have been abstract and generalised at best. To some extent, this is a product of our own trajectories and positions as academic researchers, perhaps no longer best placed to engage with such questions, but it also reflects a principled resistance to the temptation to simply prescribe practice approaches on the basis of desistance (or indeed any) research. Perhaps one of the lessons we can learn from the history of 'what works' in probation is that we should see research not as dictating practice but as a resource for practice; in the context of desistance research, a resource that challenges practitioners by elaborating our understanding of the processes it exists to support (McNeill 2009) – and our specific aspiration here has been to provide a chapter that functions more as a resource on which creative practitioners can draw than as a statement of what creative practice may be. Answering that question depends on the kind of dialogue that this book exists to stimulate.

Notes

1   www.scopic.ac.uk/StudiesSPooCS.html
2   Maruna and Farrall (2004: 28) explain that 'much criminal behaviour is maintained by rewards that are extrinsic (status, riches) or fleeting (the buzz of a drug). The discovery of an alternative, intrinsic rewarding pursuit can be a necessary, but not sufficient component of the successful abstinence from such highs'. The authors offer the example from Sennett (2003) who referred to his own cello playing in his adolescence as an example of 'craft love', describing the manner in which this activity provided him with a pleasure in itself, for itself and a sense of self-worth that wasn't dependent on anyone or anything external.

3 For many this will again evoke images of Prochaska and DiClemente's cycles of change (Prochaska *et al.* 1994).
4 Marranci's findings will be published in his forthcoming book *Faith, Ideology and Fear: Muslim Identities within and Beyond Prisons* (Continuum).
5 Many Muslim prisoners denied any difficulties they were experiencing with substance misuse for fear of rejection, which presented an additional barrier to accessing the relevant support services.

References

Barry, M. (2000) 'The Mentor/Monitor Debate in Criminal Justice: What Works for Offenders', *British Journal of Social Work*, 30 (5): 575–95.

Barry, M. (2007) 'The Transitional Pathways of Young Female Offenders: Towards a Non-Offending Lifestyle', in R. Sheehan, G. McIvor and C. Trotter (eds) *What Works with Women Offenders*. Cullompton: Willan Publishing.

Bottoms, A. and Wiles, P. (1992) 'Explanations of Crime and Place', in D. J. Evans, N. R. Fyfe and D. T. Herbert (eds) *Crime, Policing and Place*. London: Routledge.

Bottoms, A., Shapland, J., Costello, A., Holmes, D. and Mair, G. (2004) 'Towards Desistance: Theoretical Underpinnings for an Empirical Study', *Howard Journal of Criminal Justice*, 43 (4): 368–89.

Bracken, D. C., Deane, L. and Morrissette, L. (2009) 'Desistance and Social Marginalization: The Case of Canadian Aboriginal Offenders', *Theoretical Criminology*, 13 (1): 61–78.

Burnett, R. (1992) *The Dynamics of Recidivism*. Oxford: Centre for Criminological Research, University of Oxford.

Burnett, R. (2004) 'One-to-One Ways of Promoting Desistance: In Search of an Evidence Base', in R. Burnett and C. Roberts (eds) *What Works in Probation and Youth Justice*. Cullompton: Willan Publishing.

Burnett, R. and McNeill, F. (2005) 'The Place of the Officer – Offender Relationship in Assisting Offenders to Desist from Crime', *Probation Journal*, 52 (3): 247–68.

Calverley, A. (2009) 'An Exploratory Investigation into the Processes of Desistance Amongst Minority Ethnic Offenders', unpublished PhD dissertation.

Calverley, A., Cole, B., Gurpreet, K., Lewis, S., Raynor, P., Sadeghi, S., Smith, D., Vanstone, M. and Wardak, A. (2004) *Black and Asian Offenders on Probation*, Home Office Research Study 277. London: Home Office.

Calverley, A., Cole, B., Gurpreet, K., Lewis, S., Raynor, P., Sadeghi, S., Smith, D., Vanstone, M. and Wardak, A. (2006) 'Black and Asian Probationers: Implications of the Home Office Study', *Probation Journal*, 53 (1): 24–37.

Chu, D. (2007) 'Religiosity and Desistance from Drug Use', *Criminal Justice and Behaviour Online First*, 7 March 2007.

Connell, R. W. (1995) *Masculinities*. Cambridge: Polity Press.

Deane, L., Bracken, D. and Morrisette, L. (2007) 'Desistance within an Urban Aboriginal Gang', *Probation Journal*, 54 (2): 125–41.

Elliot, D. (1994) 'Serious Violent Offenders: Onset, Developmental Course and Termination', American Society of Criminology (1993) Presidential Address, *Criminology*, 32: 1–22.

Farrall, S. (2002) *Rethinking What Works with Offenders: Probation, Social Context and Desistance from Crime*. Cullompton: Willan Publishing.

Farrall, S. and Bowling, B. (1999) 'Structuration, Human Development and Desistance from Crime', *British Journal of Criminology*, 39 (2): 253–68.

Field, J. (2008) *Social Capital*, 2nd edn. London: Taylor and Francis.

Flood-Page, C., Campbell, S., Harrington, V. and Miller, J. (2000) *Youth Crime: Findings from the 1998/99 Youth Lifestyles Survey*, Home Office Research Study 209. London: Home Office.

Gadd, D. and Farrall, S. (2004) 'Criminal Careers, Desistance and Subjectivity: Interpreting Men's Narratives of Change', *Theoretical Criminology* 8 (2): 123–56.

Gelsthorpe, L. and McIvor, G. (2007) 'Difference and Diversity in Probation', in L. Gelsthorpe and R. Morgan (eds) *Handbook of Probation*. Willan Publishing: Cullompton.

Giddens, A. (1984) *The Constitution of Society*. Cambridge: Polity Press.

Giordano, P. C., Cernokovich, S. A. and Rudolph, J. L. (2002) 'Gender, Crime and Desistance: Toward a Theory of Cognitive Transformation', *American Journal of Sociology*, 107: 990–1064.

Giordano, P. C., Longmore, M. A., Schroeder, R. D. and Seffrin, P. M. (2007) *A Life Course Perspective on Spirituality and Desistance From Crime*, Center for Family and Demographic Research. Working Paper Series 07–07.

Glaser, D. (1964) *Effectiveness of a Prison and Parole System*. Indianapolis, IN: Bobbs-Merrill.

Gorman, K., Gregory, M., Hayles, M. and Parton, N. (eds) (2006) *Constructive Work with Offenders*. London: Jessica Kingsley.

Graham, J. and Bowling, B. (1995) *Young People and Crime*, Home Office Research Study 145. London: HMSO.

Healy, D. and O'Donnell, I. (2008) 'Calling Time on Crime: Motivation, Generativity and Agency in Irish Probationers', *Probation Journal*, 55 (1): 25–38.

Holt, P. (2000) 'Case Management: Context for Supervision', *Community and Criminal Justice: Monograph 2*. Leicester: De Montfort University.

Hopkinson, J. and Rex, S. (2003) 'Essential Skills in Working with Offenders', in W. H. Chui and M. Nellis (eds) *Moving Probation Forward: Evidence, Arguments and Practice*. Harlow: Pearson Education.

Hughes, M. (1997) 'An Exploratory Study of Young Adult Black and Latino Males and the Factors Facilitating their Decisions to Make Positive Behavioural Changes', *Smith College Studies in Social Work*, 67 (3): 401–14.

Hughes, M. (1998) 'Turning Points in the Lives of Young Inner-City Men Forgoing Destructive Criminal Behaviours: A Qualitative Study', *Social Work Research*, 22: 143–51.

Jamieson, J., McIvor, G. and Murray, C. (1999) *Understanding Offending Among Young People*. Edinburgh: Scottish Executive.

LeBel, T. P., Burnett, R., Maruna, S. and Bushway, S. (2008) 'The "Chicken and Egg" of Subjective and Social Factors in Desistance From Crime', *European Journal of Criminology*, 5 (2): 131–59.

Leibrich, J. (1993) *Straight to the Point: Angles on Giving Up Crime*. Otago, New Zealand: University of Otago Press.

Leibrich, J. (1994) 'What Do Offenders Say About Going Straight?' *Federal Probation*, 58: 41–6.

Lemert, E. M. (1951) *Social Pathology: Systematic Approaches to the Study of Sociopathic Behaviour*. New York: McGraw-Hill.

McCulloch, P. (2005) 'Probation, Social Context and Desistance: Retracing the Relationship', *Probation Journal*, 52 (1): 8–22.

McIvor, G. (2007) 'The Nature of Female Offending', in R. Sheehan, G. McIvor and C. Trotter (eds) *What Works with Women Offenders*. Cullompton: Willan Publishing.

McIvor, G., Jamieson, J. and Murray, C. (2000) 'Study Examines Gender Differences in Desistance From Crime', *Offender Programs Report*, 4 (1): 5–9.

McNeill, F. (2006) 'A Desistance Paradigm for Offender Management', *Criminology and Criminal Justice*, 6 (1): 39–62.

McNeill, F. (2009) *Towards Effective Practice in Offender Supervision*. Glasgow: Scottish Centre for Crime and Justice Research. Available at www.sccjr.ac.uk/documents/McNeil_Towards.pdf.

McNeill, F. and Maruna, S. (2007) 'Giving Up and Giving Back: Desistance, Generativity and Social Work with Offenders', in G. McIvor and P. Raynor (eds) *Developments in Social Work with Offenders: Research Highlights in Social Work 48*. London: Jessica Kingsley.

McNeill, F. and Whyte, B. (2007) *Reducing Reoffending: Social Work and Community Justice in Scotland*. Cullompton: Willan Publishing.

McNeill, F., Batchelor, S., Burnett, S. and Knox, J. (2005) *21st Century Social Work. Reducing Reoffending: Key Practice Skills*. Edinburgh: Scottish Executive.

Marranci, G. (2006) *Jihad Beyond Islam*. Oxford/New York: Berg.

Marranci, G. (2007) 'Faith Ideology and Fear: The Case of Current and Former Muslim Prisoners', IQRA Annual Lecture: House of Lords, 26 June 2007.

Marranci, G. (2008) 'Resettlement of Ethnic Minority Offenders', CEP Conference, 'Life After Prison: Resettling Adult Offenders', University of Glasgow (April). Available at www.cepprobation.org/uploaded_files/rep%20Gla%2008.pdf.

Marranci, G. (2009 forthcoming) *Faith, Ideology and Fear: Muslim Identities Within and Beyond Prisons*. Continuum.

Maruna, S. (1997) 'Going Straight: Desistance from Crime and Life Narratives of Reform', *The Narrative Study of Lives*, 5: 59–93.

Maruna, S. (2000) 'Desistance From Crime and Offender Rehabilitation: A Tale of Two Research Literatures', *Offender Programs Report*, 4 (1): 1–13.

Maruna, S. (2001) *Making Good: How Ex-Convicts Reform and Rebuild their Lives*. Washington, DC: American Psychological Association Books.

Maruna, S. and Farrall, S. (2004) 'Desistance from Crime: A Theoretical Reformulation', *Kolner Zeitschrift fur Soziologie und Sozialpsychologie*, 43.

Maruna, S. and LeBel, T. (2003) 'Welcome Home? Examining the "Re-entry Court" Concept from a Strengths-Based Perspective', *Western Criminology Review*, 4 (2): 91–107.

Maruna, S., Immarigeon, R., and LeBel, T. (2004a) 'Ex-Offender Reintegration: Theory and Practice', in S. Maruna and R. Immarigeon (eds) *After Crime and Punishment: Pathways to Offender Reintegration*. Cullompton: Willan Publishing.

Maruna, S., LeBel, T. P., Mitchell, N. and Naples, M. (2004b) 'Pygmalion in the Reintegration Process: Desistance from Crime through the Looking Glass', *Psychology, Crime and Law*, 10 (3): 272–81.

Maruna, S., Wilson, L. and Curran, K. (2006) 'Why God is Often Found Behind Bars: Prison Conversions and the Crisis of Self-Narrative', *Research in Human Development*, 3 (2): 161–84.

Maruna, S. and Roy, K. (2007) 'Amputation or Reconstruction? Notes on the Concept of "Knifing Off" and Desistance From Crime', *Journal of Contemporary Criminal Justice*, 23 (1): 104–24

Matza, D. (1964) *Delinquency and Drift*. New York: Wiley.

Meisenhelder, T. (1977) 'An Explanatory Study of Exiting from Criminal Careers', *Criminology*, 15, 319–34.

Pager, D. (2003) 'The Mark of a Criminal Record', *American Journal of Sociology*, 108: 937–75.

Parton, N. and O'Byrne, P. (2000) *Constructive Social Work: Towards a New Practice*. London: Palgrave Macmillan.

Prochaska, J. A., Diclemente, C. C. and Norcross, J. C. (1992) 'In Search of How People Change: Application to Addictive Behaviours', *American Psychologist*, 41: 1102–14.

Prochaska, J. O., Norcross, J. C. and DiClemente, C. C. (1994). *Changing for Good: The Revolutionary Program that Explains the Six Stages of Change and Teaches You How to Free Yourself from Bad Habits*. New York: W. Morrow.

Rand, A. (1987) 'Transitional Life Events and Desistance from Delinquency and Crime', in M. E. Wolfgang, T. P. Thornberry and R. M. Figlio (eds) *From Boy to Man, From Delinquency to Crime*. Chicago: University of Chicago Press.

Rex, S. (1999) 'Desistance from Offending: Experiences of Probation', *Howard Journal of Criminal Justice*, 36 (4): 366–83.

Rex, S. (2001) 'Beyond Cognitive-behaviouralism? Reflections on the Effectiveness Literature', in A. Bottoms, L. Gelsthorpe and S. Rex (eds) *Community Penalties: Change and Challenges*. Cullompton: Willan Publishing.

Rumgay, J. (2004) 'Scripts for Safer Survival: Pathways Out of Female Crime', *Howard Journal of Criminal Justice*, 43 (4): 405–19.

Sampson, R. J. and Laub, J. H. (1993) *Crime in the Making: Pathways and Turning Points Through Life*. London: Harvard University Press.

Sampson, R., Laub, J. and Sweeten, G. (2006) 'Assessing Sampson and Laub's Life Course Theory of Crime', in F. Cullen, J. Wright and K. Blevins (eds) *Taking Stock: The Status of Criminological Theory*. New Brunswick, NJ: Transaction.

Sennett, R. (2003) *Respect in a World of Inequality*. New York: Norton.

Sharp, D., Atherton, S. and Williams, K. (2006) *Everyone's Business: Investigating the Resettlement Needs of Black and Minority Ethnic Ex-Offenders in the West Midlands*, a report commissioned by the Prisoner Resettlement Strategy Group. West Midlands: Centre for Criminal Justice and Policy Research. University of Central England.

Shover, N. (1996) *Great Pretenders: Pursuits and Careers of Persistent Thieves*. Oxford: Oxford University Press.

Uggen, C. and Kruttschnitt, C. (1988) 'Crime in the Breaking: Gender Differences in Desistance', *Law and Society Review*, 32: 339–66.

Uggen, C., Manza, J. and Behrens, A. (2004) 'Less than the Average Citizen: Stigma, Role Transition and the Civic Reintegration of Convicted Felons', in S. Maruna and R. Immarigeon (eds) *After Crime and Punishment: Pathways to Offender Reintegration*. Cullompton: Willan Publishing.

Vaughan, B. (2007) 'The Internal Narrative of Desistance', *British Journal of Criminology*, 47: 390–404.

Chapter 4

Bringing sense and sensitivity to corrections: from programmes to 'fix' offenders to services to support desistance

Frank J. Porporino

Abstract

The search for evidence-based practices is blind empiricism unless the mechanisms of action of those practices are understood: why and how change might come about. Two paradigms (rehabilitation theories?) stand in contrast in the field of corrections at this point in time. The risk management framework, well tested and dominant, falters in some key respects since 'changeable' dynamic risk factors seem not to be that easily 'changeable'. Desistance theory and research, rich in descriptive analysis of the forces and influences that can underpin offender change, unfortunately lacks any sort of organised practice framework. Developments in motivational theory and practice, also emerging as influential in corrections, are more fully consistent with the desistance paradigm, but to date are being embraced mostly in practice as only methods for *stylistically* modifying applications of the risk management paradigm. This paper focuses on what a more *integrative* correctional practice framework might look like that aims to be more broadly evidence-based, paying proper attention to the interplay of factors that seems to assist offenders most in their ongoing and difficult struggles to desist. Though correctional practice should be obviously grounded in evidence, it should also rely on sense and sensitivity: sense in how we incorporate a broad range of evidence into the design and delivery of our services to offenders, and sensitivity in how we go about nudging change gradually but steadily rather than forcing and shaping it within time-limited interventions. Sense and sensitivity is needed as well in how we attend simultaneously to offenders' goals and preferences, what they value, what they have experienced, and their emotional, social/interpersonal and self-efficacy/ identity concerns. Practical implications are sketched out for a possible new wave of programme development in the field.[1]

Introduction

The imperative to pursue evidence-based practice has finally gripped corrections. In most progressive correctional jurisdictions internationally there is now at least the expressed intent that, as much as possible, programmes and services for offenders should be evidence-based. In an increasing number of US jurisdictions this has been entrenched in official policy and in a number of other countries (for example England and Wales, Scotland, Sweden, Denmark, Canada) this new respect for the evidence has reached new heights; only those programmers that have been thoroughly reviewed and accredited by groups of experts as meeting certain established effectiveness criteria can be implemented broadly.

Clearly, the last decade has been an especially fertile period for correctional programme development and we can now catalogue with some degree of confidence that some things work better than others in trying to reduce re-offending (Aos *et al.* 2006; Harper and Chitty 2004; MacKenzie 2006; McGuire 1995, 2002; Pearson *et al.*, 2002; Sherman *et al.* 1997; Losel 1995). The social-learning and social-cognitive frameworks within psychology have been heavily influential and the notion of targeting 'changeable' dynamic risk factors is now widely accepted, not just within correctional psychology (Andrews and Bonta 2003) but also within mainstream criminology (Farrington 2005). Programmes to help change offenders have proliferated. But a counter-movement is now also in full swing. It highlights the limitations of these approaches for reducing re-offending *on their own*, and indeed, the misplaced expectation that they could or should in view of the now growing evidence on the interplay of more subtle influences, personal/phenomenological, relational and structural, that seem to underpin desistance among offenders (Farrall 2002, 2004; Godfrey *et al.* 2008; Mair 2004; Maruna 2001; Maruna and Immarigeon 2004; McNeil 2008; Rex 1999, 2001; Ward and Marshall 2007).[2]

After three decades of determined efforts to build a knowledge base for What Works (Gendreau and Ross 1979), a new era of serious questioning of our approaches seems to be emerging that is being fuelled not by ideological cynicism but by the need for a more fundamental understanding of the actual mechanisms of action that lead to desistance; that transition from an offending to a non-offending lifestyle that sometimes seems to happen spontaneously, sometimes unexpectedly, sometimes after intervention but perhaps not because of it, and often without any obvious or formal intervention at all.

Corrections in many ways is a noble profession that has to endure shortsighted political agendas and still strive steadily to do the right thing. Under difficult circumstances, correctional practitioners are faced with the difficult challenge of managing and helping to change difficult offenders who often have lived very difficult lives. Correctional practitioners for the most part want to do this right thing and evidence-based programmes seem to offer a practical and structured way to achieve correctional aims. It is perhaps not surprising, therefore, that there has been enthusiastic endorsement of programmes and interventions as ways to correct offenders more completely, more effectively and more quickly. In this exuberant momentum towards a directed and prescriptive, *change-the-offender* agenda in corrections, however, this chapter argues that we may have blinded ourselves to other ways of approaching the challenge, ways where offenders themselves could be treated with greater respect, as the true experts regarding how they might change.

In this chapter I adopt the posture of a constructively critical friend who is also a bit apologetic. For years, I have tried to champion What Works, especially as it relates to application of good social cognitive interventions to change offenders. But I now believe that we have hit a kind of effective practice 'glass ceiling' in the field, and that further refinement, or better implementation, of our so-called evidence-based programmes will not take us much further. A clear and present danger is that we may have narrowed in on too few approaches, too prematurely, and with too much uncertainty about the real process of change that offenders move through (or don't move through).

Understanding all of the forces and influences that can nudge and maintain pro-social change for offenders is critical and the currently dominant risk/needs framework that we apply pervasively, despite its undeniable contributions, points us to only one part of the picture, the risk factors that relate to expected persistence in offending. Unattended to in that paradigm is how exactly offenders go about constructing new pro-social identities for themselves, what might spark them to do this, what are the motivational pressures that might support the change, where these pressures come from, and how is a new identity (and the future pro-social self it implies) reconciled with the criminal past it is choosing to abandon. A growing positive psychology movement argues that it is these self-determined, transformative identity motives that are central in directing and self-regulating behaviour (Patterson and Joseph 2007; Vignoles *et al.* 2008). We all, offenders included, change our behaviour when we become engaged towards achieving a desired future self, with congruent goals and values that define it.

The chapter attempts to elaborate the desistance perspective as a counterpoint to the risk/needs framework, with implications for perhaps a new era, and a new focus of development for evidence-based practice, that gets us away from a preoccupation to correct and/or fix offenders in our way for their own benefit, and to a more complete appreciation of the forces and influences that might help offenders find and follow their own way out of offending.

Interestingly, desistance findings are fully consistent with another emerging framework for working more effectively with offenders: the motivational practice paradigm, which has clear implications not just for how we might relate differently with offenders but for what sorts of strategies of influence we should choose to deploy, when, how and with what emphasis (for example to raise awareness or insight, encourage self re-evaluation, help orchestrate appropriate social support for change) (McMurran and Ward 2004; Prochaska and Levesque 2002; Porporino and Fabiano 2008). But the MI (Motivational Interviewing) paradigm, as powerful an approach as it might be, also runs the risk of being co-opted as just another method for fixing offenders if it is only superficially embedded within a broader risk/needs framework that still rules the day. A desistance perspective, on the other hand, has the potential and the breadth to guide more fundamental re-evaluation of What Works practice.

The chapter is structured as an elaboration of answers to the following questions:

1. Are the evidence-based practices we pursue (more specifically the evidence-based programmes we deliver to offenders), as evidence-based as we think?

2. What are the central themes and findings in the desistance literature that might challenge us to take another look at how we design our programmes and service delivery pathways for offenders?

3. What are some key implications for an integrated correctional practice framework that emphasises sense and sensitivity in how we might help offenders move towards desistance?

The scope and the impact of our evidence-based practice

Let's turn to the first question and try to answer it relatively quickly, since the arguments may be somewhat familiar to many readers. As a consultant, researcher and programme developer, I field calls regularly for information about one of our programmes in particular, generally acknowledged as the progenitor of the cognitive behavioural paradigm, often included in various catalogues of evidence-based programmes that are disseminated to agencies for possible consideration: the Reasoning and Rehabilitatory (R&R) Cognitive Skills Programme (Porporino and Fabiano 2000). It has been around for a while so it is kind of like the 'I'm

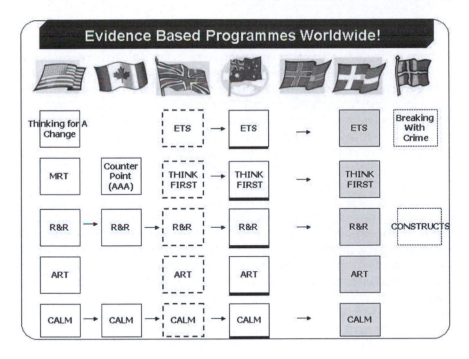

Figure 4.1 Evidence-based practices around the world

a PC' compared to the hipper 'Apple', but it still gets some attention. But that is not the point. The point is that agencies typically have no idea whatsoever why they might like to implement R&R in particular, to deliver it to whom or why or when. They are simply looking for some evidence-based practice, some special magic in a bottle!

It is quite interesting that after so many years, the scope of our evidence-based practice, at least as far as structured programmes to help change offenders, is actually fairly narrow. Figure 4.1 shows some of the major acknowledged offending-behaviour programmes that are in use worldwide as evidence-based practice.

The communality from country to country stands out (explained, of course, by the fact that we now blissfully and easily share our evidence-based practices around the world). So for example, with a few exceptions of programmes that have not really crossed international borders (like moral reconation therapy – MRT), wherever Canada, the UK and the USA have gone, so have the Scandinavian countries and Australia/New Zealand. Derivative programme development, of course, is also common, and so R&R, for example, has been morphed into Thinking for a Change in the USA, Enhanced Thinking Skills in the UK, Constructs in Scotland, Breaking With Crime in the Scandinavian countries, and Straight Thinking in New Zealand. Someone else might come up with a slightly different catalogue, but this one is certainly in the ballpark. These are all decent, generally well-evaluated, structured cognitive behavioural approaches that are delivered to thousands of offenders, who all learn the same sort of new thinking skills. But when we look at impact, even interpreting the data generously, what we see is the typically modest and conditional 10 per cent effect size, occasionally a bit more but often also less. The effect is referred to as *conditional* because our evaluation approaches usually do not really disentangle what part of that effect might be a programme effect and what part might be artifact (such as other differences between the treatment and comparison groups, principally differences in readiness to change, but this is addressed again later).

A recent meta-analysis of effective correctional strategies published by the Washington State Institute for Public Policy has received considerable exposure (Aos *et al.* 2006). Cognitive behavioural programmes came in at about an 8 per cent effect size, respectable but with apparently not much more *oomph* than the good old traditional approaches of giving offenders some vocational training, adult basic education (ABE) and maybe a decent dose of substance-abuse treatment. A recent major review of Correctional Services Canada (CSC), motivated by a conservative political undercurrent, caught wind of these findings and challenged agency defenders of programmes within CSC to prove they had done better. They couldn't, so CSC is now working towards reinvigorating the traditional emphasis on work and education and designing one efficient, super programme to target everything. 'I think therefore I'm still a criminal' is a headline that appeared in the *Sunday Times* in the UK a few years ago, paraphrasing Descartes to poke fun at the fact that the Home Office Research Unit had just released findings of no difference in re-offending rates for prisoners participating in thinking skills programmes. Though relatively progressive, the Labour Party nonetheless began to question the considerable investment that had been made to implement these programmes, and the UK as well has now re-tooled and is piloting a new and improved thinking skills intervention.

More examples could be provided but the key point is that our so-called evidence-based practices may not be as evidence-based as we think. There are some very fundamental reasons that lead to this conclusion, and weakness of clear impact on re-offending is only one.

Is our practice really evidence-based?

In clarifying a few points, it may help to refer to the simple illustration in Figure 4.2. The evidence-based practices we examine typically occur between that relatively short time-frame between A and B, and we then assess their impact on outcomes at point C. If outcomes at C show some reliable reduction in rates of re-offending (and the studies examining this

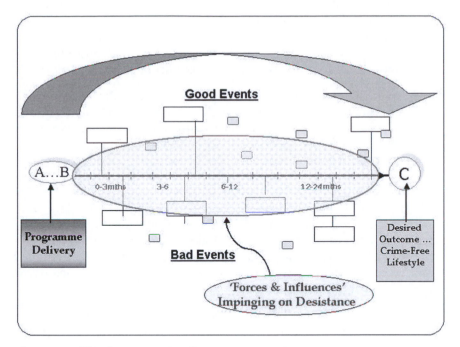

Figure 4.2   The desistance time-line

relationship are of sufficient rigour), then the intervention is deemed
· evidence-based. In fact, what we know is that whatever happened
between points A and B may have worked to some degree in impinging
on outcomes at C, but if that's what did the trick, we certainly don't know
with any degree of clarity why or how this may have happened (Pawson
and Tilley 1997).

The following is a very brief summary of some of the pieces that are
missing in our supposed scientific paradigm for assessing What Works.

1. We know very little about how intervention X delivered during the
   period A to B has any effect on changing personal circumstances, or
   changing reaction to personal circumstances, in the period A to C.
   When we ask offenders, they typically give only passing credit to these
   interventions, and much more credit to some of the things that
   happened (or didn't happen) as their lives unfolded after B and up to
   C (Farrall 2004).

2. We don't know at all precisely which dynamic risk factors we might
   need to change by how much for which offenders, so our programmes
   mostly take the scatter-gun approach: try to change as many things as
   possible and hope for the best. Moreover, when we try to measure what
   actually happened from A to B, some things seem to have changed, but

none of these things seems to be reliably related to outcomes at C (for example, interim outcome measures of how well skills have been learned or how various personality dispositions and attitudes have been affected seem completely unable to predict re-offending outcomes).

3. We target offenders for intervention based on our calibration of their risk/needs levels, but on the needs side our assessment tools are at best crude. They help identify only broad domains we could target for treatment so we use guesswork to match programme type with offender type, mismatching routinely; for example, offenders who had a substance abuse problem *once upon a time* still get substance abuse treatment, violent offenders who weren't angry when they offended get anger management, and quite cognitively skilled offenders who managed lucrative drug-dealing enterprises get our small doses of cognitive skills training. Ignored typically by programmes, and annoying to offenders when that occurs, are the myriad other more dominant and pressing personal concerns that distract them and self-consume (McMurran and McCulloch 2007).

4. Though we believe that what we target between A to B (i.e., what we try to teach) is what is making the difference, it may be something else. For example, the central process of change-inducement for the offender may be more relationship-based than it is skills-based and this relationship-based change-inducement may come from either another offender and/or the programme facilitator, or even another source all together (e.g., a family member supporting the offender's demonstrated intent to work at change, a probation officer's continued encouragement). The problems encountered with fidelity of implementation of programmes have been well documented (Gendreau *et al.* 1999; Harper and Chitty 2004; Harris and Smith 1996; Lipsey 1999; Van Voorhis *et al.* 2004), but the reasons why practitioners might resist following curricula as they are directed to by manuals seem to be less clear. Could it be that practitioners see the need to go beyond just delivering the content of structured programmes, even if they might be unsure about why or how they should do this?

5. Lots of offenders don't like what we do from A to B, and one of the most consistent findings in the field, with different programmes that address very different areas, is that programme drop-outs show considerably worse outcomes at C, much worse than programme completers and typically even worse than the comparison group who we have left alone. This is a typical, well-documented confound in evaluation studies (MacKenzie 2006) and although the generous interpretation of the phenomenon is that only the programme completers have actually changed, the equally plausible interpretation is that only the already motivated could manage to tolerate A to B.

Essentially nothing substantial may have happened between A and B other than a weeding out of the unmotivated, or alternatively, only some strengthening of what was already true at point A (the readiness to work on change). Perhaps not surprisingly, the most common reason offenders give for why they may have benefited from programme participation is that they were *ready to change* (Clarke *et al.* 2004). Offenders dropping out of programmes tend to be higher risk, have more previous convictions, are younger, less well educated, generally have less stable lives, and often come from ethnic or cultural minority groups. We could say that those offenders who might need to be engaged the most by our programmes are indeed perhaps engaged the least.

A central feature of the risk/needs paradigm is that it perpetuates the notion of fixable dynamic risk factors, and programmes become the means to that end. Unfortunately, how we can go about fixing these factors is not at all clear (Bourgon *et al.* 2008), and besides, there is at best only theoretical supposition that the same factors that might be implicated in why offending starts are also those that might underpin desistance if we reverse them. In life-course developmental work in criminology, the notion of asymmetrical causation is well accepted. Offenders might begin offending, in part at least, because of their impulsivity, failure to attend to consequences, preference for anti-social associates, unstructured lifestyles, and emerging pro-criminal sentiments . . . and so on. But it doesn't follow that a reversal in these anti-social personality traits, behaviours and attitudes is what is key in moving offenders into desistance, or even in maintaining it. The possibility has to be entertained that simply targeting (and trying to eliminate) these criminogenic risk factors may be neither sufficient nor even necessary to help offenders transition into non-offending. Indeed, when we look at offenders who are desisting they seem to be doing so without any fundamental change in their so-called anti-social personality traits and/or attitudes. Many of these ex-offenders remain, and indeed pride themselves in remaining, anti-authority, rebel-lious, adventurous and independent (Maruna 2001). What does seem to differentiate the recidivist from the non-recidivist is that non-recidivists report being much more satisfied with their lives, more optimistic, generally experiencing many more positive emotions, fewer episodes of negative emotions (depression, anxiety, loneliness, boredom or loneliness, frustration, anger), and fewer problems and worries in life (Zamble and Quinsey 1997).

Some recent findings from the Urban Institute Returning Home study in the USA are striking (Yahner *et al.* 2008). Prisoners released in Illinois, Ohio and Texas under parole supervision conditions, compared with those not under supervision, showed more likelihood of being employed and much less likelihood of substance and/or alcohol abuse. Surprisingly, though, these parolees were no less likely to re-offend, and were actually re-imprisoned at higher rates than the non-parolees (mostly due to technical violations). One can only speculate what might be going on here but perhaps it is a reflection of the fact that an unhappy, temporarily employed, struggling ex-addict might not a desister make!

Ted Palmer cautioned us years ago to focus on intermediate outcomes we might need to achieve 'with whom, when, why and under what circumstances' (Palmer 1992). We are not much closer to that ideal when we look at how our evidence-based practices have become routinised, too often inappropriately and/or unnecessarily imposed on offenders, and too often disconnected from the overriding issues and concerns that stand out as obstacles for the individual. Important to accept is that our methods (whether CBT-based or otherwise) may have only *soft power* to influence, and expecting them to, or treating them as if, they have *hard power* to change, will continue to stall us.

Themes and findings from the desistance framework

Can the desistance framework give us an alternative and possibly practical paradigm, a different kind of 'rehabilitation theory'?

As a sidetrack, it is worth noting that this literature is not neat and tidy. There is theoretical debate, inconsistency in some findings, terminology problems, loose definition of concepts, and in the tradition of ethnographic, qualitative analysis, the inevitable problems of interpretation of soft data. It is a large, growing and daunting literature to make your way through, that doesn't provide us, at least not at this stage, with nice little tools we can apply. But at the same time it is a literature that gives some perceptive new insights into what offenders think, believe, experience, try to do and try not to do, in the moment, as they live their lives. It is an important literature to attend to because the picture it paints of how offenders get out of crime is complex, interdependent, and interactive, a challenge to practice for sure, but nonetheless likely closer to reality than some of the evidence-based illusions we maintain.

So let's first clarify the term desistance. Research deals with the concept essentially as either a process or an end-state, a journey or the destination (Kazemian 2007). Treated as an empirical end-state or point in time, an offender has desisted if, for example, he/she has remained offence-free for some defined period. The developmental life-course criminology and career criminal frameworks, for example, try to determine what might predict this desistance end-state. Of course, this research has to contend with the thorny issue of when is the end really the end – two years, ten years, or a lifetime? But setting aside this little methodological problem, since desistance is treated as an end-state, the research in this tradition commonly looks for events, life circumstances or life changes (transitions) that might precede desistance. Age, of course, is the most well-established correlate of desistance, and we are all aware of the classic age/crime curve where offending peaks in early adulthood and then drops off gradually. But this leaves us only with a rather elusive maturation hypothesis where we really don't know what exactly is entailed in this growing out of crime, and especially, if it is due mostly to exogenous, social bonding experiences and/or internal changes in perception and outlook.

Desistance as an end-state has also been correlated with change in social roles and various factors that define increase in social capital. This has been a strong theme in criminological research in the last several decades (Sampson and Laub 1993; Laub *et al.* 1998), and it serves, incidentally, as the primary justification and rationale for the current Re-Entry focus in the USA. It has been referred to jokingly by Maruna (2001) as the theory of a 'steady job and the love of a good woman'. When we look for structural correlates for desistance, of course we find them, and these structural antecedents include stable employment and/or education, getting married, becoming a parent, and what Laub and Sampson (2003) have coined as the 'knifing off' of the people places and things that were intertwined with one's criminal past (such as friends, neighbourhoods and routines).

Whether talked about as triggering events (Laub *et al.* 1998) or hooks for change (Giordano *et al.* 2002), this sociogenic view sees change in circumstances as the primary driver for desistance. Laub and Sampson, for example, emphasise the power of turning points *in and of themselves*: 'Although some offenders may seek to "make good" or engage in "up-front work" to better their lives, we believe that most offenders desist in response to structurally-induced turning points that serve as a catalyst for sustaining long-term behavioral change' (Laub and Sampson 2003).

The problem, of course, is that this doesn't explain why sometimes the events serve as a catalyst or hook, but other times they don't. This is the classic person vs environment controversy that psychology abandoned long ago, looking instead at interactions as the place where the real action happens. Sociogenic views of desistance credit the offender with only a rather passive role (where good things might be happening simply randomly to bad actors; Laub *et al.* 1998), and they obviously confuse cause and correlate. Dynamic, motivational models, on the other hand, emphasise desistance as a process where the individual takes more centre stage, and where changing circumstances can be as much welcomed and sought after by the individual as an agent of their own change, the end-result of more basic cognitive transformation, as well as then received and reacted to positively (nourished and capitalised upon) as ways of trying on new pro-social identities. Change in conception of self is therefore both partly cause and partly consequence; as cause it leads to the taking on of new pro-social roles (of responsible partner at home, productive citizen at work and active participant in the community) and as consequence the experience of new pro-social roles (when experienced satisfactorily) might lead to even stronger and lasting redefinitions of self.

A more nuanced analysis of the impact of transitions supports the dynamic perspective for desistance. We know, for example, that offering work opportunities to younger offenders (less than about age 27) makes little difference when they are still uncommitted to a working lifestyle and work ethic (Bushway and Reuter 2001; Uggen 2000). Marriage similarly seems to have an age-graded impact, only clearly affecting desistance after the mid-twenties (Ouimet and LeBlanc 1996). The 'good marriage effect' takes hold, it seems, when there is more readiness and concern to partner romantically, when the quality/intimacy of the relationship becomes a priority (Shover 1996), and when that partner (and that partner's network ties) are essentially non-criminal (Giordano *et al.* 2002).

Shad Maruna, and his well-known Liverpool Desistance Study, brought the study of desistance as process to greatest prominence (Maruna 2001). Interestingly, Maruna developed his ideas for a narrative criminology from analysing common themes in dozens of published autobiographies of ex-offenders (Maruna 1997). But others have taken the same sort of in-depth qualitative look at desistance before him (Rex 1999; Shover 1996) and similar studies are ongoing; like Peggy Giordano's very methodical Ohio Life Course Study, following up a sample of male and female juvenile offenders into adulthood (Giordano *et al.* 2002); Stephen Farrall's detailed look at the problems and obstacles faced by probationers in the UK (Farrall 2002), recently replicated in Ireland (Healy and O'Donnell 2008); Janet Jamieson and Gill McIvor's study of how younger offenders in Scotland manage to desist (Jamieson *et al.* 1999), and Ros Burnett's Oxford Desistance Study of thieves and robbers just before release from prison, now followed for up to ten years (Burnett 2004; LeBel *et al.* 2008). There are some overarching themes from all of this work that are clearly important for informing practice.

First, it is clear from a number of these studies that offenders *know* when they are generally committed to desistance and/or if they're still uncertain or unwilling to try. On its own this may not sound so important, but the fact is that these desistance intentions actually predict re-offending. Offenders who express strong intent to desist, actually do (Burnett 2004). Moreover, when the offender is optimistic, and supervising officers agree that this is realistic, desistance is an even more likely outcome (Farrall 2002).

Second, desistance seems to co-occur with active, offender-led, agentic resolution of social obstacles (Farrall 2002) and this sense of agency experienced by the offender is what seems key in further strengthening of desistance motives (Maruna 2001; Burnett and Maruna 2004). Interestingly, in attempting to increase their social capital, it is the family of origin that has been found to be perhaps the strongest resource for offenders to call upon (Farrall 2002); be it for employment, accommodation or even dealing with substance abuse (Shapiro 2003; Sullivan *et al.* 2002). Our community supervision of offenders, on the other hand, seems often to make little difference since rather than recognising and working to practically supplement the efforts of offenders, it tries instead, when it tries at all, to lead with standard options rather than compliment with practical support (McNeill 2006). In the Returning Home Urban Institute Study referred to earlier, only 13 per cent of offenders mentioned that parole officers helped them with a job search, and only 3 per cent to find a drug programme. Buried in a footnote, though, is the finding that those offenders two months out who reported parole officers had done at least one specific thing to assist them were less likely to return to prison in the year following release. Not rocket science, but not the fuel we seem to rely on.

A third important finding in the desistance literature is that the concerns and preoccupations of early desisters seem to be different from those of later desisters. Perhaps not surprisingly, the concerns of early desisters seem in a sense to be more ordinary in focus, more directed to basic needs, such as employment prospects or dealing with substance abuse (Farrall 2002; Healy and O'Donnell 2008). Later desisters (like those in Maruna's Liverpool Study for example), on the other hand, seem to move towards a deeper redemptive script where strong generative concerns come to the forefront, other-centred and focused on giving back, concerns intended to satisfy both personal aspirations for new meaning and the desire to gain pro-social legitimacy.

A fourth finding, evident when we think about it, is that desistance is not linear or sequential but rather zigzag in form. As Burnett notes succinctly, 'desistance is a process which involves reversals of decisions, indecision, compromise and lapses' (2004: 169). This carries importance for practice, of course, since our reaction to setbacks and breakdowns may itself be a principal factor derailing emerging desistance (Maguire and Raynor 2006).

Finally, the fifth and possibly most important aspect of the desistance as process literature is the attempt to specify exactly what characterises the mindset of the desister; what is the precise nature of the *cognitive transformation* that takes place (Giordano *et al.* 2002), what has been referred to as a new self-narrative (Maruna 2001) or internal moral conversation (Vaughn 2007). Again there is some evidence that this may vary depending on whether we are looking at an early or later stage in the process. So, for example, in the early going there seems to be more focus on a knifing off of the past that is linked to a 'wanting to *want* to be other than the way one is, in spite of one's own resistance' (Goldie 2004). The source may be growing worries about the passage of time, more conservative views of risk and increasingly negative assessments about the prospect of being re-imprisoned (Shover 1996), all leading to some *crystallisation of discontent* (Baumeister 1994) with the realities of a life of crime. This negative reaction subsides as time passes, however, and most often discussed as fundamental for desistance to be realised over the longer haul are the positive qualities of sustaining hope, maintaining a

- *Sustaining hope* An overriding and optimistic sense of agency (locus of control shift) that internalises ultimate responsibility for the present and future.

- *Maintaining self-efficacy* An enabling sense that one has personal and/or social resources to manage obstacles and concerns, emotions and worries that might arise.

- *Experiencing adaptive shame* Re-alignment with pro-social values (but not at the expense of a changed or degraded core self); some neutralisation and/or excuse or rationalisation for past as self-protective.

- *Redefined sense of self* Able to accept 'who I was' but preferring 'who I am becoming' . . . adopting new roles and identities and differentiating oneself from criminal others (I'm not like them).

Figure 4.3   Realising desistance for the long term

strong sense of self-efficacy, experiencing adaptive shame, and redefining one's sense of self and identity (LeBel *et al.* 2008). These are elaborated in the text box in Figure 4.3.

To understand the desistance process in a different way, though, we can turn briefly to psychology where these sorts of concepts are much better developed than in criminology, studied as part of general human development, and therefore useful to show that desistance, though obviously unique in form and focus, essentially follows the same rules, and is vulnerable to the same underlying pressures, that psychologists argue impinge on all of us as we move through life and construct our identities.

Positive psychology has shown convincingly that we are more fulfilled by those aspects of our identities that better satisfy motives for self-esteem, efficacy, continuity and meaning. We all strive towards possible future selves:

1. That are personally valued and socially valued within the interpersonal and sociocultural contexts we inhabit (Self-Esteem Enhancing Motive).

2. Where we can feel competent and capable in impinging on the circumstances of our lives (Self-Efficacy Motive).

3. That bring some clear and coherent meaning to our lives (Meaning Motive).

4. Where our current self is essentially maintained . . . although not necessarily unchanged (Continuity Motive).

Added to these four central identity motives are the *Belonging Motive* (feeling accepted) and the *Distinctiveness Motive* (feeling unique), but these tend to operate through the other four core motives.

Identity motives guide the individual to behave in ways that are consistent with certain self-perceptions. But of course our automatic appraisal of more basic needs also motivates us to behave in particular ways (Deci and Ryan 2000), and this can include offending. Tony Ward's Good Lives Model (Ward and Stewart 2003), which has had some unfair knocks from proponents of the risk/needs paradigm, essentially builds on this notion and suggests that offending continues (regardless of how it originated) because offenders (1) apply inappropriate and short-sighted *means* to secure their needs; (2) lack *scope* or coherence in their overall life plan; (3) experience *conflict* among goals that they're not aware of; and (4) lack the *capacities* or skills to adjust in achieving their needs in some other ways. In other words, offenders are prone to behave in ways that forgo their basic and longer-term needs in satisfying their more immediate wants (which is clearly also a dispositional feature).

So how does all of this explain desistance? Very simply in some ways! We all oscillate between where we are and where we might like to be, and we begin to concentrate more on where we might like to be when where we are becomes especially frustrating and unsatisfying.

Desistance begins when the self-defeating process that Ward describes begins to end; when an experience, a thought, an observation, a significant other's remark, for instance registers powerfully enough to lead the offender in realising that their important and basic needs are not being met. MI has borrowed the term *dissonance* from psychology to describe this. This state of cognitive and emotional discontent orients the offender to issues or problems in their lives that they finally need to deal with. Identity motives then kick in and in moving to construct their new identity, offenders gravitate towards:

1. The trying on of new roles which are socially valued ... in the hope that they will also be personally valued (Self-Esteem Enhancing Motive).

2. The acceptance and exercise of agency in dealing with obstacles and problems that confront them (Self-Efficacy Motive).

3. The search for something beyond oneself (Meaning Motive) ... which for offenders may often involve generative commitments as a drive for 'something to show' for one's life.

4. A reframing of the past to explain and understand it (though still accept it) as 'part me' but part 'not me' (Continuity Motive) ... which for offenders may implicate some cognitive neutralisations or distortions as a helpful, self-protective mechanism.

For those readers who may be especially MI inclined, we can use the Decisional Balance as an analogy to understand this. Desistance thinking

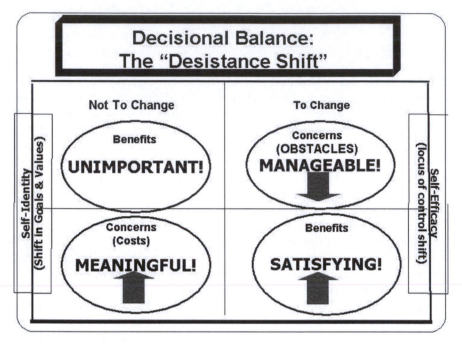

Figure 4.4   Decisional Balance

begins as the costs for 'not changing' become meaningful and acutely painful; it is supported as the obstacles in the way of change begin to be seen as manageable; it is then solidified in a sort of dual-action process where any of the possible benefits to offending become completely unimportant, whereas the benefits of non-offending become increasingly personally and socially satisfying (see Figure 4.4).

Rather than rely on the stages of change framework, it may be more useful to think of the offender as going through what we know is a natural problem-management process that we all go through, that our helping process can perhaps assist or accelerate but not replace (see Figure 4.5, adapted from Egan 1998).

Implications for practice

A psychologically informed explanation of 'desistance' is useful only if it leads to a more practically minded extrapolation of implications for practice.

The desistance perspective, and the findings to support it, has already led to a call for a more strengths-based re-entry practice (Maruna and LeBel 2002), emphasising the notions of earned redemption and treating offenders as community assets rather than 'liabilities to be supervised' (Travis and Petersilia 2001). This is a broad direction difficult to argue

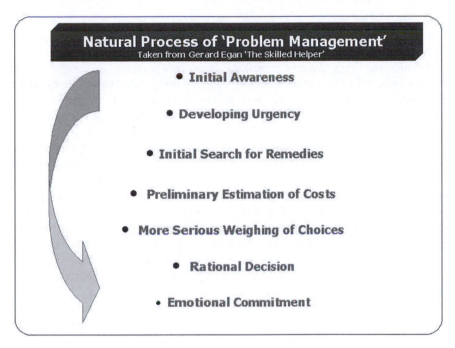

Figure 4.5 Natural problem-management process

with, even if what it might mean is not always obvious within communities that seem to be increasingly unreceptive (Bazemore and Stinchcomb 2004).

Though the language of desistance sounds as if it is perhaps a bit too imprecise to translate into practice, a psychologically minded synthesis of underlying themes points concretely to four areas where we could concentrate and redesign our efforts. In order to initiate and maintain desistance, offenders need some measure of:

- Motive (some reasons to begin considering desistance, even if only preliminarily)

- Method (some strategies and remedies that seem to address what they perceive as personal obstacles in their strivings for valued personal goals)

- Experience (of success and satisfaction in their exercising of new pro-social roles)

- Acceptance (by respected and significant others, and society more widely, for the authenticity of their change).

These four elements obviously intertwine and one or the other may be more central to opening the door to desistance for some offenders compared to others. Accepting this, the following are at least some of the things that we could do quite differently if we kept these broad aims in mind.

Within the risk/needs paradigm, we have come to assume that offenders are in persistence mode (as revealed and calibrated by their risk/needs profiles) and this directs the intensity and breadth of our services. We generally fail to attend to any 'desistance talk' (and more likely dismiss it as disingenuine). What we see as criminogenic problems becomes the foreground source for imposing our plan for change rather than the background landscape for understanding how the offender might better address their current concerns (Klinger and Cox 2004). In the process, we run the risk of pissing off offenders (therein explaining high programme attrition) since our methods seem not to match what they see as their primary needs (and most pressing goals). Our services are rejected (or don't impinge significantly) because they are not seen as driven by expressed sentiments about desistance (and how to achieve it) and don't appear to be tailored to offender's lives. There are two important things we could do instead.

One is to develop programmes that don't aim to change offenders but rather aim simply to help them explore – to look at their lives through some new lenses, sort out their needs and wants, refine their vague wishes and commit to some SMART goals, and find their own personal and interpersonal resources to stay on track (Porporino and Fabiano 2005). The other is to develop tools for the assessment of desistance sentiments that don't just pigeon-hole offenders into another category (that is, pre-contemplative) but actually provide us with some insight into the strength and nature of their identity motives and how this relates to their concerns and goals; e.g., change beliefs, self-efficacy appraisals (Serin and Lloyd 2009; McMurran et al. 2008; Ward and Marshall 2007).

In a curious reversal, we tend to work harder to change the still committed offender rather than those who show signs of some emerging interest in desistance. But there is not just an issue of priority in our efforts (is it right?) but one of approach that needs to be considered (might it be too narrow?).

Developments in motivational practice have been important in pointing to the benefits of a different style and focus of interaction with offenders (Prochaska and Levesque 2002), even if this is sometimes applied only tenuously and perfunctorily.[3] But our mostly rational attempts to elicit some initial readiness for change (empathic 'talking therapy' and exercises to help direct consideration for change) may not be enough, or at least not enough for some offenders. Relatively unexplored, and generally not considered as appropriately evidence-based, may be more powerful ways of *nudging* increased awareness or insight at the emotional level, either through building on the impact of some intense experience (Baim et al. 2002), or building on the more gradual impact of some different experience (such as rewarding volunteerism or community service). We know, for example, that there is documented impact on re-offending with community service work (McIvor 1992; Uggen and Janikula 1999), but this experience seems to have impact only when offenders come to perceive the work as (1) useful in employing some of their skills or providing opportunity for new learning; (2) involving a reciprocal relationship where they gain the trust and confidence of other people to whom they are giving something back to; and/or (3) giving them some insight into other people's struggles and some different understanding of their own. Community service as a sanction can be used to help clean our dirty roads, or it can become part of evidence-based practice if we just learn to apply some basic matching principles.

Let's turn now to implications for some of the other favored methods we use to encourage desistance. We teach offenders problem-solving, coping and planning skills in our programmes, but we teach these skills mostly in the abstract (to help them prepare for and anticipate difficulties) rather than 'in the moment' when offenders are in the thick of things, facing up to and having to resolve their actual problems. We teach, in a sense, theoretical reasoning skills rather than potentially more valued practical reasoning – which we know is always muddier and more difficult unless we keep our eye on personally meaningful goals, aspirations and intentions (Ward and Nee 2009). A consistent finding in positive psychology is that 'implementation planning' (the how, when and where of goal pursuits) works only when there is strong autonomous motivation to strive for the goal, and works better when approach-oriented strategies are applied.[4] In working with offenders, it means that we should be helping them with their problem-solving, coping and planning skills, practically and concretely, not intellectually, and we should be by their side as their approach-goals emerge, not just to admonish them in advance about what they should avoid.

Of course, we also spend loads of time trying to change offenders' criminal thinking or those elements of this thinking that we have determined will maintain offending. Unfortunately, we don't at all try to discern whether some of this thinking (neutralisations/excuses/justifications) may actually be serving an important self-protective function, part and parcel of the desistance process. Though we may see it for what it is, thinking that has some element of distortion, the old adage applies well: why fix it if it ain't broke?

We teach offenders skills for self-regulation (for example emotional, impulse and habit control) to help them deal with urges/temptations and avoid the hot emotions (such as frustration and anger). By contrast, since we've come to regard personal distress as not especially criminogenic, we focus much less on how to contend with what may be the more primary debilitating emotions (depression, anxiety, worry, confusion) that we know can spiral offenders easily into re-offending (Zamble and Quinsey

1997). Again, we know from positive psychology that positive emotions broaden one's awareness and encourage novel, varied and exploratory thoughts and actions (which builds skills over time). Negative emotions, on the other hand, mostly prompt narrow, survival-oriented behaviours (Patterson and Joseph 2007). When we go out of our way to make offenders miserable, then both they and we may suffer the consequences.

We teach an array of social, vocational, academic, parenting and relationship skills to offenders as well, which is clearly in the interest of increasing their social capital. But curiously we then fail to monitor (and respond appropriately by topping-off or reinforcing with the support that may be necessary) to ensure these skills are actually helping to engender more enjoyment, satisfaction and sense of fulfilment in offenders' lives (in the workplace, family, in their relationships and in the community more broadly). We seem to believe that once they have the recipe, the meal they cook will be tasty automatically. Work with families in this regard may be especially important since well-functioning families may be the best resource to influence better functioning in offenders.

Finally, we know that desistance as process happens over time, but inevitably our own process takes over, and we seem inflexibly accustomed to throwing most of our services at offenders in a concentrated manner, mostly at the beginning. As some offenders begin to do well, we tend to pull back rather than orchestrate ways to step-up (whenever needed). Moreover, when we pull back, typically it is without any real acknowledgement of success (without recognising at all significantly any of the offender's efforts at reform). Indeed, the slightest slip-up becomes a call for re-condemnation, not an opportunity for re-energising agency through recognition of actualised effort. Our casework with offenders should follow a timeline as well, that meets the offender where they are and takes this notion of 'responsivity' seriously, as something that needs time to grow (Porporino and Fabiano 2008).

Let me end with some observations from a desistance study of offenders on probation that was done some ten years ago, before the rise of the MI and pro-social modelling practice frameworks. This is what Sue Rex (1999) noted as 'what worked' in community supervision (see text box in Figure 4.6). This may all sound familiar, perhaps because it always has been and always may be what Don Andrews keeps highlighting as Core Correctional Practice.

If we distil it to the bare bones, what this chapter has argued is that perhaps we may be more successful, offenders and our communities may be better served, if we get past our programme fetishism, casework managerialism, and our compliance-on-demand syndromes when working with offenders. The desistance paradigm suggests that we might be better off if we allowed offenders to *guide us* instead, listened to what they think might best fit their individual struggles out of crime, rather than continue to insist that our solutions are their salvation. Where we can help

- Supervision that focuses on encourageing offenders to arrive at sensible and reasonable conclusions (through analysis of their own decisions/thinking).

- Provides 'critical and 'problem-solving' advise *when it seems welcomed* . . . but grounded in a 'demonstrated understanding of the offender's situation'.

- A demeanour that shows sensitivity and appreciation of the offender's viewpoints (without collusion).

- An ability to negotiate *active* participation.

- An attuned sense of how offenders may tend to *react to and/or reject* what is proposed to them.

- Can talk convincingly about the consequences of and alternatives to offending.

- Provides encouragement that is preceived as genuine . . . coming from a desire for 'wishing you make a success of your life'.

- Attends to promoting self-determination . . . and change in the offender's 'self-identity and sense of maturity and responsibility'.

Figure 4.6   What works in community supervision

meaningfully is in working with offenders to clarify their goals and what they value in life, help them realise that there may be competing agendas and a real price to pay for change, focus on strategies that can work for them, refine and shape their plans to get to where they want, and finally, and eventually, learn to get along without us. Perhaps corrections need not be reinvented, only reoriented towards sense and sensitivity that seriously allows and supports skilled staff to become truly skilled helpers.

Notes

1   Preparation of an earlier version of this paper was funded by the US National Institute of Corrections. The paper was delivered as an invited plenary presentation to the Research Conference of the International Community Corrections Association in October of 2008.
2   Desistance is defined in this paper in the manner highlighted by Maruna (2001) as maintenance of relatively 'long-term abstinence from crime among individuals who had previously engaged in persistent patterns of criminal offending'.
3   For example, there seems to be new and growing fad in correctional programming which suggests that motivation can be easily fixed as well (e.g., front-end modules to programmes with a little discussion of stages of change,

a decisional balance, and maybe a value sort . . . so that – *voilà* – the offender is no longer pre-contemplative).
4   For example, in controlling weight, attending to the quality of food rather than the quantity we consume.

References

Andrews, D. A. and Bonta, J. (2003) *The Psychology of Criminal Conduct*, 3rd edn. Cincinnati, OH: Anderson Publishing Co.

Aos, S., Miller, M. and Drake, E. (2006) *Evidence-Based Adult Corrections Programmes: What Works and What Does Not*. Olympia: Washington State Institute for Public Policy.

Baim, C., Brookes, S. and Mountfard, A. (eds) (2002) *The Geese Theatre Handbook: Drama with Offenders and People at Risk*. Winchester: Waterside Press.

Baumeister, R. F. (1994) 'The Crystallisation of Discontent in the Process of Major Life Change', in T. F. Heatherton and J. L. Weinberger (eds) *Can Personality Change?* Washington, DC: American Pschological Association.

Bazemore, G. and Stinchcomb, J. (2004) 'Rehabilitating Community Service: Toward Restorative Service Sanctions in a Balanced Justice System', *Federal Probation*, 58: 24–35.

Bourgon, G., Hanson, R. K. and Bonta, J. (2008) 'Risk, Need and Responsivity: A Heuristic for Evaluating the "quality" of Offender Interventions', *Proceedings of the North American Corrections and Criminal Justice Psychology Conference*. Ottawa: Public Safety Canada.

Burnett, R. (2004) 'To Re-offend or Not to Re-offend? The Ambivalence of Convicted Property Offenders', in S. Maruna and R. Immarigeon (eds) *After Crime and Punishment: Pathways to Offender Reintegration*. Cullompton: Willan Publishing.

Burnett, R. and Maruna, S. (2004) 'So "Prison Works", does it? The Criminal Careers of 130 Men Released from Prison under Home Secretary Michael Howard', *Howard Journal of Criminal Justice*, 43: 390–404.

Bushway, S. and Reuter, P. (2001) 'Labor Markets and Crime', in J. Q. Wilson and J. Petersilia (eds) *Crime: Public Policies for Crime Control*, 2nd edn. Oakland, Ca: ICS Press.

Clarke, D., Simmonds, R. and Wydall, S. (2004) *Delivering Cognitive Skills Programmes in Prison: A Qualitative Study*, Home Office Research Findings 242. London: Home Office.

Deci, E. L. and Ryan, R. M. (2000) 'The "What" and "Why" of Goal Pursuits: Human Needs and the Self-determination of Behaviour', *Psychological Inquiry*, 11: 227–68.

Egan, G. (1998) *The Skilled Helper: A Problem-Management Approach to Helping*. Pacific Grove: Brooks/Cole Publishing Company.

Farrall, S. (2002) *Rethinking What Works With Offenders: Probation, Social Context and Desistance from Crime*. Cullompton: Willan Publishing.

Farrall, S. (2004) 'Supervision, Motivation and Social Context: What Matters Most When Probationers Desist', in G. Mair (ed.) *What Matters in Probation*. Cullompton: Willan Publishing.

Farrington, D. P. (ed.) (2005) *Integrated Developmental and Life-Course Theories of Offending*. New Brunswick: Transaction Publishers.

Gendreau, P. and Ross, R. R. (1979) 'Effective Correctional Treatment: Bibliotherapy for Cynics', *Crime and Delinquency*, 25: 463–89.

Gendreau, P., Goggin, C. and Smith, P. (1999) 'The Forgotten Issue in Effective Correctional Treatment: Program Implementation', *International Journal of Offender Therapy and Comparative Criminology*, 43: 180–7.

Giordano, P., Cernkovitch, S. A. and Rudolph, J. L. (2002) 'Gender, Crime, and Desistance: Toward a Theory of Cognitive Transformation', *American Journal of Sociology*, 107: 990–1064.

Godfrey, B. S., Cox, D. J. and Farrall, S. (2008) *Criminal Lives: Family Life, Employment, and Offending*. Oxford: Oxford University Press.

Goldie, P. (2004) *On Personality*. London: Routledge.

Harper, G. and Chitty, C. (eds) (2004) *The Impact of Corrections on Offending: A Review of 'What Works'*, Home Office Research Study 291. London: Home Office.

Harris, P. and Smith, S. (1996) 'Developing Community Corrections: An Implementation Perspective', in A. T. Harland (ed.) *Choosing Correctional Options That Work: Defining the Demand and Evaluating the Supply*. Thousand Oaks, CA: Sage.

Healy, D. and O'Donnell, I. (2008) 'Calling Time on Crime: Motivation, Generativity and Agency in Irish Probatiuoners', *Probation Journal*, 55: 25–38.

Jamieson, J., McIvor, G. and Murray, C. (1999) *Understanding Offending Among Young People*. Edinburgh: HMSO.

Kazemian, L. (2007) 'Desistance from Crime: Theoretical, Empirical, Methodological, and Policy Considerations', *Journal of Contemporary Criminal Justice*, 23: 5–27.

Klinger, E. and Cox, W. M. (2004) 'Motivation and the Theory of Current Concerns', in W. M. Cox and E. Klinger (eds) *Handbook of Motivational Counselling: Concepts, Approaches and Assessment*. Chichester: John Wiley.

Laub, J. H. and Sampson, R. J. (2003) *Shared Beginnings, Divergent Lives: Delinquent Boys to Age 70*. Cambridge, MA: Harvard University Press.

Laub, J. H., Nagin, D. S. and Sampson, R. J. (1998) 'Trajectories of Change in Criminal Offending: Good Marriages and the Desistance Process', *American Sociological Review*, 63: 225–38.

LeBel, T., Burnett, R., Maruna, S. and Bushway, S. (2008) 'The "Chicken and Egg" of Subjective and Social Factors in Desistance from Crime', *European Journal of Criminology*, 5 (2): 131–59.

Lipsey, M. (1999) 'Can Rehabilitative Programs Reduce the Recidivism of Juvenile Offenders? An Inquiry into the Effectiveness of Practical Programs', *Virginia Journal of Social Policy and the Law*, 6: 611–41.

Losel, F. (1995) 'The Efficacy of Correctional Treatment: A Review and Synthesis of Meta-evaluations', in J. McGuire (ed.) *What Works: Reducing Re-Offending – Guidelines for Research and Practice*. Chichester: John Wiley.

Maguire, M. and Raynor, P. (2006) 'How the Resettlement of Prisoners Promotes Desistance from Crime: Or Does it?, *Criminology and Criminal Justice*, 6: 19–38.

Mair, G. (ed.) (2004) *What Matters in Probation*. Cullompton: Willan Publishing.

Maruna, S. (1997) 'Going Straight: Desistance from Crime and Self-Narratives of Reform', *Narrative Study of Lives*, 5: 59–97.

Maruna, S. (2001) *Making Good: How Ex-Convicts Reform and Rebuild Their Lives*. Washington: American Psychological Association.

Maruna, S. and LeBel, T. P. (2002) 'Revisiting Ex-prisoner Re-entry: A Buzzword in Search of a Narrative', in S. Rex and M. Tonry (eds) *Reform and Punishment*. Cullompton: Willan Publishing.

Maruna, S. and Immarigeon, R. (eds) (2004) *After Crime and Punishment: Pathways to Ex-Offender Reintegration*. Cullompton: Willan Publishing.

MacKenzie, D. L. (2006) *What Works in Corrections: Reducing the Criminal Activities of Offenders and Delinquents*. New York: Cambridge University Press.

McGuire, J. (ed.) (1995) *What Works: Reducing Re-Offending: Guidelines for Research and Practice*. Chichester: John Wiley.

McGuire, J. (2002) 'Criminal Sanctions Versus Psychologically-based Interventions with Offenders: A Comparative Empirical Analysis', *Psychology, Crime and Law*, 8: 183–208.

McIvor, G. (1992) *Sentenced to Serve: The Operation and Impact of Community Service Orders*. Aldershot: Avebury.

McMurran, M. (ed.) (2002) *Motivating Offenders to Change: A Guide to Enhancing Engagement in Therapy*. Chichester: John Wiley.

McMurran, M. and McCulloch, A. (2007) 'Why Don't Offenders Complete Treatment? Prisoners' Reasons for Non-completion of a Cognitive Skills Programme', *Psychology, Crime and Law*, 13 (4): 345–54.

McMurran, M. and Ward, T. (2004) 'Motivating Offenders to Change: An Organizing Framework', *Legal and Criminal Psychology*, 9: 295–311.

McMurran, M., Theodosi, E., Sweeney, A. and Sellen, J. (2008) 'What do Prisoners Want? Current Concerns of Adult Male Prisoners', *Psychology, Crime and Law*, 14: 267–74.

McNeill, F. (2006) 'A Desistance Paradigm for Offender Management', *Criminology and Criminal Justice*, 6: 39–62.

McNeill, F. (2008) 'Giving Up and Giving Back: Desistance, Generativity and Social Work with Offenders', in G. McIvor and P. Raynor (eds) *Developments in Social Work with Offenders*. London: Jessica Kingsley.

Ouimet, M. and LeBlanc, M. (1996) 'The Role of Life Experiences in the Continuation of the Adult Criminal Career', *Criminal Behavior and Mental Health*, 6: 73–97.

Palmer, T. (1992) *The Re-Emergence of Correctional Intervention*. Newbury Park: Sage.

Patterson, T. G. and Joseph, S. (2007) 'Person-centered Personality Theory: Support from Self-determination Theory and Positive Psychology', *Journal of Humanistic Psychology*, 47: 117–39.

Pawson, R. and Tilley, N. (1997) *Realistic Evaluation*. London: Sage.

Pearson, F. S., Lipton, D. S., Cleland, C. M. and Yee, D. S. (2002) 'The Effects of Behavioural/Cognitive-behavioural Programmes on Recidivism', *Crime and Delinquency*, 48 (3): 476–96.

Porporino, F. J. and Fabiano, E. (2000) *Theory and Application Manual for the Reasoning and Rehabilitation Programme Revised*. Ottawa: T3 Associates Inc.

Porporino, F. J. and Fabiano, E. (2005) *The Focusing on Re-Entry Programme (F.O.R.): Theory and Conceptual Overview*. Ottawa: T3 Associates Inc.

Porporino, F. J. and Fabiano, E. (2008) 'Case Managing Offenders Within a Motivational Framework', in G. McIvor and P. Raynor (eds) *Developments in Social Work with Offenders*. London: Jessica Kingsley.

Prochaska, J. O. and Levesque, D. A. (2002) 'Enhancing Motivation of Offenders at Each Stage of Change and Phase of Therapy', in M. McMurran (ed.) *Motivating Offenders to Change: A Guide to Enhancing Engagement in Therapy*. Chichester: John Wiley.

Rex, S. (1999) 'Desistance from Offending: Experiences of Probation', *Howard Journal*, 38 (4): 366–83.

Rex, S. (2001) 'Beyond Cognitive-behaviouralism? Reflections on the Effectiveness Literature', in A. Bottoms, L. Gelsthorpe and S. Rex (eds) *Community Penalties: Change and Challenges*. Cullompton: Willan Publishing.

Sampson, R. J. and Laub, J. H. (1993) *Crime in the Making: Pathways and Turning Points Through Life*. Cambridge, MA: Harvard University Press.

Serin, R. and Lloyd, D. (2009) 'Examining the Process of Offender Change: The Transition to Crime Desistance', *Psychology, Crime and Law*, 15 (4): 347–64.

Shapiro, C. (2003) *Families: A Critical Resource for New Jersey Prisoner Reentry Strategy*. Newark, NJ: New Institute for Social Justice.

Sherman, L., Gottfredson, D., McKenzie, D., Eck, J., Reuter, P. and Bushway, S. (1997) *Preventing Crime: What Works, What Doesn't, What's Promising*. Washington, DC: Office of Justice Programmes.

Shover, N. (1996) *Great Pretenders: Pursuits and Careers of Persistent Thieves*. Boulder, CO: Westview Press.

Sullivan, E., Milton, M., Nelson, K. and Pope, J. (2002) *Families as a Resource in Recovery from Drug Abuse: An Evaluation of La Bodega de la Familia*. New York: Vera Institute of Justice.

Travis, J. and Petersilia, J. (2001) 'Re-Entry Reconsidered: A New Look at an Old Question', *Crime and Delinquency*, 47: 291–313.

Uggen, C. (2000) 'Work as a Turning Point in the Life Course of Criminals: A Duration Model of Age, Employment and Recidivism', *American Sociological Review*, 65: 529–46.

Uggen, C. and Janikula, J. (1999) 'Volunteerism and Arrest in the Transition to Adulthood', *Social Forces*, 78: 331–62.

Van Voorhis, P., Spruance, L. M., Ritchey, P. N., Listwan, S. W. and Seabrook, R. (2004) 'The Georgia Cognitive Skills Experiment: A Replication of Reasoning and Rehabilitation', *Criminal Justice and Behaviour*, 31 (3): 282–305.

Vaughn, B. (2007) 'The Internal Narrative of Desistance', *British Journal of Ciminology*, 47: 390–404.

Vignoles, V. L., Manzi, C., Regalia, C., Jemmolo, S. and Scabini, E. (2008) 'Identity Motives Underlying Desired and Feared Possible Future Selves', *Journal of Personality*, 76 (5): 1165–200.

Ward, T. and Marshall, B. (2007) 'Narrative Identity and Offender Rehabilitation', *International Journal of Offender Therapy and Comparative Criminology*, 51: 279–97.

Ward, T. and Nee, C. (2009) 'Surfaces and Depths: Evaluating the Theoretical Assumptions of Cognitive Skills Programmes', *Psychology, Crime and Law*, 15 (2–3): 165–82.

Ward, T. and Stewart, C. (2003) 'Criminogenic Needs and Human Needs: A Theoretical Model', *Psychology, Crime and Law*, 9: 125–43.

Ward, T., Melser, J. and Yates, P. M. (2007) 'Reconstructing the Risk-Need-Responsivity Model: A Theoretical Elaboration and Evaluation', *Aggression and Violent Behavior*, 12: 208–28.

Yahner, J., Solomon, A. L. and Visher, C. (2008) *Returning Home on Parole: Former Prisoners' Experiences in Illinois, Ohio, and Texas*. Washington, DC: Urban Institute.

Zamble, E. and Quinsey, V. L. (1997) *The Criminal Recidivism Process*. Cambridge: Cambridge University Press.

Part Two

Overview

In Part One the scene was set. The uncertainty of the future for the probation service was a theme clearly identified. While Vanstone talked of a past probation service with a rich history full of creativity and experimentation, he sees this attitude and approach being squeezed out with the move towards a law enforcement and management agency that would do little more than assess risk and sequencing of interventions. One may think, therefore, that the flexibility and innovation in a struggle to develop better and more effective ways of supervision has been stifled!

The theoretical aspects of desistance have been explored by Weaver and McNeill, which further helps our understandings of the processes through which people come to cease offending. Officer–offender relationships, social contexts and issues of identity and diversity are significant issues that will impact on offending behaviour and desistance from it. As such their chapter provides a resource on which creative practitioners can draw rather than providing a prescription of what creative practice might be.

Porporino followed on and talked about sense and sensibility. He questioned past correctional ways of working with offenders and asked a very pertinent question: has the directed and prescriptive change-the-offender agenda in corrections blinded us to other ways of approaching the challenge? His chapter presented a new and exciting way of thinking that moved us away from a preoccupation on correction to a more complete appreciation of the forces and influences that might help offenders find and follow their own way out of offending.

Part Two of this book highlights that creativity has not been stifled. Practitioners, policy-makers and academics variously discuss the creative ways in which they are working with offenders or other socially excluded people or ways in which this could happen. Even within, or perhaps because of, the current focus on risk, risk management, the meeting of

National Standards and targets, there are some exciting and creative things going on. Creativity cannot be stifled; human beings are very resourceful. Many of the initiatives documented are not new and can be traced back through history, while others represent new ways of working or thinking. What all the chapters have in common is a desire to work with offenders and other socially excluded people in ways that make a difference to people's lives including offenders, victims and society.

Chapter 5 by Jenny Roberts focuses on women offenders and recognises their specific and often unmet needs. The Asha Women's Centre, one response to these unmet needs, is a rare and creative example of a women-centred one-stop shop that was set up with the aim of reaching women who are isolated by disadvantage and providing them with access to resources to help them achieve their social and economic potential. Roberts points out that one of the main statutory agencies (the probation service) that might have been expected to address the needs of women has generally failed to do so. This is especially contradictory given that the probation service is mainly made up of women probation officers, and as such this is one of the tensions highlighted in this chapter.

Chapter 6 continues to explore facilities for offenders and other socially excluded people but looks at a very different form of provision: hostels and approved premises. Cowe and Cherry argue that these are at risk of becoming 'warehouses' that merely manage and contain offenders notion-ally 'in the community'. This chapter explores another more humanitarian and creative way of working with high-risk offenders, and this is to develop more of a 'greenhousing' approach. The authors set out the key elements to such an approach and suggest that this creative way of working may enable individual change and growth alongside the contri-bution to risk management and public protection, and indeed may be more efficacious in protecting the public.

Attention then turns to creative ways in working with minority ethnic offenders. Durrance, Dixon and Bhui begin with a question: why is it important to find creative ways of working with black and minority ethnic offenders? The authors set about answering this question by looking at the history and current approaches of working with minority ethnic offenders. They also look at challenges and the need for innovation. Interestingly a worry is identified at the outset, and this is one that emerges as a concern for many of the authors in this book: that the many recent changes in probation practice and the subsequent reduction in face-to-face work may undermine the energetic creativity of some of the historically creative initiatives developed by probation staff. This is all the more worrying with regard to issues of race and diversity given the lack of any substantial body of research in this area and the lack of reassurance that these issues will be given sufficient attention by what they refer to as the 'troubled' National Offender Management Service. With these issues in mind they argue for a desistance-focused practice that respects the multifaceted identities of minority ethnic offenders and encourages creative ways of reinforcing those that are most positive.

Following on from this is a chapter that focuses on youth justice. Drakeford and Gregory argue that the hallmark of a successful society, in relation to young people and the criminal justice system, is achieved when the former have as little as possible to do with the latter. Again we see an argument put forward against the top-down authoritarianism that has been the watchword of New Labour, stifling local resourcefulness and imagination in the enthusiastic embrace of its popular punitivism. Attention is directed to localism, and more specifically the new Child Trust Fund, credit union development and time banks, which are all assets that can be exploited by young people. These are indeed innovative and creative ways in which young people can harness and draw on assets to help them take control and create opportunities previously prohibited due to lack of income.

While some of the issues in this text – minority ethnic offenders, 'race' and diversity, and gender being the most obvious – cross local, national and international boundaries, there are different political boundaries in England and Wales. Chapter 9 touches upon some of these differences but the focus remains on youth justice. Attention is given to the transition of young people from custody to the community. The project discussed is an initiative developed by the Welsh Assembly Government (WAG) and was set up as one creative way in which to work with Welsh young offenders, many of whom were serving a custodial sentence in England and then resettling back in Wales. The project employed youth workers rather than youth justice workers and this represented a creative departure from the orthodox as it worked through a voluntary relationship that is at the heart of youth work. Brayford and Holtom argue that while projects of this nature may be costly, the benefits far outweigh the wider human and financial costs of future offending behaviour.

Chapter 10 examines sex offender provision. The authors argue that although CBT approaches can help to reduce recidivism, other more creative ways of working with this group of offenders should be explored. The chapter explores two new innovative conceptual approaches: the Good Lives Model (GLM) and Circles of Support. The two approaches offer different but very interesting methods of working with sex offenders. The GLM looks at the causes of sex offending and incorporates risk management principles into a more holistic strengths-based approach to sex offender rehabilitation. Circles of Support, on the other hand, developed in Canada but exported to the UK, is rooted in the community and consequently focuses attention on the management of sex offenders in the community using volunteers.

Chapter 11 presents another very different creative way of working. It charts the territory and benefits to some prisoners and probationers who are working in, and having contact with, nature in forest and conservations management environments. Building upon the work of McNeill (2006, and Chapter 3 in this book) Carter and Pycroft argue for a new paradigm that focuses on processes of change rather than modes of intervention. More specifically they argue for a move away from 'desistance-impeding interventions' towards a 'desistance-enhancing interventions' (Maruna 2007). Working in forest management and conservation enhances personal health and well-being as well as helping offenders to develop social capital. As such these meaningful work placements adopt a biopsychosocial approach to desistance and symbolise a big step from feeling and being seen as an offender or ex-offender to feeling and taking one's place as a citizen.

The book would feel incomplete without a look at the problems and possibilities for offender management and Maguire and Raynor provide this in Chapter 12. They review the National Offender Management Model (NOMM) implementation process, revisit some early concerns about its implementation, review progress and consider whether or not the model shows any signs of fulfilling its potential. As Maguire and Raynor argue, the probation service is hostage to political will as well as being increasingly reliant on other organisations to provide the necessary services required for effective supervision with offenders.

While Chapter 12 focuses specifically on the current state of play for NOMS, the concluding chapter looks at the wider implications for offenders and other socially excluded people. Chapter 13 does not repeat the arguments already made, but draws upon the central themes made in earlier chapters. In so doing it provides discussion of some of the tensions and problems that are evident, and reviews potential theoretical and policy implications. As such the authors move away from the What Works agenda and open up a dialogue for further discussion and debate about creative work, that has been, and is still, going on outside of this agenda.

References

Maruna, S. (2007) 'After Prison What? The Ex-prisoners Struggle to Desist from Crime', in Y. Jewkes (ed.) *The Handbook on Prisons*. Cullompton: Willan Publishing.

McNeill, F. (2006) 'A Desistance Paradigm for Offender Management', *Criminology and Criminal Justice*, 1: 39–62.

Chapter 5

Women offenders: more troubled than troublesome?

Jenny Roberts[1]

I have been dismayed at the high prevalence of institutional misunderstanding within the criminal justice system of the things that matter to women and at the shocking level of unmet need. Yet the compelling body of research which has accumulated over many years consistently points to remedies. Much of this research was commissioned by government. There can be few topics that have been so exhaustively researched to such little practical effect as the plight of women in the criminal justice system. The volume of material might lead one to suppose that this is a highly controversial area, which might account in some way for the lack of progress and insight in the way women continue to be treated. This is not the case. There is a great deal of evidence of fundamental differences between male and female offenders. (Corston 2007: 16)

Baroness Corston had been commissioned to conduct 'an independent review of "vulnerable" women offenders and other vulnerable women who come into contact with the police or courts, identifying gaps in provision for their needs within the criminal justice system and related health services'. The review was to be 'focused on the group of women offenders who have multiple needs, particularly those women whose risk factors could lead them to harm themselves in prison, and take fully into account existing and planned work' (Corston 2007: Terms of Reference, Appendix B). The review was often presented to the public as having been triggered by a sequence of six suicides in a single year by women prisoners at HM Prison Styal, but the terms of reference above, defined by Baroness Scotland, a Home Office Minister, envisaged a broad investigation that went beyond prisons and even offenders, and also pointed clearly to the part that mental health problems play in the lives of vulnerable women.

The question implicit in Jean Corston's observation (why criminal justice policy does not flow logically from research findings) is important, but equally important is the fact that a compelling body of research alone was insufficient to remove the barriers to the provision of appropriate methods of dealing with women offenders. Since the 1990s, research had identified that women offenders needed specifically women-centred provision, but the policy climate only began to thaw sufficiently when campaigning organisations (especially the Prison Reform Trust and the Fawcett Society) raised the public profile of women offenders. The disproportionate rise in the women's prison population in England and Wales provided an important focus for their campaigns. Gelsthorpe and Morris (2002) reported that receptions of women into prison had increased by 142 per cent between 1990 and 2000, compared with a 34 per cent increase in male receptions in the same period, and they provide a useful analysis of this trend, and a discussion of women's pathways to offending. In this chapter, it is my intention to discuss the development of a more appropriate manner of intervening with women offenders in the community, with specific reference to one such project, the Asha Centre, Worcester.

Several reports (such as Prison Reform Trust 2000; Esmée Fairbairn Foundation 2004; and Fawcett Society 2003–2009) essentially reiterated the same arguments and ensured that the issue was rarely out of the limelight. It could be argued that any serious opposition to a different approach to women offenders had been thoroughly tested. The commissioning of Jean Corston's review by the Home Secretary in November 2005 signalled that the government was receptive to recommendations for change (senior politicians and officials had been members of the other reporting bodies). It was framed as a review of current initiatives relevant to women offenders 'with particular vulnerabilities'; including the recently proposed 'Together Women' demonstration projects (see below). A number of its recommendations echoed those of an earlier report on women's imprisonment (the Wedderburn Report: Prison Reform Trust 2000).

The current policy context: a need is recognised

In March 2005, shortly before commissioning the Corston Review, the then Home Secretary Charles Clarke announced an investment of over £9 million in

radical new approaches to help reduce women's offending. The new initiatives will be set up in two areas and will include women's community supervision and support centres, where female offenders can access a whole range of services and support designed to meet their needs. They will provide women with the help and support they need to tackle issues such as drug abuse, mental health problems, housing, childcare, domestic violence and other issues that can affect why women offend. These 'one-stop-shops' will learn from the experiences of existing projects such as the Asha Centre in Worcester and the 218 Project in Glasgow, both of which already offer an innovative range of services to women in the community. By tackling these problems more effectively in the community the aim is to reduce the use of custody for women offenders. (Home Office 2005)

The new projects were called the Together Women projects, and the funding was allocated to the North West and the Yorkshire and Humberside National Offender Management Service (NOMS) regions. The projects comprised five 'one-stop' shops for women offenders and women at risk of offending, operated by voluntary organisations and coordinated through the regional offices of NOMS and through the Women's Policy Team at the Ministry of Justice.[2]

The two models cited by the Home Secretary were in some respects very different. The 218 Project in Glasgow was the product of a policy debate that led to substantial funding being allocated by the Scottish Office, the NHS and Glasgow Social Services to Turning Point Scotland,[3] to offer an alternative to custody for women offenders affected by substance misuse. The Project offers a 14-bed residential unit and 50 non-residential places (Loucks *et al.* 2006).

The second model was the Asha Women's Centre in Worcester. This was (and remains) a voluntary organisation that offers a one-stop shop for women referred by local agencies, including offenders but not exclusively so. Its aim is to reach women who are isolated by disadvantage, providing access to a range of resources (but not residential accommodation) that will help them to achieve their social and economic potential. What both centres had in common is that they were rare examples (at that time) of women-centred one-stop shops that provided for or included offenders. There were at the time very few other such examples in the UK. It is upon the development and operation of the Asha Centre that this chapter is focused.

The Together Women projects were initially funded until 31 March 2009. An initial evaluation (Hedderman *et al.* 2008) reported favourably on the way the projects had been implemented, and their costs will continue to be met. In February 2009 Maria Eagle, Minister at the Ministry of Justice, announced that £15.6 million would be invested over the next two financial years:

in the provision of additional services in the community for women offenders and women at risk of offending. The new funds will be directed towards building capacity of specialist provision for women in the community and developing bail support services. We propose that some of the funding will be used to invest in existing third sector providers, enabling them to work with courts, police, probation and other statutory agencies to provide support and services to vulnerable women in the criminal justice system. (Eagle 2009)

The first £4 million tranche of that funding has been awarded to seven providers: Anawim in Birmingham; Asha Women's Centre; Peterborough Women's Centre and Cambridge Women's Resource Centre (partnership bid); Tyneside Cyrenians (Newcastle upon Tyne); Safer Wales (Women's Turnaround Project); Women in Prison (London); and WomenCentre (Calderdale and Kirklees). The decision to provide funding for the continuing development of Together Women and similar projects was remarkable because of the pressures upon public spending at the time, and may be construed as firm evidence of the government's commitment to a women-centred approach to women offenders.

The Asha Centre: some background

Before moving to discuss in detail provision for women offenders, at this point it would be useful to briefly review some of the background to the development of the Asha Centre and its links to developments with working with women offenders in one particular probation service. Prior to the setting up of the National Probation Service for England and Wales (NPS) in 2001, local probation services had a history of *ad hoc* developments in interventions targeted upon and designed for various minority groups within the criminal justice system, including women. Prompted by a thematic inspection report on women offenders (HM Inspectorate of Probation 1991), the Hereford and Worcester Probation Service had developed a women-centred approach to women offenders, including a group programme that was multi-modal and could also be delivered one to one. Alongside the general group programme, an additional module dealing solely with offending behaviour was employed, to meet the needs of the relatively small proportion of women offenders considered by local practitioners to have more substantial cognitive behavioural problems. When the Home Office moved to only allowing the new probation areas in the NPS to use accredited programmes, the Hereford and Worcester programme was put forward for accreditation but refused, although it had been accepted as a 'pathfinder' programme. The establishment of the Asha Centre as a voluntary organisation offering a generic one-stop shop to women referred by other agencies should not be viewed as a reaction to the Home Office refusal to accredit the programme for women offenders. That move was initiated in 1997, in recognition of the response of a number of agencies to the existence of the Asha Centre, which enabled them to use its facilities to reach socially excluded women.

The main obstacle to accreditation appeared to relate to the requirement that accredited programmes dealt primarily with cognitive behavioural deficits that were viewed as susceptible to correctional treatment. The women's programme, by contrast, was a multi-modal programme, which assumed a weakness or breakdown in capacity to meet demands that could be counteracted by a range of techniques very similar to those used in other programmes, but with an emphasis on empowerment, and on improving access to community resources. When Home Office officials stated, with apparent conviction, that it was preferable to offer women offenders programmes based on what was known to be effective (*sic*) with male offenders, than to pursue other options, any reconciliation of views was considered unlikely (see Carlen 2002 for a fuller discussion).

The views of Home Office officials reported above were put into question by Home Office Research, Development and Statistics Directorate publications in 2003 and 2006 (Falshaw *et al.* 2003; Cann 2006). These found no statistically significant differences in one and two-year reconviction rates between (respectively) male and female offenders who participated in two accredited cognitive behavioural programmes and control groups. The more recent report observes that the programmes were developed around the known needs of male offenders and observes (inaccurately) that there had been little research into the needs of female offenders until recently. In particular it concludes that there is no clear evidence for a link between cognitive deficits (weaknesses in understanding the link between thoughts, actions and consequences) and women's offending: the presumed link upon which the entire body of cognitive behavioural programmes as developed for use by HM Prison Service in England and Wales was based.

At the time the programme was selected as a pathfinder, the Probation Studies Unit at the University of Oxford was commissioned to undertake an evaluation of the programme as it was being delivered in Hereford and Worcester Probation Service prior to the development work associated with the accreditation process (2000). Samples comprising 591 women who had either attended the programme or been sentenced to other disposals were drawn up. To ensure reliability, it was necessary to match the women's criminal records on both the Offender Index and the Police National Computer, and the researchers found an unusually high level of non-matches. The final sample of 575 women was achieved by identifying matches between the PNC and the service's own information system (IOSS). Table 5.1 shows the construction of the sample.

The evaluation found that 70 per cent of women who completed one session of the group work programme went on to complete the whole programme. It also found statistically significant differences in reconvictions between programme completers and non-completers at 12, 18 and

Table 5.1 Available data on women offenders in the Hereford and Worcester evaluation

Dates	Types of cases	Sampled cases	Women occurring more than once	Missing cases	Source of reconviction data		
					PNC	IOSS	Recon cases
1994–96	Women's programme attenders	110	0	0	56	54	110
1997–98	Women's programme attenders	96	14	0	42	40	82
1994–98	Women's programme attenders	206	14	0	98	94	192
1997–98	Custody sentences	26	0	0	26*	26*	26
1997–98	Probation and combination orders	209	26	1	92	90	182
1997–98	Community service orders and other disposals	289	99	15	94	81	175
	Total	730	139	16	310*	291*	575

*The PNC and IOSS custody samples comprise the same women offenders.

24 months after completion suggesting that the results were not due to a selection effect, and therefore indicating the possibility of a treatment effect (Probation Studies Unit 2000).

When women involved with the programme were compared with those who were otherwise dealt with by the courts, it was reported that:

> The differences between the programme completers and both the custody and probation/combination order groups just failed to reach significance (p>0.1) at the twelve, eighteen and twenty-four month stage. A significant 'treatment' effect for the women's programme is not clearly established by this particular data, but the small differences are all marginally in favour of programme completers over any of the other disposals. (See Figure 5.1)

The report of the evaluation by the Probation Studies Unit was completed in September 2000, but not formally considered by the Accreditation Panel that had decided to refuse accreditation to the programme in August 2000.

This was the only quantitative study of the Hereford and Worcester work with women offenders. However, in 2004 the Asha Centre published

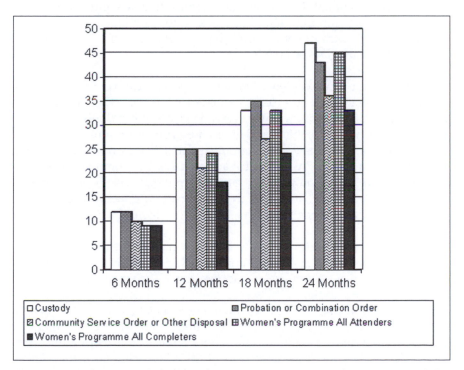

Figure 5.1 Proportion of women offenders reconvicted over four time periods by the type of sentence, and attending or completing the women's programme

a qualitative evaluation undertaken to mark the end of a period of West Midlands Government Office funding for the new one-stop shop (Rumgay 2004a). This was an unusual study because the women offenders who participated had undertaken the programme either before or after the new centre was established (between 2000 and 2003). The sample was very small (19 women), illustrating the difficulty for voluntary organisations in following up their service users; but the study also included an important and unusual element – a survey of the partner organisations linked to the centre, which produced universal approval of the work of the centre. In discussing the views of the women offenders, Rumgay observed 'their frequent claim to have "taken control", to be "in charge", and to feel increased confidence in problematic situations'. She links this with Maruna's (2001) finding that the 'active voice' distinguished desisting from active offenders:

> The changes reported by women were of kinds that aligned them more closely with conventional lifestyles. Their attachment or re-attachment to conventional citizenship was demonstrated through their connection to relationships and statuses that supported their identities as conforming individuals, such as mother, daughter, employee or student. Moreover, these connections gave them 'something to lose' through slipping back into previous behavioural patterns, or 'stakes in conformity' that supported their maintenance of change. (Rumgay 2004a: 29)

The programme for women offenders was not delivered after 2003, because, as mentioned, the local probation area was then required to deliver an accredited programme (Enhanced Thinking Skills) to women offenders. For two years this was delivered by probation staff at the centre, but attrition of participant numbers meant that it was rarely completed. Meanwhile, staff at the Asha Centre adapted the programme for women offenders into an empowerment programme that has been delivered successfully to its users and it is this, alongside a general discussion of might work with women offenders, that is the focus for the rest of this chapter.

Her Majesty's Inspectorate of Probation conducted a thematic inspection of women offenders in 1991 that included analysis of probation reports on women sentenced to imprisonment, and made a number of recommendations designed to secure 'substantive equality'. The Inspectorate recognised that women offenders could not be expected to benefit from provision designed for male offenders, and the development of methods other than traditional one-to-one supervision (community service orders, schedule 11 requirements of the 1982 Criminal Justice Act to attend group programmes, in particular) had highlighted the absence of women-centred options for courts (HMIP 1991).

Whether traditional one-to-one supervision also demonstrated substantive equality is open to debate: one curiosity of the legal framework for the probation service is that until the 1967 Criminal Justice Act was implemented, all women and children were supervised by women probation officers. This necessitated the appointment of at least one woman probation officer to every petty sessional division and ensured that supervision was women-friendly. An observation in King (1969) suggests that it may have been repealed because of the difficulty of providing women supervisors in some parts of the country.

At the time of publication of the Inspectorate's report in 1991, the Hereford and Worcester Probation Service had articulated a commitment to delivering programmes that drew upon academic research and evaluated offender treatment methods.[4] It also aimed to provide local courts with group programmes designed for specific groups of offenders, such that courts had the opportunity to order up to 90 per cent of offenders who were sent to custody to attend such a programme as an alternative. This policy had developed following the remarkable apparent success (in the 1980s) of a multi-modal group programme for young adult offenders in reducing reconvictions (C. Roberts 1994; J. Roberts 1994). Building on this success, other programmes had subsequently been developed for sex offenders, drink drivers, anger management, adult property offenders and other groups. The Hereford and Worcester Service was one of two probation services that took a lead role in establishing and delivering the What Works conferences that brought together leading academics from many countries with managers and practitioners to support developments in this field. In this context, the challenge posed by the Inspectorate's recommendation that probation services make specific provision for women offenders led to the approval of an anti-sexism strategy by the local Probation Committee in 1992, and the development of the group work programme for women offenders (PWO) based on what was known from research about what might work with women offenders.

Some other probation services also responded to the original challenge from the Inspectorate, but not all. In 1996 HM Inspectorate of Probation found that: 'a minority of probation areas had strategies, action plans or practice guidelines to help ensure that women had equal access to community sentences'.

Developing a programme for women offenders: identifying needs

In Hereford and Worcester, two probation staff were tasked with finding out what was known about the needs of women offenders and designing a programme to meet those needs. One of them was experienced in delivering some of the other group programmes offered to courts locally, but they also researched and visited women-centred provision (not solely for offenders) elsewhere in the United Kingdom. One of the local teams had also been operating its own group programme for the women on their caseload, and this was influential in shaping the design of the programme. The staff involved quickly came to the view that a separate women-only centre was necessary for delivery of the programme, and the first Asha Centre was established.[5]

It was decided that an external consultant be appointed to support the development of the work. Dr Judith Rumgay worked with the team from 1995, and made an influential contribution to the development of the theoretical basis for their work (Rumgay 2000), including an audit of reports written about women offenders by local probation officers. Rumgay referred to specific levels of need described in the reports:

- Almost universal poverty

- Current involvement in abusive relationships or intimidating relationships with a male person

- Child abuse survival

- Alcohol and drugs

The 12-session programme for women offenders (later adapted to be delivered one-to-one and with additional specialised modules for specific issues and an induction module delivered in local teams) was designed around issues that a literature review had shown to be relevant to women, including debt management, domestic violence, employment and training, assertiveness, relationships and women's health; where relevant the sessions were co-led by an expert from a relevant community organisation. Indeed, the involvement of community organisations in the work of the original probation centre was both very productive and influential in the subsequent decision to develop a generic voluntary organisation.

The programme sessions dealing with relevant needs were firmly placed in the context of developing strategies to avoid offending. The programme was delivered through a single centre (the original Asha Centre) and locally by specialist women supervising officers.

Subsequently the identification and analysis of women offenders' needs that underpinned the programme was supported by the use of the ACE[6] system. A later analysis by Simon Merrington (2001a) of a sub-sample of ACE reports completed in the Hereford and Worcester and Greater Manchester areas in 1999 and 2000 demonstrated the marked contrast between the offending-related needs of male and female offenders. The main analysis is reported in ACE Practitioner Bulletin 4 (Merrington 2001b).

Table 5.2 is an extract, and all the differences shown were statistically significant as factors identified in pre-sentence reports as related to offending. The only statistically significant problem that applied only to

Table 5.2 Comparative prevalence in court reports of problems linked to offending

Problems linked to offending	Female n=180 (%)	Male n=1117 (%)
Accommodation problem	+10*	
Looking after home	+22**	
Financial problem	+22**	
Living alone with children	+23**	
Family/relationship problems	+19*	
Alcohol (offence-related)		+13*
Physical health problem	+14*	
Mental health problem	+36***	
Interpersonal skill problems	+13*	
Self-esteem problem	+39***	
Taking responsibility/control	+11*	

*Level of significance of association with offending behaviour

Table 5.3 Extract from OASys records of 22,000 offenders in an English region in 2005–06

Criminogenic needs	Male offenders (%)	Female offenders (%)
Accommodation	35	39
Education/employment	55	62
Financial management/income	22	30
Relationships	37	60
Lifestyle/associates	40	36
Drugs	27	31
Alcohol	42	30
Emotional well-being	36	60
Thinking and behaviour	56	45
Attitudes	26	17

male offenders was use of alcohol. The most prevalent problems for women were mental health problems and self-esteem.

A more recent and detailed analysis from the Yorkshire and Humberside region of NOMS is shown in Table 5.3, and is summarised from OASys records. The language used to describe the needs is different, in some instances because the ACE system had been modified to include needs specific to women offenders. However, the gender variations recorded by Merrington in the ACE analysis are mirrored in the OASys summary, albeit less markedly in some instances.

Although Tables 5.2 and 5.3 only provide lists of individual needs, it will be evident that some offenders must feature complex combinations of needs. This is an issue that was addressed by the definition of a model of change to explain women's offending and that also provides a classification of needs.

Defining the model of change

In 1998 the Hereford and Worcester programme for women offenders was identified as a Pathfinder for the new system of accreditation of group work programmes by a Home Office panel. There had been an earlier attempt to have it accredited as a prison programme, and two practice runs had been completed at the local women's prison (HMP Brockhill). Now considerable further work was undertaken by a group of probation staff to develop and manualise the programme and supporting supervision methods, and in particular to define the model of change that underpinned the design of the programme. Individual supporting modules were also developed for use in one-to-one supervision. One member of staff undertook a more detailed literature survey at the Institute of Criminology at Cambridge, under the supervision of Dr Loraine Gelsthorpe.

The model of change was required by the accreditation panel to account for women's offending behaviour and is briefly described in the following extract from the programme theory manual (Hereford and Worcester Probation Service 1999: 3), which contains the findings of the literature survey about offending by women and how women are affected by a range of social issues and role expectations:

The model explains offending by women as the product of a breakdown in their ability to hold in balance:

- the demands upon them (deriving both from their position as women and from their specific circumstances)

- the external resources and legitimate opportunities available to them

- and their capacity/functioning (which is assumed in the model usually to be impaired usually as a result of their history and experiences).

Other crises may also occur when they cannot maintain that balance. Within that broad account, the model accommodates the behaviour of both late-onset and persistent women offenders, those who have adopted a criminal lifestyle as their preferred method of maintaining that dynamic

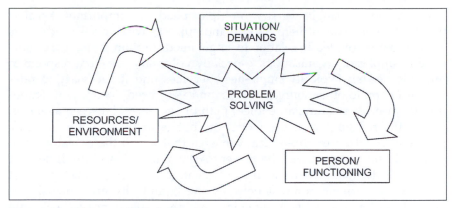

Figure 5.2   The model of change

balance; and those who feature recognisable cognitive-behavioural deficits.

A pictorial version of the model illustrates its dynamic nature (see Figure 5.2). In this model, offending is seen as a failure of 'problem-solving' and other types of crisis (some mental illness, self-harm) may also be explicable as a failure of problem-solving.

The model also organises or classifies the needs of offenders into three groups:

- Person/functioning can include mental health, substance misuse, low self-esteem, eating disorders, skills deficit, low confidence and self-esteem.

- Demands can include being a lone parent or carer, domestic violence and other forms of victimisation, childcare, caring for a home, responsibility for family budget.

- Resources can include (lack of) family or social support, unemployment, poverty, inability to access services, poor housing.

The dynamic nature of the model is important. Disadvantage in a single area of the model is probably very widespread. Disadvantages in two or three areas interact to compound the effects of each, to the point where in extreme cases women may be enmeshed in a complex web of disadvantage from which it is impossible to extricate themselves. A common example is a lone parent with young children and no family support, low skills and earning capacity, in receipt of benefits and under pressure from a drug pusher and/or a pimp, and often also a victim of physical or sexual abuse and affected as a consequence by mental health problems and low self-esteem.

The issue of single versus multiple needs is important because traditionally sources of help, advice and support with social needs have tended to be provided in relation to single needs (although there are some good examples of organisations, especially voluntary ones that respond to multiple needs). Typically single-need services find it necessary to refer their users on to other sources of help, and very needy people sometimes find themselves treading an endless path of re-referral between agencies. It was the recognition in the model of change of the difficulties facing people affected by multiple disadvantages that led to the one-stop shop approach that characterises the present Asha Women's Centre. Indeed, it was explicitly noted when the model of change was being developed that there was a striking contrast between the complexity and intensity of needs found among women offenders and their reluctance to seek help from agencies relevant to needs.

Many vulnerable women have been victims of male violence and abuse, and many are afraid of officialdom, afraid of being branded as poor mothers, possibly even quite simply unwilling to deal with rejection of their attempts to seek help. They are often the targets of policies that isolate and stigmatise them as a group and reinforce their lack of self-esteem: lone parents, undereducated, unemployed, unskilled, in receipt of benefits, mentally ill. Their functioning is impaired by their past experiences, and they may regard themselves as deserving little in the way of resources to help them deal with the demands they must meet. In particular, and given the positive way such women have responded to women-only, women-centred provision such as the Asha Centre, their reluctance may be described as a simple lack of confidence that their needs as women will be understood or accepted.

It is also evident that disadvantaged women often live in very disadvantaged areas, with little in the way of local resources to be accessed easily, and the added demands of protecting themselves and their dependents from high levels of crime. When low income, lack of personal transport and the demands of small children are factored in, it is perhaps not surprising that few of them have the resources required to seek the support and advice that might benefit them. Society demands that they give priority to home and children over their own needs, and they accept this. Yet the (lack of) resources element of the model is particularly important, because their needs in all areas of the model require effective access to support, advice and other resources.

The Joint Prison/Probation Accreditation Panel (since renamed the Correctional Services Accreditation Panel) declined to accredit the programme, but the model of change that had offered the framework for intervention with women offenders under probation supervision in Hereford and Worcester also profoundly influenced the development of the Asha Women's Centre as a voluntary organisation.

Women-centred, women-only provision for offenders and generic one-stop shops

There is a considerable amount of women-centred provision in the United Kingdom in the form of women's centres (Gelsthorpe *et al*. 2007) and women's organisations (such as the Women's Institute, Soroptimists, Mothers' Union, Women's Royal Voluntary Service), but relatively few examples of women-centred provision specifically for offenders or that accepts offenders. In addition to the Asha Centre, examples include the following:

- Adelaide House in Liverpool is one of very few surviving women's approved hostels.

- Trevi House in Plymouth offers residential places for women (who can be accompanied by their children) with alcohol and drug problems.

- The 218 Project in Glasgow is funded by the Scottish Office and provides both residential and non-residential facilities mostly for women whose offending is drug-related.

- Anawim was established in Balsall Heath, Birmingham initially for women involved in the sex industry but has broadened its intake to include other offenders. It operates as a one-stop shop.

- The Calderdale Centre in Halifax (and a linked centre in Kirklees) did not originally provide for offenders but now does so.

- The Together Women projects in Liverpool, Salford, Leeds, Doncaster and Bradford are funded by the Ministry of Justice (initially as demonstration projects). They provide primarily for offenders but also for vulnerable women at risk of offending.

- There are also a number of voluntary organisations that support women prisoners during sentence and following release (for example Women in Prison, Hibiscus).

The benefits of women-centred provision (that is, provision explicitly designed to respond to the needs of women) have already been identified in the context of needs. The benefits of one-stop shops are also evident given the complexity of needs identified among women offenders and other women isolated by disadvantage, and the interactive nature of those needs. This is defined by the model of change described above, which also points to the importance of tackling such needs simultaneously.

However, one of the main statutory agencies that might have been expected to address the needs of women in such a manner has generally failed to do so. Why the probation service has been unable to develop women-centred provision is difficult to explain, particularly in a service where over 67 per cent of probation officers are women (NOMS Human Resources Workforce Profile Report Issue 4 September 2007). Women represent between 10 and 20 per cent of the convicted offender population, but they are on average a lower risk group than the male offender population, and the resources of the probation service are increasingly applied to the management of higher risk offenders. This may explain why women's specific needs have been neglected. Nevertheless, for nearly a decade it was possible to operate a dedicated system of supervision for women offenders in a dispersed rural area like Hereford and Worcester with a single centre as the focus for practice excellence. This did not require substantial additional resources, only the support of management and the probation committee for some reorganisation of resources.

Women-only provision can be justified on separate grounds from women-centred provision not only because women who have been marginalised are more likely to believe that their needs will be understood and accepted, but also because women work particularly well together in women-only systems. This has long been discussed in relation to single-sex schools: it is known that boys and girls learn differently, and develop their abilities over different timescales. Most women work well together in groups, and at the Asha Centre the mutual support that women offer each other in group situations (courses, programmes and social events) is a powerful tool in helping them to achieve their goals.

One example of one-stop shop provision: the Asha Women's Centre

The current Asha Women's Centre in Worcester is a voluntary organisation with the explicit aim of providing vulnerable women (including offenders) referred by other agencies with a single access point to the range of services they need:

> The Asha Centre aims to benefit women who are isolated by disadvantage from resources that will help them to achieve their potential. Through the provision of information, advice and opportunities it will strengthen their social and economic proficiency and reduce the risk of offending and exclusion. (Asha Centre mission statement, June 2002)

As described above, the centre is a direct development from the work undertaken by the Hereford and Worcester Probation Service with women offenders until 2001. In that year, the Crime Reduction Director at the Regional Office for the West Midlands responded positively to an application for funding to establish an independent generic centre, and the new centre opened in May 2002. From the outset a high level of referrals was established, from both statutory and voluntary organisations. On average, between 250 and 300 referrals are received each year of women from Worcester and the surrounding towns. Worcester is not a severely deprived area (Department of Communities 2009) and it can be assumed that much higher levels of needs would be found in some urban areas.

As a generic centre it had the important advantage that it was not associated with any particular need and therefore being referred to or from the centre carried no stigma. This also enabled staff to focus on what the users had in common as women, rather than giving what may be undue weight to a specific need. Funding limitations meant that the willingness of the local college and the WEA (Workers' Educational Association) to offer free courses ensured that learning became an important element of centre provision. The considerable appetite that women referred to the centre showed for courses and groups was unexpected. Together with the generic intake and the focus on issues relevant to women, the acquisition of skills and knowledge was thought to have a normalising effect for socially excluded women. This may also explain why other needs, particularly substance misuse, were less often identified by the users than might be expected; and as a generic voluntary agency, the Asha Centre is under no obligation to detect or meet needs that the users themselves do not wish to nominate. As a voluntary organisation, the Asha Centre is able to learn from experience and to innovate to an extent that is no longer possible in the statutory sector.

At an initial interview, women referred to Asha are encouraged to identify the obstacles in their lives that prevent them from achieving their potential, and to develop a personal plan to use the resources that can be mobilised for them, to overcome those obstacles and take control of their lives. Monitoring of obstacles identified by the women regularly produces a pattern not unlike that found among women offenders, although only a minority of Asha Centre users are known offenders and some categories of need are not included in earlier examples of offender monitoring (see Table 5.4).

On average, each women identified 3.8 issues, but it is likely that this under-reports the complexity of their needs given that this was their first contact with the centre (and also that there are likely to be inconsistencies in practice between interviewers). Sometimes traumatic experiences are not disclosed during such early contacts; but other women feel sufficiently safe in this setting to disclose immediately experiences that were not previously disclosed to any other agency.

Responding to women's complex needs

A simple list of the provisions available to women at the Asha Women's Centre would not necessarily explain how and why these respond to the

Table 5.4 Obstacles identified by women referred to the Asha Women's Centre

	2007 (%)	2006 (%)		2007 (%)	2006 (%)
Abuse	34	38	Jobs/training/education	37	55
Legal	10	9	Drug/alcohol abuse	27	26
Housing	31	26	Mental health	51	64
Children	48	36	Bereavement	32	34
Partner	40	34	Isolation	55	64
Money/debt	33	34	Domestic violence	28	30
Self-harm	27	18	Low confidence/self-esteem	60	98
Eating disorder	7	16	Anger	37	28

complex needs identified above. It is equally important to identify the ethos within which it is delivered, and the key elements on which that ethos is based. Rumgay suggests that successful desistance from crime may involve recognition of an opportunity to claim an alternative, desired and socially approved personal identity, readiness for change, peer support, and access to pro-social community role models: 'The evidence for the crucial role of support networks for women's resilience to personal and social hardship implies that rehabilitation efforts should not focus solely on "fixing" individual shortcomings' (2004b: 415). Rumgay's analysis is primarily concerned with women offenders' desistance from offending, but the methods that flow from that analysis are equally relevant to other women who may not have offended but who are trapped by complex needs in situations from which they cannot extricate themselves.

The key elements of one-stop shops that provide women with an opportunity to claim an alternative identity are, first, that provision is women-centred, such that staff develop expertise in working with women, and women recognise that their needs will be understood. Provision of a crèche and of transport support for those otherwise unable to access the centre is evidence of that recognition. Second, empowering women is a fundamental aim of the centre, from the first contact at an assessment and planning interview. Women identify the obstacles they wish to overcome and are helped to translate these into an initial plan for using the resources of the centre. The provision of courses that lead to qualifications, or enable the acquisition of key skills such as use of computers, of an empowerment programme, and of opportunities to contribute to the work of the centre through fundraising or becoming a volunteer or mentor all contribute to the building of an alternative identity.

Peer support is an important tool that is applied by bringing women together in small groups at the earliest possible stage. Some women are too lacking in confidence and self-esteem to face others and need individual support first, but the majority gain courage from discovering that what they perceive as their own failures are shared by many other women. Mutual support and exchanging strategies for survival become the informal currency of such groups, whatever their formal aims. The provision of social outings and groups open up new experiences, such as art, singing and dance; books may provide quite complex benefits in terms of the resilience of a new identity, of social support and of access to role models and constructive scripts.

Flexibility is allied to individualisation of the centre's response to need. Although centre provision can be viewed as responding to needs in the three areas of the model of change (person, resources, demands) women are encouraged to choose their own route through what is on offer, and at their own pace. Fixing individual shortcomings is one of the choices that is available to women, but not imposed upon them.

On one level, one-stop shops offer a relatively obvious and straightforward mix of provision. The challenge lies in engaging with complex needs and this requires staff who are appropriately qualified, skilled and experienced. In addition, women staff provide role models, as do tutors, advisers, volunteers and mentors; and because the setting is informal, centre users may approach any of them for advice or support, and receive it. At times a very complex mix of subject expertise, educational and social work skills is required. Courses and programmes where disclosure or recall of past trauma is likely to occur must be staffed jointly by tutors and social work staff to ensure that the emotional impact can be appropriately handled while learning and empowerment proceed.

Similarly, engaging with complex needs requires a high level of competence in partnership work with other agencies that respond to specific needs. At any one time the staff of the Asha Centre in the small city of Worcester must maintain effective relationships with around 40 other organisations, that themselves may change or develop over time.

The effectiveness of a one-stop shop for women isolated by disadvantage

The complexities of evaluating provision designed to reduce re-offending pale alongside those of evaluating non-statutory provision designed to improve the social and economic functioning of women and delivered through individually tailored interventions. As Judith Rumgay found, tracing and engaging with women who are no longer in contact with the Asha Centre is not easy. It is also not easy to determine what effects can be attributed to the interventions and over what period of time. In addition, individual funders may require specific evaluation of the particular work they have funded; a current example relates to funding for work with women referred by mental health services, where a bespoke set of soft measures of progress has been required.

In practice, the Asha Women's Centre applies a number of methods of measuring effectiveness, and in particular a set of 'soft' measures of distance travelled. This involves self-assessment by service users at their first assessment and planning interview, and again at regular review interviews. The self-rating ('How do I feel?') is made by identifying a score on a 1 to 10 point scale on nine measures:

- Physical health

- Mental health

- Enjoyment of life

- Coping/problem-solving

- Assertiveness

- Confidence

- Self-esteem

- Motivation

- Relationships

The results are primarily used by support coordinators with individual service users, but when collated they tend to show average improvements of up to 12 points across all the measures in a three-month period, with an average of more than one point per measure. Service users do not, however, invariably report positive change, for life events can affect them adversely even if they find the centre helpful. In some respects, especially mental health, deterioration may be reported because users have become more aware of their own needs.

An independent evaluation (Jones 2007) of a specific 27-month project to enable socially excluded women to gain accredited qualifications found that over 70 per cent of participants gained a credit or award (and in addition some participants continued on relevant courses after the end of the project funding). Around one-third of participants progressed to employment, training, further and higher education and voluntary work. Many of the women were lone parents with young children, and could aspire to only part-time employment, if at all. The emphasis of the project was on recruiting the women to lifelong learning, and to identifying long-term development and progression goals, and these short-term achievements were viewed as very encouraging by project staff.

An entirely different test of the effectiveness of the Asha Centre can be found in the Together Women demonstration projects – to a substantial extent a replication of the work of the centre (albeit rather more generously funded). A report by Maura Jackson (2009) to the Together Women Board on lessons learned from the projects illustrates clearly that replication was achieved, and that despite the fact that the projects are more closely linked to the criminal justice system than is the Asha Centre, a very similar style of operation was achieved with a higher concentration of women offenders. The report also noted that where probation staff had been seconded to the projects to enable women to meet compliance expectations without making an additional journey to a probation office, no woman was breached as a result of non-attendance. This needs to be seen alongside Jean Corston's observation (Corston 2007) that at the time of her report, 50 per cent of new receptions of women offenders at Holloway Prison were for breach of requirements of a court sentence.

It was also reported informally at a Project Board meeting at the Ministry of Justice that self-reported re-offending rates over a period of up to two years in the North West region Together Women Projects had been 7 per cent, and in the projects in the Yorkshire and Humberside region 13 per cent in the first year (Jackson 2009, personal communication). In comparison, reconviction rates for women offenders in the first quarter of 2006 and published by NOMS in 2007 were around 33 per cent. A full reconviction evaluation is being undertaken by the University of Leicester.

Conclusion

The title of this chapter is taken from Gelsthorpe and Loucks' (Home Office 1997) discussion of magistrates' views about sentencing women offenders, the publication of which gave considerable encouragement to the probation staff who were developing and delivering the Hereford and Worcester Programme for Women Offenders. Their needs-based approach was quite explicitly marketed to magistrates' courts in the area and was well received. The idea of transferring the approach to a generic women-centred one-stop shop pre-dated the selection of the programme as a Pathfinder, for the charity was registered in 1997 by a steering group that formed in 1995. The Asha Women's Centre therefore owes its origins to the recognition of the importance of a multi-agency approach to the needs of socially excluded women.

The failure to secure accreditation by the Home Office Joint Prison/Probation Panel in 2000 undoubtedly led to the eventual demise of women-centred practice in the local probation service. Ultimate recognition of this approach by the Home Office (later Ministry of Justice) was not awarded because it reduces reconvictions (although it may do so); it was gained through pressure from campaigning organisations and the tenacity of key individual academics, civil servants and politicians, especially Baroness Corston. As Worrall argued: 'justice for women offenders will not be achieved through What Works programmes or conventional equal opportunities policies, unless there is a recognition of the particular social injustices with which many still have to contend' (2002: 148).

Economic arguments may also have played their part. In a recent publication by the New Economic Foundation (2008: 4) it was argued that:

> there are huge benefits from investing in alternatives to prison. Even small reductions in re-offending translate into significant savings. Traditional cost/benefit analysis only looks at narrow returns to one stakeholder, under-representing the real value of these initiatives. Taking an SROI approach shows us that because of their special position as primary carers, the costs of locking up women offenders will also have long-term consequences that will be felt by future generations.

The government decision to fund the Together Women projects represented the first step towards mainstreaming an approach that might have been mainstreamed earlier as a result of accreditation as a programme for offenders. However, the process of accreditation is likely to have reduced the scope for any subsequent creative developments in women-centred practice. The Ministry of Justice decision in 2009 to continue to fund both those projects and other existing voluntary sector projects may be construed as evidence of government commitment to this approach to offenders. Arguably, because it responds to women offenders as socially excluded, rather than solely to the offending that is the product of their needs, the development of the one-stop shop approach to work with women offenders may prove more relevant and effective than the original probation service methods on which it is based. It raises the question of whether a similar approach might be pursued with other groups of lower risk offenders.

The Ministry of Justice decision to support the voluntary sector in delivering services to offenders is by no means unprecedented. In the past, much of the provision of approved premises (also known as probation hostels) was originally made by voluntary organisations, as were drug and alcohol treatment services for offenders. What is unusual is the policy decision to restrict the funding of women-only one-stop shops to the voluntary sector, and the associated decision to include funding for women at risk of offending as well as for women offenders. The multiple disadvantages that affect women offenders and those at risk of offending not only justify the one-stop shop approach, but also point to the absence of appropriate women-centred provision in other services. The Criminal Justice Women's Strategy Unit has a cross-departmental remit, as described by Maria Eagle in the final written statement about implementation of the Corston Review in December 2008:

The Cross-departmental Criminal Justice Women's Strategy Unit now includes representatives from the Attorney General's Office, Government Equalities Office and the Department of Health, and we are continuing to negotiate with other departments to contribute resources. The Unit informs the work of the Ministerial Sub-Group on Implementation of the Government'sresponse to Corston; which has recently expanded its membership to include Ministers from both the Department for Innovation, Universities and Skills and Department for Children, Schools and Families. (Eagle 2008)

This multi-departmental approach to the resourcing of work with women offenders and those at risk of offending is perhaps more ground-breaking than the work itself, as it seeks to allocate responsibility for dealing with the causes of offending, or at least the disadvantages that are associated with offending, across a number of government departments. Something like this has been tried before in the public sector: the establishment of youth justice teams was achieved by directing relevant public sector agencies (police, probation and local authorities) to contribute resources to create multi-disciplinary teams; and a similar approach was taken to the establishment of drug intervention programmes. The decision to pursue implementation of the Corston Review *via* the voluntary sector implies a different balance between a criminal justice response to offending and a wider response to the factors associated with it. This is reflected in the allocation of responsibility for work with women offenders. The National Offender Management Service will continue to carry primary responsibility for higher risk women offenders who are subject to supervision in the community and following a custodial sentence, although probation and prison staff will be expected to make full use of the services offered from one-stop shops for such women; and the one-stop shops are expected to intervene directly with women offenders who are low risk, and therefore not a priority for probation service intervention (as well as with women at risk of offending).

The creativity and commitment that characterise the best voluntary sector services are not always sufficiently respected by funding bodies, who often levy demands that can distort the services that they are purchasing. The one-stop shop approach to women offenders is still in its infancy, with much yet to be learned about how to ensure it is effective, and it is important that it is able to retain the flexibility that will allow this to take place.

Notes

1 The author has been associated with the Asha Centre since it was first established in the Hereford and Worcester Probation Service and is currently Chair of Trustees of the Centre.

2 The Ministry of Justice was created in April 2007 and took over responsibility for much of the criminal justice system from the Home Office.
3 Turning Point Scotland is a voluntary organisation established to provide services for people with alcohol addictions, and later extending these to include those with drug addictions, mental health problems, and learning disabilities.
4 The author was Chief Officer of the Hereford and Worcester Probation Service at the time and this account is based upon personal knowledge.
5 The first Asha Centre was named by probation staff in tribute to the Asha project created in 1988 in Delhi by Dr Kiran Martin, the aim of which was to motivate, unite and empower poor people and especially women from slum districts. Asha means 'hope' in Hindi.
6 ACE is a case management assessment that provides a structured assessment of problems that research has shown to be related to offending ACE measures, the extent to which a problem exists, and also whether it is thought to be a contributory factor in offending. It was introduced in Hereford and Worcester in 1998, and featured some additional elements relevant to women offenders. It generates an offending-related score, and was superseded by OASys in England and Wales, but is still used in some other jurisdictions.

References

Cann, J. (2006) *Cognitive Skills Programmes: Impact on Reducing Reconviction Among A Sample of Female Prisoners*, Home Office Findings 276. London: Home Office.

Carlen, P. (ed.) (2002) *Women and Punishment: The Struggle for Justice*. Cullompton: Willan Publishing.

Corston, J. (2007) *A Report by Baroness Jean Corston of a Review of Women With Particular Vulnerabilities in the Criminal Justice System*. London: Home Office.

Department of Communities (2009) *Tracking Neighbourhoods: Economic Deprivation Index 2009*. Available online at www.communities.gov.uk/documents/commu nities/zip/1126210.zip

Eagle, M. (2008) *Final Written Ministerial Statement of Progress on the Government's Response to the Corston Review*. London: Ministry of Justice.

Eagle, M. (2009) Written Ministerial Statement, *Hansard*, 3 February. London: House of Commons.

Esmée Fairbairn Foundation (2004) *Crime, Courts and Confidence: Report of an Independent Inquiry into Alternatives to Prison*. London: Esmée Fairbairn Foundation.

Falshaw, L., Friendship, C., Travers, R. and Nugent, F. (2003) *Searching for 'What Works': An Evaluation of Cognitive Skills Programmes*, Home Office Findings 206. London: Home Office.

Fawcett Society (2003) *Report on Victims and Witnesses: Interim Report by the Commission on Women and the Criminal Justice System*. London: Fawcett Society.

Fawcett Society (2005) *Commission on Women and the Criminal Justice System: One Year On Report*. London: Fawcett Society.

Fawcett Society (2006) *Justice and Equality: Second Annual Review of the Commission on Women and the Criminal Justice System*. London: Fawcett Society.

Fawcett Society (2007) *Women and Justice: Third Annual Review of the Commission on Women and the Criminal Justice System*. London: Fawcett Society.

Fawcett Society (2009) *Engendering Justice: From Policy to Practice. Final Report of the Commission on Women and the Criminal Justice System*. London: Fawcett Society.

Gelsthorpe, L. and Morris, A. (2002) 'Women's Imprisonment in England and Wales: A Penal Paradox', *Criminal Justice*, 2 (3): 277–301.

Gelsthorpe, L., Sharpe, G. and Roberts, J. (2007) *Provision for Women Offenders in the Community*. London: Fawcett Society.

Hedderman, C., Palmer, E. and Hollin, C. (2008) *Implementing Services for Women Offenders and Those 'At Risk' of Offending – Action Research with Together Women*. Ministry of Justice Research Series 12/08. London: Ministry of Justice.

Hereford and Worcester Probation Service (1999) *Programme for Women Offenders Theory Manual*. Unpublished, available from the author.

HM Inspectorate of Probation (1991) *Report on Women Offenders and Probation Service Provision*. London: Home Office.

HM Inspectorate of Probation (1996) *A Review of Probation Service Provision for Women Offenders*. London: Home Office.

Home Office (1997) *Understanding the Sentencing of Women*, Home Office Research Study 170. London: Home Office.

Home Office (2005) *Announcement by the Home Secretary at the Launch of 'One Year On', a Report by the Fawcett Commission*. Home Office Press Release, March. London: Home Office.

Jackson, M. (2009) *Together Women Project: Key Lessons Learned to Date*, personal report to the Together Women Board at the Ministry of Justice.

Jones, I. (2007) *GQ – Get Qualified! An Evaluation*. Worcester: Asha Women's Centre.

King, J. (ed.) (1969) *The Probation and After-Care Service*, 3rd edn. London: Butterworths

Loucks, N., Malloch, M., McIvor, G. and Gelsthorpe, L. (2006) *Evaluation of the 218 Centre*. Edinburgh: Scottish Executive Justice Department.

Maruna, S. (2001) *Making Good: How Ex-Convicts Reform and Rebuild Their Lives*. Washington, DC: American Psychological Association.

Merrington S. (2001a), *ACE Profiles for Female, Ethnic Minority and Young Offenders*, Unpublished paper available from Probation Studies Unit, University of Oxford.

Merrington S. (2001b) *Emerging ACE Data: Further Analysis of Needs and Risk*, ACE Practitioner Bulletin 4. Oxford: Probation Studies Unit, University of Oxford.

New Economic Foundation (2008) *Unlocking Value: How We All Benefit From Investing in Alternatives to Prison for Women Offenders*. London: New Economic Foundation.

NOMS (2007) *Human Resources Workforce Profile Report Issue 4*. London: Ministry of Justice.

Prison Reform Trust (2000) *Justice for Women: The Need for Reform. The Report of the Committee on Women's Imprisonment*. London: Prison Reform Trust.

Probation Studies Unit (2000) *Report on the Retrospective Study of the Hereford & Worcester Probation Service Women's Programme*. Centre for Criminological Research, University of Oxford.

Roberts, C. (1994) 'Study of the Comparative Effects on Criminal Careers of Custodial Sentences and Community Sentences', paper presented to the Academy of Criminal Justice Sciences Annual Meeting, Chicago (March). Available from the author.

Roberts, J. (1994) 'Long Term Evaluation: Outcomes and Implications of the Young Offender Project', paper presented to the What Works conference, University of Salford. Available from the author.

Rumgay, J. (2000) 'Policies of Neglect: Female Offenders and the Probation Service', in H. Kemshall and R. Littlechild (eds) *User Involvement and Participation in Social Care: Research Informing Practice*. London: Jessica Kingsley.

Rumgay, J. (2004a) *The Asha Centre: Report of an Evaluation*. Worcester: The Asha Women's Centre.

Rumgay, J. (2004b) 'Scripts for Safer Survival: Pathways Out of Female Crime', *Howard Journal*, 43 (4): 405–19.

Worrall, A. (2002) 'Missed Opportunities: The Probation Service and Women Offenders', in D. Ward, J. Scott and M. Lacey (eds) *Probation: Working for Justice*. Oxford: Oxford University Press.

Chapter 6

Residential work with adult offenders: greenhouses or warehouses?

Francis Cowe and Sally Cherry

'Approved premises' (hostels for adult offenders) are a unique resource in the community[1] interventions field. They offer the possibility of interaction between staff and residents 24 hours a day, seven days a week, while being located in the community and this is key to their rehabilitative and dynamic risk management potential. Apart from a custodial sentence, criminal justice staff have no other measure in their public protection toolkit that affords the opportunity for such intensive, focused and potentially individually tailored change orientated intervention(s). The current stated purpose of approved premises is the provision of enhanced supervision as a contribution to the management of offenders who pose a significant risk of harm to the public (Home Office 2005).

This chapter argues that hostels/approved premises are at risk of becoming 'warehouses' focusing exclusively on risk and risk management. A shift towards a more control-focused practice is detectable in hostels. Their purposes are becoming redefined and remoulded into a form of 'new punitiveness' (Feeley and Simon 1994). Theory and engagement with hostel staff and residents suggest that a more creative model of the hostel as 'greenhouse' is possible. This chapter explores a 'greenhousing' approach (Cowe 2008)[2] arguing that work with high-risk offenders need not exclude the possibility of a creative and humanitarian practice. It sets out proposed key elements of such an approach suggesting how a creative hostels practice may enable individual change and growth alongside contributing to risk management and public protection. It also suggests that some recent risk-driven practices are in fact counterproductive to good risk management.

It will be argued that offender management that is devoid of the possibility of and a focus on change and reintegration risks moving towards an administrative 'warehousing' approach that manages and contains offenders, notionally 'in the community'. Communities may find an exclusionary approach appealing as it ignores the 'offenders are us' reality of who hostel residents are and places the responsibility for offenders within the criminal justice system (Gorman *et al.* 2006). However, this strategy creates a discourse of stigma and exclusion that stifles creative practice, thus reducing the possibility of reintegration.

The policy and practices of a society towards its offenders may end up being more revealing of society and policy-makers than the offenders it purports to be tackling. As Young notes (2001: 30), 'To successfully essentialise oneself it is of great purchase to negatively essentialise others.' A hostels policy that is built upon an essentialist ideology of residents as both other and risky will inevitably deny or denigrate the potential for those 'others' to change and ignore the creative potential that may come from engaging with the common humanity of 'residents', 'staff' and the 'wider community'. A brief overview of hostels past will demonstrate that an exclusive focus on 'care' or 'control' has been shown to be both counterproductive and ineffective. A consideration for policy-makers and practitioners in exploring hostels and their possible futures should include attention to previous research in this area. Cowe (2008) and Barton (2005) suggest that 'looking backwards to look forwards' may be underutilised as an approach by policy-makers keen to launch 'new' and 'improved' criminal justice services.

Looking backwards to look forwards

In the period between 1970 and the mid to late 1990s probation underwent considerable political and organisational transformation (Chui and Nellis 2003; Whitehead and Statham 2006) with the ripples of that change more recently resulting in the creation of the National Offender Management Service (NOMS) and the development of a more centralised and publicly visible service. In this period the service has shifted from a treatment and rehabilitation focus towards a public protection and offender management paradigm. A brief résumé of hostels' history in this period traces the impact of that shift on their purposes.[3]

Hostels and hostels policy have been through many changes in the last 40 years. A common thread throughout these changes has been a clear focus on the dual aims of transformation and resettlement. The former focused on enabling the individual to change or address specific problems; the latter on enabling those individuals who, as a result of their behaviour, addiction, social circumstance, imprisonment and or offending, were at the edges of or standing outside mainstream society to renegotiate a role and identity that allowed them to return to the community. How hostels have attempted to achieve these purposes and who this activity has been focused on has changed over time.

From Trotter's work *No Easy Road* (1969) it is clear that early pre-release hostels (linked to a prison) performed a testing-out role and flagged at an early stage the possibility of the coexistence of care and control functions. Although located within the prison boundary, once an inmate was accepted into the 'hostel' he ceased contact with the prison regime and other 'inmates', focusing his time on employment outside the prison and on resettlement work with the hostel staff.

The prisoner in effect became an 'outmate', being tested out for eventual freedom in the community. Such early hostel practices explicitly acknowledged the need to assess prisoners for their suitability for such regimes and supervised 'outmates' in a way that was realistic about the potential for re-offending. Engaging offenders in meaningful activity and wherever possible getting them into employment – making them active and productive social agents – was core to their purposes.

Rolph (1971), as part of a 1965 committee commissioned to look into the needs of homeless discharged prisoners, identified five distinct possible types of adult hostel: multipurpose; bedsitter; hostel for 'alcoholics'; hostel for 'aged offenders'; and work restoration therapy unit. He referred to these as 'halfway houses' (1971: 5): that is, for their residents they were halfway back into the community either from prison, their addiction or disenfranchised status. Although not strictly 'approved probation hostels', their work was supported by the Home Office and local probation areas and their staffing included probation staff on secondment as wardens or as members of the hostels' governing committee. A focus on enabling residents to resettle in the community was core to their identity. That is, it was hostels' role in this period to re-engage those whom society might find easier to leave in institutions back into normative and productive social relationships. Individual hostels' policy and focus appear to have been driven by the wider needs of the criminal justice system and at times a selective focus on a particular 'client' or 'social problem' grouping. Cook *et al.* (1968: 40) highlighted the ability of a hostel: 'to build up long standing relations with men who had previously been estranged from normal social contacts for long periods . . .'

Despite the focus on different potential resident populations, a common aspect has been an explicit focus on the potential care–control dynamic in the resettlement role of hostels and their relationship with residents and the communities in which they are located. This has been core to hostels' identity and function. Hostels constructed as places of control and separation from the community, primarily as places to warehouse 'risks', are a more recent addition to the hostel story. A potential role as a place of secure separation may have an initial appeal for some but it will later be argued that such a *cordon sanitaire* may be of limited social (and economic) value to communities and offenders.

When considering the change in the focus of hostels working with offenders it is important to note that from the mid-1970s to the 1980s a 'new' group of victims and offenders were being 'uncovered' or 'rediscovered'. Colton and Vanstone (1996: 2) note: 'In Britain, the number of children on the NSPCC register under child sexual abuse rose exponentially from 7 in 1977 to 527 in 1986.' Although sex offenders in hostels' current populations are often presented as a completely 'new' group offering uniquely different challenges from those faced by hostels in the past, discussions with those who were working in probation in this period suggest that the hostel estate housed a small but regular number of such offenders. By 1993 it was estimated that 260,000 men in England and Wales had a conviction for a sexual offence of which 110,000 were for an offence against a child (Calder *et al.* 1999: 4).

The development of regimes that can hold and purposefully direct a creative practice with the individual resident that is both change-focused and risk aware is not a new challenge. In the 1980s, Hampshire Probation Area trialled hostel approaches that separated out care and control, setting up one hostel that was very much control-focused with limited external community contact and another where the residents had almost complete freedom and involvement in running the hostel and deciding the rules.

Carlisle House had a regime devised by the warden Steve Essex, described as 'a radical and pioneering experiment in the therapeutic use of freedom' (Fisher and Wilson 1982: 11). It was informed by principles of having few rules, minimal use of staff authority and a democratic approach to day-to-day living. It was suggested that freedom from control and rules could be used to promote self-control and self-awareness. Such freedom was supposed to prepare the resident for a life of free choices in the community. Care, challenge, demand and stimulation were the four drivers.

Culverlands, on the other hand, 'subjected the resident to a formal structure with a rigid hierarchy and strict discipline requiring him to work his way up the hierarchy by demonstrating a willingness to develop and grow' (Fisher and Wilson 1982: 14). Culverlands was unique in the probation hostel work of its day for its explicit experimental work in creating a regime that explicitly sought to: (a) convert recidivists into law-abiding competent citizens; (b) achieve that aim by means of a comprehensive programme of communal therapy; and (c) unequivocally accept the control/punishment implications of treating clients sentenced by the courts (Fisher and Wilson 1982: 108). Culverlands focused on changing the individual with regard to their 'deviant lifestyles' and not just on meeting or assisting with their social or personal needs. It did not shy away from the imposition of a controlling regime: 'The resident is not permitted contact with any relative, friend or associate outside the community until he has become fully integrated into the programme and has shown that he can cope effectively with his own problems within the house' (Fisher and Wilson 1982: 112).

Both Culverlands and Carlisle House were deemed a failure and closed down. It is of note that the more controlling regime had the least success, with high levels of absconding and re-offending. Hostel residents who were left to make the decisions for themselves, however, were repeatedly frustrated at trying to understand what the hostel was for and what staff wanted them to do. Successful hostels need to be explicit about their values and ethos.

The experimental 'freedom' and 'authority' regimes showed that care implemented in isolation from control (or vice versa) and without reference to the individual residents' needs and risk creates a one-sided regime that has limited impact on residents. Hostels and their regimes can increase the risk of absconding and create stress and dissatisfaction for both staff and residents.

Brown and Geelan (1998: 13), exploring Elliot House in Birmingham, opened in 1994 for 'mentally disordered offenders', noted the role that residents can play in supporting each other. A focus on offenders as high risk or in need of constant monitoring may ignore the potential benefits (and risks) that exist in resident-to-resident interactions and the overall ethos and culture of the hostel.

In the 1990s hostels emerged with a focus on a range of diverse resident populations, including resettlement, bail, probation orders, licence release, women offenders and residents with drugs, alcohol and mental health problems. Their focus was often driven and shaped by a mixture of local probation area interests and a particular policy change or shift. Through-out this period the wider probation service had seen a shift from a treatment approach towards a more managerial and administrative processing and risk-focused practice (James and Raine 1998).

By the end of the twentieth century hostels presented a range of resettlement and rehabilitation specialisms for offenders (around 2,200 residents). Across England and Wales hostels took referrals on a local and national basis. They often became known individually for their particular specialism or as a place that would or would not take particular offence or offender referrals. Table 6.1[4] summarises some of the key features of hostels and hostel practice up to the mid 1990s and contrasts this with the emerging hostel policy and practice in today's hostels. Like all definitions of practice-focused reality, the extent to which this can be applied to each individual hostel will vary.

Within a revised public protection focused paradigm modern hostels risk becoming places that are halfway out as opposed to halfway in. In an ethnographic study, Cowe (2008) found that for some residents and staff hostels could be places of social exclusion and suggests that an overly risk-focused practice may be emerging. As Barton (2005) suggests, hostels can be damaging and excluding places. Without a renewed focus on hostels' rehabilitative and reintegrative potential they risk becoming warehouses: places where instead of working towards saving, developing

Table 6.1 Key features of hostel practice

Hostel	Old penology: 1960s–late 1990s	New penology: late 1990s onwards
Focus	Individuals Guilt responsibility Diagnosis Treatment	Managing groups Risk identification Risk classification Risk reduction
Themes	Transformation of the individual Change	Managing risk Protecting the public
Practices	Rehabilitative programmes Needs-based work Preparation for freedom Welfare Therapy	Actuarial profiling Preventative/pre-emptive incapacitation programmes Case management
Workers	Relative independence Professional discretion Welfare/change oriented Positivist outlook To the side of mainstream practice	Monitoring Managing Prescribed practice Administration/classification monitored Centrally defined purposes
Role of institution	Rehabilitation Care/control Assistance Reintegration/resettlement	Punishment Control often prioritised over change Public protection Safeguarding the community
Status of individual	Client Rehabilitated/recidivist In need of help, support and direction Possibly homeless or alcohol problems Released from prison or ... on probation	Offender Possible risk/danger In need of monitoring Subject to punishment and control

or reclaiming the individual the institution is now part of a wider policy shift that recycles, contains and manages 'offenders' as risk entities in need of monitoring, control and surveillance. Their safe containment or warehousing becomes the primary object.

The modern approved premise – reality and challenges

In 2000 the National Probation Service was established, and this led to a more centralised management of policy and practice through national standards and performance targets in the probation service in general and approved premises (AP) in particular. A change in policy emphasis means that approved premises engage with a resident population defined more by its level of risk than of need. Some of these residents are the most potentially dangerous and risky adults living in the community; some have committed extremely serious offences in the past and could potentially do so again, while others are prolific offenders often committing multiple offences in order to support an addiction.

At the same time public concern about risky adults and particularly child sex offenders living in hostels has been rising. This is partly fuelled by a series of high-profile offences, some involving people under the supervision of the probation service, which led to damning inspection reports (for example HMIP 2006). It has also been exacerbated by a continued media campaign (for instance *News of the World* 2006 and BBC *Panorama* 2006). In the public (media) domain hostel residents are presented more readily in terms of their deficits and stigma than their potential as constructive and productive citizens, or, as in the 1970s, as ex-prisoners in need of support and accommodation. The media campaigns also constantly fail to remind people that most risky adults are living in the community with no supervision from the probation service or any other agency.

Cowe (2008) notes that there has been a clear shift away from hostels being heavily used for bailees and community punishment orders towards a much greater focus on licensees and in some instances longer periods of residence. Hostels have the potential to offer phased and supervised reintegration of high-risk or high-need offenders from custody to the community.

Given that the probation service and NOMS is concerned with end-to-end offender management – from the point of court appearance to sentence expiry – it would appear that the modern hostel now functions mostly at the latter end of this spectrum – at the point of licensed release.

Nimbyism (not in my back yard) appears live and well. The perception and construction of residents as both 'other' and potentially 'high risk' has perhaps not surprisingly encouraged the Ministry of Justice, NOMS, the local probation areas and AP management and staff to adopt practices that 'ensure' that residents do not go out from the hostel and commit offences.

In days gone by running the hostel was just about successful reintegration within communities, that is still our aim, our target, whether it is as important as enforcement or public protection I am not sure, there is a real sense of a duty to protect the public and that is how it should be. As a manager there is always the pressure of an enquiry if something goes wrong. I bear the burden of responsibility. Generally we are pretty isolated from the rest of the service. We need to provide a balance between public protection and reintegration.

Most Offender Managers seem only interested in Public Protection and don't see that successful reintegration protects the public. (Hostel Manager)

The research and evaluation carried out in hostels during the 1970s and 1980s repeatedly demonstrated the central impact of the hostel manager or warden on residents' success (Sinclair 1971; Fisher *et al.* 1980). Sinclair's early findings confirmed the role of staff in shaping and determining the ethos and efficacy of a hostel regime. The power of staff should not be underestimated.

An easy option for managers would be to adopt a warehousing approach and make approved premises a place where risk is managed by monitoring and surveillance alone, but to do this is to miss the myriad opportunities presented in daily interaction between staff and residents for staff to develop working relationships that model pro-social behaviour and contribute in a much more lasting and meaningful way to risk management. The management of risk by, for instance, implementation of a curfew or making a child sex offender sign in hourly is only ever as good as the last time the resident was seen; it has no impact on what they do in between signing in or on changing behaviour except that they are restricted in how far they can travel in a short period of time. The resident learns nothing except to be compliant at 'checking' times and it could be argued that the greatest risk that is being managed is the probation services' accountability if something goes wrong: 'At the end of the day we are not their friends and we are here to do a job ... apart from keywork I have little other contact with the residents perhaps only 10–15 minutes twice a day ... any more than that would blur the lines of the job' (Hostel keyworker).

A loss of relational-focused practice reduces the opportunity for creativity and honesty between staff and residents. Managing relationships with residents in a short-term and instrumental way can mean ignoring a more sophisticated risk management approach that pays attention to what happens to both risk and need in the moment and with a view to what will happen once the resident has moved on. Staff who have worked in hostels prior to the shift towards a public protection paradigm may be more equipped to 'keep faith' with the rehabilitative potential of hostels albeit tempered by an acute awareness of the changed population and policy contexts. Some are able to offer a more sophisticated perspective on hostels revised role and the implications for practice:

The work is still about getting at the person behind the offence, find out how they got to be here – assist them with accommodation, employment, benefits, welfare, health, mental health. It needs though to be a holistic approach, at times some offence work – you need a sense of process and check out the regulation, attendance, conditions, etc. too, and work to help them move on. We need to protect the public and helping residents change is a big part of this. (Hostel worker)

Short-term 'guarantees' of public protection may be of limited long-term value without a focus on what happens next. Indeed, Cowe (2008) found that some residents responded to such approaches by adopting an approach that encouraged them to see the hostel as an extension of custody and to disengage from and distrust telling staff about what was happening in their lives and 'in their heads' in case they were breached or treated more severely.

Risk and public protection have the potential to be constructed as immediate and short-term concerns that are measured in relation to whether a re-offence or incident 'happens on my watch'. A culture that becomes shaped by this can lead to processes and interactions that enable and facilitate residents to take responsibility for themselves and those actions staff take to demonstrate their management of residents' risk to the public can become compartmentalised and fragmented. Such fragmentation may not be conducive to promoting change-focused practice:

National Standards frameworks and structures can make it difficult to work with the chaotic and difficult ones. There is a real danger of creating a revolving door for residents. I think this group of residents are more likely to be recalled now because of their risk and links to MAPPA. Everyone is watching them closely . . . if they cough they are straight back in . . . (Hostel worker)

In a more holistic regime, where staff engage with the residents on a day-to-day basis, risk management is enhanced by the fact that when staff get to know the residents they are may be able to notice changes in behaviour and mood that indicate a change in level of risk. For instance, they are likely to spot increasing depression, change in patterns of alcohol or drug use, change in associations with others, change in patterns of going out or staying in. Also, in the short and longer term staff will have a chance to affirm, support and encourage positive efforts by the offender; this will have the effect of decreasing the level of risk, for instance avoiding undesirable associations, striving to reduce or abstain from alcohol and or drug use, or simply recognising a criminogenic need and asking for help over a period of time. Focused motivational work, encouraging the development of problem-solving skills through pro-grammes such as Living Here Moving On (LiHMO) (Cherry 2004) and pro-social modelling, all have the potential to discourage anti-social behaviour and encourage pro-social behaviour, which may lead to a reduction in risk both of harm and of re-offending (for a summary of the evidence base for the impact of pro-social modelling on offending behaviour, see Cherry 2005). Add to this other rehabilitation work such as helping the offender with longer-term accommodation needs, improving education, and the chances of reducing risk of re-offending increase even more (for example, HMIP 2005 demonstrated that the re-offending rate of offenders with accommodation needs was 36.3 per cent and those identified as not having an accommodation need was 19.6 per cent).

A shift away from relational-focused practice undermines good risk assessment. Ethnogrophic studies (Ditton and Ford 1994; Wincup 2002; Cowe 2008) have found that offenders tend to readily identify those staff they believe are genuinely interested in them and communicate less with those they see as instrumental in their relationships with them. Moreover, if the opportunity for a change-focused practice that is narrative based is removed or reduced, practice can become reduced to a series of alleged risk reduction and resident control interactions.

Are there any alternatives to a protectionist warehousing approach?

The NPS Approved Premises Pathfinder 2001–05 demonstrated that staff trained in pro-social modelling and motivational work can exert a positive influence on residents (Wincup *et al.* 2005). The concept that rehabilitative work will support risk management because the offender is more likely to be motivated to become more pro-social is supported by research findings in various fields. For instance, Sinclair (1971) demonstrated that regimes that were 'firm but fair' had the best outcomes; Trotter (1999) demonstrated that working pro-socially reduced breach rates considerably. Further support for the idea that engagement is an effective way to manage difficult and dangerous people comes from the work on 'dynamic security' in prisons.

The term 'dynamic security' was coined by Ian Dunbar, former Director of Inmate Security in the wake of the prison riots and disturbances of the 1970s and 1980s (see Dunbar 1985 in Parker 2007). Dynamic security refers to the practical management of safety through interaction and negotiation between individuals (staff and prisoners).

Dunbar identified the aspects of dynamic security as follows (Parker 2007: 234):

- Staff and prisoners treated as individuals

- Staff member/prison officer relationships characterised by fairness and decency

- Sufficient purposeful and meaningful activity to occupy prisoners

- All bounded by effective security.

This has developed over the years and has become an accepted way of working that relies on prison officers developing good working relationships with prisoners. In an atmosphere of trust and mutual respect and open communication, prison officers should be able to make good decisions about meeting individual needs. Additionally, in everyday interactions there are multiple opportunities for information to be shared and an increased likelihood that prisoners will let staff know 'what is going on' and/or prison officers will sense that something 'is not right'. When Whitemoor Prison changed the regime in its segregation unit from very strict control (with very little interpersonal contact between prisoners and prison officer) to a regime that the unit manager calls a 'therapeutic alliance type environment', this 'transformation' (Fenwick 2005: 10) resulted in a large reduction in the number of times extreme force (mechanical and/or physical restraints or the use of force) was used.

Twenty-first century hostel staff are operating in a more dynamic and visible context than prison service staff. They need to respond to the presenting factors of risk, needs, motivation and consider the rehabilitative and risk potential of engaging a particular offender in a local community. Alongside this they need to proactively plan for the residents' eventual departure and 'move on' from a hostel.

> It is an important point that most offenders are released from prison at some stage. Only those serving life or detained in secure psychiatric units are detained indefinitely, should they be assessed as posing continuing high risk of harm. This applies to very few cases. The majority of prisoners serve determinate sentences and will be released. (HMIP 2008: 23)

This is equally true of approved premises residents, most of whom will not stay very long in the hostel.

A key overarching dynamic that informs change-focused practices is the ability to enable the individual, as a social actor, to counteract previous disadvantage and harm and to clearly discourage and deter further offending. The relationship between risk, needs and reintegration is a complex triad. At its centre is the active pursuit of discourses of transition. Like all social actors, residents need room to foster, rehearse and try out new scripts, role-playing and testing out new identities (starting from a stigmatised and excluded identity is problematic – see Goffman 1990). Hostel staff who employ a greenhousing approach will be encouraging individual growth, have a clear focus on development, present an outward-facing perspective and actively check for signs of problems and the need for additional support (or censure). Staff who can act in this way have potential to enable residents to prepare for their eventual inclusion and engagement as individuals living in the wider world. Reintegration and rehabilitation require the possibility of social inclusion.

Social inclusion for hostel residents, in order to gain public acceptability, may need to be restructured as social integration, making explicit the twofold aim of increasing social agency and deterring particular anti-social actions and choices. Levitas (2005) cautions against developing integrative discourses that focus exclusively on individual actors and their pathologies, while ignoring wider social factors. An exclusively risk (stigma) centred approach is unlikely to encourage communities or individuals to engage with offenders just as a naively risk-myopic approach is likely to be unconvincing to the public and potentially collusive with offenders who may not be committed to change.

In the criminal justice context, the development of a reintegrative discourse appears less problematic if workers are able to balance the explicit roles of control and empowerment demanded of them. In relation to the hostel regime it may be useful to recognise the potential for negative role modelling and mixed messages. Ethnographic research (Cowe 2008) suggests that creating a broad context for change in hostels relates to three key dynamics:

- The belief by staff that offenders could change.

- The development of a pro-social context that supported integration in society.

- The provision of support in developing and transiting to a pro-social lifestyle.

A greenhousing approach in hostels must be risk aware but not risk or stigma driven. It requires:

- A regime and staffing that shows sensitivity and understanding of residents' perspectives.

- An ability to negotiate participation with residents.

- An understanding of how and why residents may engage with interventions.

- Staff training in specific sex offender and serious violent offender issues.

- A regime that encourages residents to think through and articulate their reasons for action.

- Regular consistent advice *via* keywork and offender management that works with where residents are at and draws and explains appropriate boundaries and sanctions.

- Trained and committed staff who are able to talk about, explore and assist transition to non-offending identities, making use of appropriate community and personal resources.

- Staff who come across as genuinely interested and committed to offenders' change.

- A regime that promotes appropriate responsibility-taking, encouraging residents to become active social agents in their lives, developing non-offending focused activities and interests.

- Staff recognition of risk factors, support in this and explicit discussion of these with residents and, where appropriate, MAPPA.

- Reintroducing pro-social work for residents that allows them to experience being active social agents, benefiting others.

- Pro-social use of monitoring, surveillance and appropriate restriction of liberty.

- Purposeful engagement in the community.

(This list is adapted from Cowe 2008; Porporino and Fabiano 2007; Ditton and Ford 1994; Trotter 1999; Cherry 2005.)

None of the staff behaviours described above precludes day-to-day risk management, but set it in a context of a more holistic approach, helping individuals to change and thereby become less risky. By revisiting the focus, themes and practices previously associated with hostels and by considering how these might relate to a 'new' revised hostel role and resident group, one can map a set of desired relationships between staff and residents and hostels and the community, suggesting a role for hostels that recognises both care and control functions but refuses to set these against or above one another. Such a greenhousing approach requires a regime that is creative, constructive, dynamic, risk-engaged and change-focused.

For this to be effective in hostels a practice framework is required that sets out, for each offender and the regime as a whole:

- A planned and purposeful use of the period of residence.

- A focus on pro-social and motivational work.

- A regime ethos that balances risk management and change-focused practices.

- A more reasoned and mature relationship between hostels, the community and policy-makers.

It is argued that such an approach has implications for how hostels (and policy-makers) conceive of public protection and engage with and resettle offenders in the community. This will impact on hostels, residents and communities. A degree of trust and reciprocity is required between all parties, which can never be risk-free. 'Dangerisation' (Douglas and Lianos

2002) is too easy an option, which plays on communities' fears, individual risk and (media) constructed stigma, serving to justify and reinforce warehousing approaches. However, if residents are engaged in a way that is neither naive nor superficial, then both residents and communities may benefit. Ethnographic work by the authors and their involvement in the training of hostel workers suggests that in reality in many hostels this is being done by some staff but may not be fully supported by current policy contexts.[5]

Greenhousing: an alternative penology?

This work suggests that hostels need not end up being yet another penal *cul de sac*; however, it cautions against the assumption the hostel story will of itself have a happy ending worked out on the back of 'our belief that reason, justice, sciences and human nature will ultimately prevail' (Pratt 2002: 192). Pratt cautions against ignoring the 'dark side' of our ability to treat people in harmful ways. By focusing on the risk of hostels moving completely away from their rehabilitative and reintegrative past we hope to draw policy-makers' and practitioners' attention to what is happening and what could be possible. There are constructive and creative ways of engaging with hostels' current context and clientele.

As has been noted earlier, hostels now appear to be at risk of becoming a 'transcarceral system of control' (Pratt *et al.* 2005: xiii). Surveillance and public protection concerns may not only overshadow rehabilitative practices in hostels but risk undermining and excluding them *per se*. If this process continues unabated, while ignoring the more complex and inter-related dynamic that exists between ostensibly 'caring' or 'human' rehabilitative functions and robust risk assessment/public protection activity, then in the hostel domain 'new penology' may be becoming less of a hypothesis and more than just the warning that some have previously suggested (Cheliotis 2006: 313).

An alternative penology is possible. A practice that retains hostels' longer rehabilitative and reintegrative past need neither exclude nor undermine hostels' potential to engage with their more recent public protection and risk reduction roles. Indeed they may prove to be theoretically and practically of mutual benefit. Hostels are changing but we have a choice as to whether they become greenhouses or warehouses. These choices may say as much about the kind of society, policy-makers, managers and practitioners 'we' are, as the kind of residents 'they' are in hostels. An alternative penology for hostels would learn from previous research, policy and practice while acknowledging the reality of degrees of change that the current context and clientele entails.

Raynor and Robinson (2005: 28) have revisited Garland's (2001) suggestion that a focus on public safety and public protection has shifted the rationale of rehabilitation from being for the benefit or restoration of the offender towards the benefit of the victim/potential victim and/or the wider community. A framework for developing a new alternative creative hostels practice now requires a reorientation away from a 'new penology' approach towards a more creative and constructive policy paradigm. Juxtaposing rehabilitative and reintegrative practices against public protection and risk/stigma-focused credentials may achieve a visible 'get tough' look and feel but in the end it is argued that such approaches give an appearance of risk management but achieve little for offenders or communities in the longer term.

In addition to the implications warehousing has for residents, a retreat from rehabilitation has the potential to see a transfer of resources (and values) from activities that co-constructed rehabilitative opportunities in the community to more segregated and potentially 'private' spaces. If communities and policy-makers believe that such 'protection' is in their long-term interests, voices of dissent may be few and far between. Hostels today currently mirror well a wider emerging precautionary approach suggested by Nash: 'Criminal Justice Legislation . . . appears to single out and isolate certain groups of offenders for special treatment, with common themes of restricted or non-release and intermediate detention' (2006: 69). An exclusively risk-driven practice may perversely end up putting communities and offenders at greater risk by removing attention away from how residents live their lives after the hostel period to controlling, monitoring and containing them within the hostel.

Ross and Fabiano, who have been associated with the rise of accredited programmes and the growth of cognitive behaviourist informed practice in probation in fact suggested in their work (1985) that probation embrace a more holistic practice than that which has been allowed to develop. Indeed they suggest that for probation practice more generally, pro-social behaviour needs to be reinforced and practised by offenders and not just modelled by staff. Informal activities with 'offenders' and their engagement in appropriate voluntary work, which were seen as key to this and underpinning much of their approach to change-focused practice, are conspicuous by their absence in current probation policy and practice.

From a theoretical and practice perspective this is a concern, as a selective engagement of what hostels are and can be now appears to be impacting on understandings of their future role. As probation remains poised to become more aligned as part of a 'corrections service' under NOMS, hostels in England and Wales risk being reconstructed with little reference or understanding of their potential as resettlement and rehabilitative mechanisms. As Maguire notes of probation more generally:

> if the wrong choices are made about contestability, centralisation and enforcement, we could move quite quickly towards a situation where little is left of the Probation Service of the past 100 years. An

important vehicle for dialogue and reconciliation between society and its delinquent members will then be lost, and the necessary work of supervising offenders and helping them to stop offending will be done, if at all, by others. Such an outcome would be both extraordinary and perverse. (Maguire 2007: 81)

Research and theorising that ignore the holistic nature of offenders' lives may lose sight of those very mechanisms that a creative practice can engage to enable change and transition. If the concept of end-to-end offender management and the larger NOMS model that develops ignores change-focused practice as a key part of risk assessment and risk management, the efficacy of hostels' potential impact on residents' current and future risks may be seriously undermined. Much of the NOMS model appears relevant and pertinent to hostels, with its policy focus on rehabilitation and resettlement in the community and its practice focus on relational work with offenders. Indeed, the more negative practices that this model seeks to tackle include notions of poor transition from institution to society and a lack of continuity of caseworkers.

HMIP (2007: 83) notes that: 'the hostel is currently the junior partner in the offender manager relationship but could do much more with better and not just more resources. We do not criticise probation areas for prioritising restrictive interventions over constructive measures if resources do not stretch to them both.'

Residents require the provision of support in developing and transiting to a pro-social lifestyle. The authors are critical realists, acknowledging that enabling a change-focused practice is not without theoretical or practical challenges. We are not naive as to what the challenges are. Developing a creative and constructive practice base for hostels may sit uneasily within a service that has more recently been at ease with a compartmentalised engagement with 'offenders'. Attention to distinct activities of risk assessment, intervention, case management, programmes, contracting out and partnership approaches may sit uneasily with those who are now unfamiliar with the 24-hour nature of their offenders' lives. Policy-makers, practitioners and researchers risk losing an awareness of the overall dynamic created by the 'system' as a whole.

Maintaining hope for offenders appears core in desistance research (Maruna 2000). However, this hope needs to be both realistic about offenders' potential risks and acknowledging of the very real harms they may have caused. Staff too require 'hope' to maintain a changed-focused practice. The potential for the demise of such hope in hostels and a lack of moral commitment to a creative change-focused practice by government and the probation service (who at a policy level now appear indistinguishable) could see a very real and lasting shift in hostel values.

A greenhousing approach offers practitioners and policy-makers an alternative strategy from a risk-driven approach. It suggests that key to realising hostels' rehabilitative and public protection potential is the nature of the relationship between staff and residents and a commitment to change-focused practice. Core to this is how staff and regimes relate to and engage with residents.

Key to an effective change-focused regime is an explicit opportunity for residents to learn to behave differently and a supporting ethos. Hostels should be explicit and mindful of risk. However, an exclusive focus on this either in terms of constructing the regime or in the nature of the relationships between staff and residents is likely to lead to poor risk assessment and management, as offenders will say less and staff will learn less about their individual stories and recognise fewer individual offenders' risks and opportunities.

If policy-makers and managers fail to recognise and engage with their resettlement function with the same vigour as their public protection function they risk changing hostels' role to that of a human warehouse and transforming staff roles to that of warehouse managers and 'risk' controllers.

Conclusion

The holistic realities of residents' lives are presented to those who work in hostels in a way that appears to be now much more hidden in other interventions. Offender management at its best would work to regain insight into and leverage on offenders' lives in much more joined-up ways. Hostels provide a unique setting in which to build up research and practice skills in working with offenders in the community in a holistic and intensive setting.

A key issue for the modern hostel is the extent to which this work to 'contain' residents while they are there impacts on the quality, content and scope of practice focused on enabling long-term change and reintegration into society. If normal choices and responsibility-taking are removed from residents this has the potential to undermine their resettlement afterwards.

An oversimplification of risk of harm and offender categorisation/ stigmatisation means that hostels' potential impact on residents is diminished. An exclusive focus on control, surveillance and monitoring mechanisms will tend towards keeping residents separate from the wider community. This is a questionable long-term strategy, as in almost all hostels offenders will eventually be released to the community. An oversimplified attempt to reduce 'risk to the public' (and avoid the media spotlight) is likely to undermine resettlement and place some in vulnerable positions both during their residence and afterwards.

What is now of critical importance is how the wider service understands its role and purpose and how hostels in particular encourage staff to re-engage with 'offenders'. A shift towards playing up the services' exclusive public discourses around 'high-risk' offenders and 'public protection' particularly surrounding 'sex offenders' is somewhat asynchronous to the dominant themes and paradigms that are associated with the history of probation in general (see Whitehead and Statham 2006) and the practices and purposes of hostels. Hostels have previously housed serious sexual and violent offenders. However, it is only relatively recently (Home Office 2005) that their stated purposes aligned such work as its main focus and that the media have attacked the presence of hostels in general.

While the authors acknowledge that hostel regimes and staff competencies need to reflect the 'changed' clientele that hostels take and align this with some shifts in the purpose(s) of hostels, we contend that the ascendancy of risk-focused practice, a fear of a public (media) focus on 'sex offenders' and probation's wider desire to be seen to be 'effective' at such 'risk management' may be overly dominant in shaping a much narrower and ineffective practice and purpose. In fact, some current approaches may actually undermine both good risk assessment and public protection as well as mitigate against a creative and change-focused practice with residents.

Kemshall and Wood (2007: 393) note the impact of probation's wider work with high-risk offenders but suggest that practice now 'requires a move from a "zero risk" position to a position of acceptable risk, acknowledging that nothing is risk free and that the role of the Probation Service is to work with manageable risks in the community, not to manage risks away.'

The mechanisms through which (all) staff engage with offenders are primarily dependent on constructive and creative one-to-one relationships with individual residents and the overall ethos and routines that the team of staff create. Approved premises managers and deputies are key to setting out and modelling a constructive regime. However, in order to achieve this they need a policy and management context that has the courage to go beyond surveillance and risk-driven policies and once again engage with rehabilitation as core to risk reduction.

A failure to do this may initially draw approval of those who see the need to 'get tough', 'protect the public' and 'reduce risk'. However, a growing body of theory, research and practice experience suggests that the resultant practices may in fact lead to less accurate risk assessments and a false sense of being able to control, monitor and predict residents' behaviour.

Control and public safety in relation to hostels can be best ensured by a dynamic regime that remains committed, in a realistic fashion, to the long-term goals of risk reduction and resettlement. Hostels that fail to engage with their resettlement and rehabilitative function may end up presenting longer-term risks and costs for society as well as reducing their potential efficacy with the individuals they capture. As Gorman *et al.* (2006) note, change-focused practice requires both sites of engagement and a context that is supportive of constructive practice with offenders. Hostels offer a unique resource for a creative and constructive practice with offenders.

This chapter reflects the personal opinions of the authors.

Notes

1   Throughout this work the use of the word community is used as an essentially contested notion particularly in its alleged relationship(s) to crime, disorder and safety. Young (2007) makes a convincing argument for critical criminologists to problematise and question the use of this word and its meanings.

2   All quotes from staff and residents of approved premises come from Cowe (2008) and the primary ethnographic material underpinning this. Details of individuals and dates have been excluded to protect anonymity.

3   Cowe (2008) sets out a much longer 'hostel story' that traces their origins back to the use of early sailing ships, training, industrial schools and reformatories.

4   This table is from Cowe (2008: 141).

5   For the last three years probation circulars have been published (Home Office 2006, 2007, 2008) on the implementation of Performance Standards in approved premises. The Performance Standards almost entirely refer to process matters, emphasise risk much more strongly than resettlement and do not attempt to measure the quality of staff–offender interactions.

References

Barton, A. (2005) *Fragile Moralities and Dangerous Sexualities: Two Centuries of Semi-Penal Institutionalisation for Women*. Aldershot: Ashgate.

BBC *Panorama* (2006) 'Exposed: The Bail Hostel Scandal', 8 November.

Brown, G. and Geelan, S. (1998) 'Elliot House: Working with Mentally Disordered Offenders', *Probation Journal*, 45 (1): 10–14.

Calder, C., Hampson, A. and Skinner, J. (1999) *Assessing Risk in Adult Males Who Sexually Abuse Children*. Dorset: Russell House Publishing.

Cheliotis, L. K. (2006) 'How Iron is the Iron Cage of New Penology?', *Punishment & Society*, 8 (3): 313–40.

Cherry, S. (2004) *Living Here, Moving On (LiHMO): A Group Work Programme for Offenders in Hostels*. Birmingham: MPTC.

Cherry, S. (2005) *Transforming Behaviour: Pro-Social Modelling in Practice*. Cullompton: Willan Publishing.

Chui, W. H. and Nellis, M. (2003) *Moving Probation Forward: Evidence, Arguments and Practice*. London: Pearson.

Colton, M. and Vanstone, M. (1996) *Betrayal of Trust: Sexual Abuse by Men who Work with Children . . . In Their Own Words*. London: Free Association Press.

Cook, T., Morgan, H. G. and Pollok, B. (1968) 'The Rathcoole Experiment: The First Year at a Hostel for Vagrant Alcoholics', *Probation Journal*, 14 (2): 40–4.

Cowe, F. (2008) 'Greenhouses or Warehouses? An Ethnographic and Theoretical Study of the Origins, Development and Purposes of Approved Premises', PhD thesis, Cardiff University.

Ditton, J. and Ford, R. (1994) *The Reality of Probation: A Formal Ethnography of Process and Practice.* Aldershot: Ashgate.

Douglas, M. and Lianos, M. (2002) 'Dangerization and the End of Deviance: The Institutional Environment', in D. Garland and S. Sparks (eds) Criminology and Social Theory. Oxford: Clarendon Studies in Criminology.

Dunbar, I. (1985) *A Sense of Direction.* London: HMSO.

Feeley, M. and Simon, J. (1994) 'Actuarial Justice: The Emerging New Criminal Law', in D. Nelken (ed.) *The Futures of Criminology.* London: Sage.

Fenwick, S. (2005) 'Achieving Change in Whitemoor Segregation Unit', *Prison Service Journal*, March: 9–11.

Fisher, R. and Wilson, C. (1982) *Authority or Freedom.* Aldershot: Gower.

Fisher, R., Wilson, C. and Germann, O. (1980) 'Adult Probation Hostels: A View from the Field', *Probation Journal*, 27 (1): 18–21.

Garland, D. (2001) *The Culture of Crime Control: Crime and Social Order in Contemporary Society.* Oxford: Oxford University Press.

Goffman, E. (1990, originally published 1963) *Stigma: Notes on the Management of Spoiled Identity.* New Jersey: Penguin.

Gorman, K., Gregory, M., Hayles, M. and Parton, N. (2006) *Constructive Work with Offenders.* London: Jessica Kingsley.

HMIP (2005) *An Essential Element of Effective Practice – An Inspection of National Probation Service Work on Offender Accommodation*, Inspectorate Findings 03/05. London: Home Office.

HMIP (2006) *An Independent Review of a Serious Further Offence Case: Damien Hanson and Elliot White.* London: Home Office.

HMIP (2007) *Not Locked Up but Subject to Rules: An Inquiry into Managing Offenders in Approved Premises (Hostels) Following the Panorama Programme Broadcast on 8 November 2006.* London: HMIP.

HMIP (2008) *Probation Hostels: Control, Help and Change – A Joint Inspection of Approved Premises.* London: HMIP.

Home Office (2005) *The Role and Purposes of Approved Premises*, Probation Circular PC37/2005. London: Home Office.

Home Office (2006) *Implementation of Approved Premises Performance Improvement Standards*, Probation Circular PC19/2006. London: Home Office.

Home Office (2007) *Approved Premises Improvement Standards: Guidance on Second Round of Audits*, Probation Circular PC20/2007. London: Home Office.

Home Office (2008) *Approved Premises Improvement Standards: Guidance on Third Round of Audits*, Probation Circular PC13/2008. London: Home Office.

James, A. and Raine, J. (1998) *The New Politics of Criminal Justice.* London: Longman.

Kemshall, H. and Wood, J. (2007) 'Beyond Public Protection', *Criminology and Criminal Justice*, 7 (3): 203–22.

Levitas, R. (2005) *The Inclusive Society? Social Exclusion and New Labour*, 2nd edn. London: Palgrave Macmillan.

Maguire, M. (2007) 'The Resettlement of Ex-Prisoners', in L. Gelsthorpe and R. Morgan (eds) *Handbook of Probation.* Cullompton: Willan Publishing.

Maruna, S. (2000) *Making Good: How Ex-Convicts Reform and Rebuild their Lives.* Washington, DC: American Psychological Society.

Matthews, R. and Pitts, J. (eds) (2001) *Crime, Disorder and Community Safety*. London: Routledge.

Nash, M. (2006) *Public Protection and the Criminal Justice Process*. Oxford: Oxford University Press.

News of the World (2006) 'The Hidden Evil Revealed – Secret Hostels where Paedophiles Lurk in our Midst – Monsters on Our Streets', 23 March. www.the.sun.newsint-archive.co.uk

NOMS (2006) *NOMS Offender Management Model*. London: Ministry of Justice.

Parker, M. (2007) *Dynamic Security: The Therapeutic Community in Prison*. London: Jessica Kingsley.

Porporino, F. and Fabiano, E. (2007) 'Case Managing Offenders Within a Motivational Framework', in P. Raynor and G. McIvor (2007) *Developments in Social Work with Offenders*, Research Highlights 48: London: Jessica Kingsley.

Pratt, J. (2002) *Punishment and Civilisation*. London: Sage.

Pratt, J., Brown, D., Brown, M., Hallsworth, S. and Morrison, W. (eds) (2005) *The New Punitiveness: Trends, Theories, Perspectives*. Cullompton: Willan Publishing.

Raynor, P. and Robinson, G. (2005) *Rehabilitation, Crime and Justice*. Basingstoke: Palgrave Macmillan.

Rolph, C. H. (1971) *Homeless from Prison – A Report on Five Hostels set up by the Special Aftercare Trust*. London: Riverside Press.

Ross, R. and Fabiano, E. (1985) *Time to Think: A Cognitive Model of Delinquency Prevention and Offender Rehabilitation*. Johnson City, TN: Institute of Social Sciences and Arts.

Sinclair, I. (1971) *Hostels for Probationers*, Home Office Research Unit Report. London: HMSO.

Trotter, C. (1999) *Working with Involuntary Clients*. London: Sage.

Trotter, S. (1969) *No Easy Road: A Study of the Theories and Problems Involved in the Rehabilitation of the Offender*. London: Allen and Unwin.

Whitehead, P. and Statham, R. (2006) *This History of Probation: Politics, Power and Cultural Change*. Glasgow: Shaw and Sons.

Wincup, E. (2002) *Residential Work with Offenders: Reflexive Accounts of Practice*. Aldershot: Ashgate.

Wincup, E., Nettelton, A., Oldfield, M., Buckland, G., Saunders, R., Cockcroft, T. and Fenyo, A. (2005) 'Evaluation of the Approved Premises Pathfinder', unpublished report for the Home Office.

Young, J. (2001) 'Identity, Community and Social Exclusion', in R. Matthews and J. Pitts (eds) *Crime, Disorder and Community Safety*. London: Routledge.

Chapter 7

Creative working with minority ethnic offenders

Pauline Durrance, Liz Dixon and Hindpal Singh Bhui[1]

Introduction

Why is it important to find creative ways of working with black and minority ethnic offenders? There is, after all, little evidence that they themselves want specific approaches distinct from those that apply to all offenders (Calverley *et al.* 2004); and similarly minimal evidence that addressing the effects of racial victimisation among offenders has a noticeable impact on offending (Powis and Walmsley 2002). The answer to this question is as unsatisfactory as it is persuasive: the generic approach to work with minority ethnic offenders is also severely lacking in convincing evidence. It does not engage adequately with diversity within black and minority ethnic groups, or between them and white British offenders. It has also been argued that approaches that are not in line with cognitive behavioural orthodoxy have been prematurely dismissed without adequate research into their potential effectiveness (Durrance and Williams 2003).

Once it is accepted that distinct approaches to work with minority ethnic offenders should be researched at all, the picture becomes less rather than more clear. Articulating what it means to be from a black and minority ethnic group in Britain today is an ever more complex task. It demands recognition of various intersecting identities drawing on ethnic, religious, national and cultural reference points. In an era of global communication, identities are also influenced by the media and political discourse like never before; one of the major strands of that discourse relates to concerns about terrorism and violent extremism, ostensibly inspired by religious belief, and perpetrated by people of different nationalities, but predominantly of Asian or African/African Caribbean appearance. An additional consideration is then the impact of layers of discrimination, disadvantage and, conversely, advantages conferred by membership of different identity groups in our contemporary society. At first sight, therefore, there is little sense in attempting to construct theories and develop practice models that focus on 'race'[2] without reference to dimensions such as religion and, to a lesser extent, nationality; nor, in broad terms, can we develop meaningful practice models unless they incorporate research on the diversity of experiences among people from minority ethnic groups.

However, practitioners are charged with moving towards both creative and effective practice in the absence of any substantial body of such research. It is encouraging that the probation service has a history of producing creative ground-level initiatives, generated by practice insights built on engagement with offenders, some of which are described in this chapter. The worry is that the many recent changes in probation practice and subsequent reduction in face-to-face work may undermine the energetic creativity that has led to some of these initiatives. The troubled history of the National Offender Management Service has certainly not provided reassurance that issues of race and diversity will be given sufficient attention (Bhui 2006).

This chapter reflects on the past tendency in the probation service toward practice-led thinking and local initiatives, and the value of a humanitarian probation ethos to the development of this work. The effects of the profound changes in probation practice and increasing managerialism are explored, along with recent attempts to develop work specifically aimed at minority ethnic offenders. We discuss the results of the black and Asian offender Pathfinders, and current debates and initiatives, including the validity or otherwise of cognitive behavioural and other approaches, mainly black empowerment/self-development work with minority ethnic offenders.

The main part of the chapter discusses the new challenges that are impacting on work with minority ethnic offenders, and how these may require a different approach. In particular, we consider the new focus on preventing extremism/radicalisation; the impact this has on minority ethnic offenders' perceptions of criminal justice agencies, including probation; and the response needed to new communities of migrant workers, refugees and asylum seekers. All contribute to a need for a broader conceptualisation of 'what works' and for a sensitivity to race and diversity issues. The value of desistance theory and the way that this approach is being and can in future be applied to work specifically with minority ethnic offenders is considered in detail.

Brief history of work with minority ethnic offenders and current approaches

The Probation Inspectorate's Thematic Review of race issues (HMIP 2000) noted the probation service's loss of direction on anti-discriminatory practice during the 1990s, although it had been a leading light in the criminal justice field in the previous decade. Although matters had improved to some degree by the time of the follow-up report (HMIP 2004), the ongoing direction of probation in relation to race equality is of considerable concern. The National Offender Management Service was created with little consideration given to its impact on the culture of a service with a strong humanitarian ethos. But it is this ethos that underpins the essential foundation for generating creative anti-discriminatory initiatives, which are at root a recognition of individuality (Bhui 2006). Vanstone (2006: 18) argues that 'the history of the Probation Service on anti-racism is not a glorious one, but it is at least characterised by a propensity for self-scrutiny not always so evident in other government agencies and the private sector'. Such self-scrutiny needs time and an openness to new thinking that is rarely seen in the current climate of managerialist excess (Bhui 2006), but which characterised earlier initiatives designed to address the needs of minority ethnic offenders.

The history of work with minority ethnic offenders within probation reflects a tendency toward practice-led initiatives and local small-scale research. The creativity and commitment to equality of probation practitioners and researchers is evident from the various articles and studies that have appeared in the pages of the *Probation Journal* since the 1980s looking at the needs not just of minorities, but of sub-groups within them. For example, an interesting early paper is Carrington and Denney's (1981) research on practice with Rastafarian offenders. The authors explore the history and perspectives of this group in some detail and consider lessons for practice, calling essentially for a more thorough-going commitment to diversity that is responsive to the changing nature of probation work. In common with other local studies of intervention with minority ethnic groups, the authors also concluded that a 'client-centred and community-based form of intervention' (1981: 117) was to be desired. Similarly, Ahmed et al. (1998) discuss work with young Bengali offenders in Tower Hamlets, and stress the importance of a focus on identity issues, family and community. In these studies we see findings that anticipate those emerging from current desistance literature. However, the pleas of such early studies for greater research on the needs of minority ethnic offenders have been met with mixed results.

Black self-development programmes

In a critique of the focus on cognitive behavioural programmes, Durrance and Williams (2003) discuss black self-development groups, which grew from local initiatives but, in common with other approaches, generated limited evidence of effectiveness in terms of reducing re-offending. Such 'empowerment' approaches are based on various theoretical rationales. One, control theory, instead of focusing on why people offend, asks what makes most people stay within the confines of the law. It asserts that the existence of certain characteristics, for example meaningful roles and relationships, a sense of belonging and identity, goal orientation, the ability to tolerate frustration and a strong self-concept as a law-abiding person, far better predict non-offending than criminogenic factors predict offending. Initiatives, therefore, focus on fostering positives rather than dwelling on negatives. This perspective involves looking toward the future, defining where the offender would like to be, and fits with the rehabilitation approach. It also acknowledges the agency of the offender rather than regarding the individual as a passive recipient of 'treatment'.

In practice, completion rates for black self-development groups were excellent despite attendance being voluntary, and interviews carried out with all completers suggested a significant impact of the material (Durrance and Williams 2003). Interestingly, offending did not appear to be central to participants' sense of identity. This augurs well for offenders being able to build a positive self-image in which continued offending does not feature and, again, fits well with desistance thinking. Maruna (2000) has described how successful desisters often do not deny their past but see it as a stage they have gone through and on which they can build. In keeping with this idea group members were able to identify how skills involved in offending could be used in more constructive ways. The group worked because both staffing suitability and offender selection were closely controlled. Offenders were only accepted if the group was felt to address their offending-related needs and (time-intensive) open days were held to allow them to decide whether it was for them. The programme aimed to provide a framework within which group members could begin to understand how their experience of racism had affected their own behaviour. In turn this process provided a foundation upon which a sense of self, conducive to law-abiding behaviour, could develop.

There have also been attempts at a strategic level to explore better ways of working with minority ethnic offenders. However, probably the most prominent of these ended in disappointment. The black and Asian offender Pathfinders established four models based on the principle that general offending behaviour programmes could be adapted for use with minority ethnic groups. They included group work designed to prepare black and Asian offenders for the Think First cognitive behavioural programme, volunteer mentors supporting offenders through Think First, and the Drink Impaired Drivers programme delivered to Asian offenders (Stephens *et al.* 2004). The whole pathfinder enterprise was dogged by problems, including shortages of staff and of suitable offenders, variations or failures in implementation. Lewis (2009: 116) summarises it thus:

> It is difficult not to feel disappointment with the Pathfinder enterprise, which promised so much but produced so little. Problems of implementation, data collection and throughput meant that the models were never properly tested. The final evaluation reports ... appear to be gathering dust. It seems that we know little more at the end of the Pathfinder enterprise about what works with black and Asian offenders than we did at the outset.

More fundamentally, any findings from this research could only ever have been inconclusive given the decision to exclude approaches that did not fit within a cognitive behavioural framework. To some degree this decision was understandable; only areas with large numbers of minority ethnic offenders would have been likely to allocate resources to specialist programmes and there are undoubtedly methodological issues around researching such programmes. But if creative work is to be developed, the onus should be on identifying research methodologies appropriate to the nature of interventions rather than excluding interventions because they do not fit within given parameters of research design.

Today empowerment programmes are uncommon, despite the encouraging results of evaluations (Durrance and Williams 2003). We would speculate that they do not fit within what McCullough and McNeill (2007) call 'commodified' public services. The latter describe a process of 'substantive commodification' under which services offered by probation are seen as 'discrete units of output that can be produced and packaged in a more or less standard way' and 'offered to an open market' (2007: 206). Following the manufacturing analogy, more faith is placed in the 'products' of probation such as assessment tools and programmes, than in the skill of the practitioner (2007: 235). Compare, for example, the professional judgements underpinning the selection for empowerment group members described above, with allocations informed by locating an individual within a targeting matrix. The downgrading of the skills and training required of front-line probation practitioners appears to support concerns that individual practitioner knowledge and creativity are not viewed as being as important as was previously the case (Davies and Durrance 2009).

The advent of modernisation and commodification, McCullough and McNeill argue, has been mirrored by a lack of clarity within the service itself as to what it is ultimately trying to achieve; to adopt marketing terminology, what is its unique selling point? 'Although rehabilitative and socially inclusive probation practices survive, these are increasingly subsumed by and subordinated to policy discourses that increasingly stress that probation's intended purpose is "reduced reoffending" . . . and reassuring consumers' (2007: 227). It is doubtful if a view of rehabilitation as a means to an end rather than being an end in itself can provide the foundations on which to build effective relationships with offenders.

New challenges and the need for innovation

One of the most prominent new challenges impacting on work with minority ethnic offenders is the focus on preventing and challenging extremism and radicalisation, primarily among Muslims from minority ethnic groups. Another prominent and linked area is that of new communities of migrant workers, refugees and asylum-seekers, who are to some extent conflated in public and media debates with terrorists and Muslims (Cooper 2009). Cooper highlights what she terms 'the hostile and racialised nature of debates around asylum, immigration and crime' that ensure that 'Refugees and asylum seekers remain one of the most vulnerable groups in society today victimised because of their ethnicity and/or nationality and excluded from mainstream society' (2009: 149). She suggests that refugees and asylum-seekers have been subjected to a labelling process similar to that experienced earlier by black communities, and there seems to have been some displacement of racist attitudes toward these groups.

All such issues contribute to a need for a broader conceptualisation of 'what works' and a broader sensitivity to diversity issues that go beyond race. It is worth remembering that both religious discrimination and xenophobia have substantially deeper historical roots than the relatively recent concept of racism (Smith 2009), and the powerful hold of 'Islamophobia' in western societies (Spalek et al. 2009) is perhaps not surprising in this context.

There is evidence of a strong link between ethnic and religious identities: the 2001 Home Office citizenship survey (Attwood et al. 2003) revealed that religion played an important role in the self-identity of Asian respondents (61 per cent)[3] and black respondents (44 per cent), compared to only 17 per cent of white respondents. At the same time, the terrorist attacks of September 2001 and July 2005 have substantially increased the spotlight on Islam and Muslim offenders, which has translated into probation work focused on work with terrorism-related offenders, nearly all of whom are from Muslim minority ethnic groups. As in the prison context (see Bhui 2009), this has given rise to concerns that the focus on extremism will undermine attention to minimising discrimination and lead to abuses.

If Muslim prisoners feel they are no longer subject to the basic protections of a race equality focused approach in prisons, and feel they are being seen primarily as potential terrorists, this will do little to create the right conditions to maintain the information flow that might help staff to identify and tackle extremism, and may instead create the conditions to exacerbate alienation and encourage poor relations. (Bhui 2009: 91)

A similar problem applies to work in the community, where criminal justice practitioners are grappling with the challenge of supervising 'extremists'[4] who have been convicted under new terrorist-related legislation, primarily those offenders considered to be 'Al Qa'ida inspired' (Home Office 2009). They are predominantly male, Muslim and black or Asian. The need for creative work with this group is particularly evident given the need to consider multiple issues in order to forge productive working relationships. Practitioners need simultaneously to consider identity factors, including feelings of vulnerability as a result of racial or religious discrimination, alienation due to a hostile and suspicious media and political climate in relation to Muslims, and the anger created by this. This in a context where practitioner confidence in working with minority groups has been found to be wanting (HMIP 2000, 2004).

Probation staff (and those in other agencies) currently have a limited though developing knowledge base regarding risk assessment and practice with extremist offenders. The experience in the London Probation Area is that staff have found it challenging to gain 'legitimacy' with the offenders, which increases the difficulty of supervision and provokes anxiety about work with a generally high-profile and high-risk group. The cases are subject to multi-agency public protection arrangements with extensive surveillance requirements. A variety of government bodies are involved in the management of the cases which increases the workload involved in supervision. These challenges and complexities have led to the formation of a specialist unit that manages those charged under the terrorist legislation. In practice this usually means working with minority ethnic people who are Muslims, although there are some white offenders. Practitioners are positively encouraged to look to community resources and think 'outside the box', constructing in-depth and time-consuming individualised interventions that integrate community groups and resources, as the following case example shows:

Mr M was a 23-year-old young man convicted under the terrorist legislation and was on licence following a period of imprisonment. He was of previous good character. The offender manager together with the specialist probation officer planned a programme of work that involved identity exercises adapted from the service's Diversity Awareness Programme. In supervision key elements in his identity were explored, these included his ethnic, cultural, class religious as well as his offending identity. They also explored the impact of critical world events, such as conflicts in Iraq, Afghanistan and Palestine, 9/11 and 7/7 and the staff helped him reflect on how these incidents impacted and shaped his identity and his views. The aim was to establish how he came to be who he was and to help him reflect upon the pathways that led to his offending. The exercises then focused on his actual offending and what had helped him to avoid such offending subsequently. The probation officers referred him to an established community faith group that works with young vulnerable Muslims on the edge of gang culture or violent extremism. Mr M found this community group invaluable and aspires to becoming a community outreach worker with them.

Desistance thinking was used throughout the intervention planning process, as this was considered to be the most effective means of developing the crucial level of legitimacy needed to engage positively with this man. The individualised approach encouraged by desistance thinking is necessarily creative as it is responsive to need.

The importance of a good and developing knowledge base and the confidence that flows from it is illustrated by the debates about the legitimacy of such work within the probation service. The challenge of engaging with politically or religiously motivated offending became apparent as an issue when dealing with sectarian violence in Northern Ireland. Both NAPO – the professional association and trade union for probation staff – and individual probation officers expressed reluctance to work with politically motivated offenders. This was partly because of the incompatibility of offering a criminal justice intervention when the issue was political ideology, and partly, in the case of racially motivated offenders, because the 'repugnance' of far right sympathisers affected staff 'motivation' (Dixon and Okitikpi 1999). The theory is that those who break the law because of their ideological beliefs are less likely to be receptive to these interventions; they do not accept that what they have done is 'wrong'. Nonetheless, criminal justice workers do engage with politically and religiously driven offending and can be highly effective in terms of protecting victims and containing offending. In some cases the links to the ideologies are quite tenuous and pro-social modelling and appropriate mentoring alongside other intervention can be effective in fostering more positive identities.

In some respects, all work with extremists is creative as a wide range of criminal and community justice agencies and Muslim community groups seek constantly developing solutions to counteract the threat. The government's 'CONTEST' strategy for working with extremism (Home Office 2009) has evolved rapidly and raises awareness about the sensitivity of language, stereotyping and labelling. It encourages all agencies to attend to those who are vulnerable to recruitment, namely the disaffected and excluded and those who fit the profiles of others who have been radicalised in this country. There is a huge current investment in establishing pathways into extremism and supporting Muslim community groups and initiatives that can communicate with vulnerable Muslims and prevent violent radicalisation

Recognising individuality: desistance models and creative work

The importance of desistance theory to the work outlined above and to the future of creative and effective work with minority ethnic offenders is worth elaborating on. The slow development of research and practice with those offenders has tended to lead to limited attention being focused on issues around complex individual identities. Identifying commonalities that can generate analytical categories is a valid endeavour and there are evidently some psychological, economic and social factors that distinguish between black and minority ethnic and white groups: it would clearly be crass and counter-productive to deny the value of assigning explanatory categories to groups of offenders. However, for practice to evolve, differences between minority ethnic offenders also need to be considered as far as possible. Walmsley and Stephens (2006: 175) point out that: 'there are also important differences within the BME group with respect to a range of factors that may be indirectly related to offending and order compliance. These factors may include culture and religion, educational background and achievement, language use and competence, employment status, and so on.' Similarly, Calverley's recent work (2009) suggests there may also be substantial differences in patterns of desistance in offenders from different ethnicities.

The development of desistance theory is addressed in more detail elsewhere in this book, but in our view it has a particularly important part to play in creative work with minority ethnic offenders: what distinguishes the concept of 'diversity' from the earlier 'equal opportunities' is the tailoring of provision to the needs and circumstances of the individual. Any move that individualises the process of assessments and interventions would appear to bode well for work with minority ethnic offenders as it places the world view of offenders at the centre of the process, thereby minimising the potential for stereotypical assumptions.

In contrast to cognitive behavioural approaches that stress the importance of thinking processes in the aetiology of offending, desistance models suggest a need for holistic, offender-focused interventions that examine individual characteristics, social environments and the interactions between the two. Interventions should take account of strengths as well as needs, be forward-looking and seek to help the individual build a new identity. Williams (2006: 160) has asserted that 'it is exposure to the empowerment process that can facilitate the desistance process', a statement with which we would agree. What would interventions aimed at empowering offenders to move on from offending look like for the broad range of offenders who come from ethnic minorities, and how might these be facilitated within existing probation structures?

Starting at the first stage, assessment, while the male white bias of current assessment tools (Shaw and Hannah-Moffat 2000) is problematic, another, perhaps more fundamental, criticism might apply to the problem-focused nature of current psychometric approaches to assessment. While the assessment of risk obviously has to remain central, this should not override a parallel need to explore offenders' values, goals and strengths, their vision of a 'good life', and how this might be achieved (Ward and Maruna 2007; Maguire 2007). Desistance models stress the importance of 'approach goals'; where the offender would like to get to, and how these might be reached. Moreover, an essential part of working through how these goals can be achieved will involve an exploration of the social networks of family and community as potential supports and possible dangers are identified, features that are not central to current assessment tools.

For all individuals there is a need to explore areas that fall outside the standard tools if staff are to understand the social context within which offenders find themselves. We cannot assume that offenders will spontaneously mention important issues. They may have reasons for wanting to withhold significant factors or may not fully understand the parameters of what it is acceptable to discuss in supervision. In the case of individuals from minority ethnic groups, these reasons may be different from white offenders, relating, for example, to their experience of racism or religious prejudice, or for people new to the country, issues around living in an alien culture or dealing with the aftermath of trauma. Offender managers need to be both sensitised to the type of issues that may be relevant and supported in developing the skills required to deal with the potentially emotive areas of people's lives. It is unclear if such skills are given the space to develop and flourish in the structured and time-constrained world of modern probation practice. Changes in the nature of probation training and the structure of the workforce, the target-focused nature of supervision and a focus on programmes may all affect the confidence levels of staff faced with this type of work.

While many staff are likely to have developed their own techniques, those who are less experienced may find it easier to work with more structured approaches such as the Wheel of Life, a practice tool developed in relation to the Good Lives model (Ward and Maruna 2007). This presents the offender with 'eight goods' which any individual needs to balance in order to achieve a 'good life', that is, one that they would define as personally satisfying. It is then possible to explore what 'good' the individual was trying to achieve by their offending and what may need to be changed if they are to move toward a more satisfying life. One aim of discussions is to help offenders think through the interrelatedness of different aspects of their lives and how decisions taken in relation to one domain impact on others. Another is to define goals and identify both the resources and strengths offenders already have and those they would need to develop in order to achieve them, and also what behaviours they would need to avoid. Inevitably this forward-looking approach involves discussing the offender's social context, their family, peers and the larger community as strengths and pitfalls are identified. There is no reason why this approach cannot be used with minority ethnic offenders, though it is to some extent reliant on cultural knowledge and practitioner confidence.

A further feature of desistance models focuses on the importance of developing social capital on which the offender is able to draw. In his recent research into desistance in minority ethnic offenders, Calverley (2009) compares the accounts of black and dual heritage offenders with those from Indian and Bangladeshi backgrounds and uncovers differences in the way cultural and religious values, family structures and social resources may interact and support different pathways out of crime. The actions of families to minimise stigma, access to economic opportunities, the availability of ongoing support and the promise of reacceptance into the community tended to differ depending upon the ethnic background of the individual. While offenders from Indian and Bangladeshi backgrounds could often rely on the support of family and the broader community, Calverley found that this was less likely to be available to black and dual heritage offenders whose experience was generally of 'a much lonelier journey' (2009: 299). This led him to comment on Sampson and Laub's earlier assertion that ethnicity does not constitute a causal factor in desistance thus:

> ethnicity is highly relevant as a dependent variable which indexes significant structural differences. These differences have implications for the operation of processes of desistance by affecting the availability of resources, opportunities and pathways out of crime which, in turn, affect the expectations and actions of desisters themselves. (Calverley 2009: 300)

Interestingly, the impact of families acting to minimise stigma differed depending upon the motivation of the offender to stop offending. When the offender was motivated it was generally positive, being linked to reacceptance into the community. Conversely, shielding individuals from some of the adverse effects of conviction could limit their motivation to change (Calverley 2009). While this type of research-generated information could be important for sensitising offender managers to the variations in resources that may be available to offenders, this needs to be balanced against the dangers of stereotyping and making ungrounded assumptions.

A rigorous assessment process should leave both offender and offender manager with a clearer understanding of needs and strengths and consequently help them make informed choices around what should happen next. In the past, to offenders in the large metropolitan services, this may have involved participation in the type of empowerment group-work programmes described above. These, with the possible exception of those linked to Think First pre-programme work, were largely swept away by the advent of accredited programmes. While a lack of demonstrated effectiveness was undoubtedly one factor underlying this decision, others were more concerning, in particular the fact that services were not allowed to include completion of any non-accredited programmes toward achieving government-generated targets (Durrance and Williams 2003).

A further reason for discontinuing empowerment programmes related to differences in opinions expressed by ethnic minority offenders. While many reported feeling that racism had an impact on their lives, most expressed little interest in attending black-only groups and others were positively antagonistic to the idea (Jeffers 1995). We would suggest that this limited interest is what would be predicted from the heterogeneity of views likely to be held within any group. What should be available is a broad range of interventions, some involving group work, some one-to-one approaches. In other cases it may be that community resources are best employed in dealing with an individual's needs.

It is also important to recognise and understand the limitations of these interventions. Empowerment groups, though ostensibly designed to address the needs of black and Asian offenders, tended to find it easier to recruit black offenders than members of other minority ethnic groups. At the time it looked like this might be due to a match with the ethnic background of staff running the groups and their ability to identify material that appealed to the world-view of black offenders. Calverley's research, however, suggests that black offenders might be more likely to look to this type of group for the support that Asian offenders may get from family and/or their broader communities. Calverley suggests that one way of providing support would be to 'establish networks of like-minded black and dual heritage desisters' (Calverley 2009: 312). Arguably this is one important function that empowerment groups were providing and one that may have had less resonance for members of other ethnic groups.

There may also be advantages in developing Campbell and Johnson's suggestion for mixed ethnicity empowerment groups which split along racial lines when issues relevant to race are discussed (Campbell and Johnson 2000). This could address the needs of those ethnic minority offenders who argue that black-only groups are inherently racist or who feel that, for them, racism is not a central concern. This model could also provide a safe space within which white offenders could deal with perceptions that their own culture is undervalued or even pathologised.

Appreciating that all offenders may have issues around culture in its broadest sense or may struggle to cope with pressures from the societies in which they find themselves may limit the tendency of the members of any group to see themselves as victims. Issues around identity are considered central to desistance. As Maruna states:

> ex-offenders need to develop a coherent, pro-social identity for themselves. As such they need to account for and understand their criminal pasts . . . and they also need to understand why they are not like that anymore . . . Ex-offenders need a coherent and credible self-story to explain (to themselves and others) how their chequered pasts could have led to their new reformed identities. (Maruna 2000: 7)

Sen's discussion of the multifaceted nature of identity and our flexibility in moving different aspects either to the fore or into the background depending upon the situation is useful here (Sen 2006). This highlights the importance of helping individuals recognise and develop a range of identities that can be employed in different situations and also to understand the links between these different aspects of themselves.

Desistance models also highlight the significance of the offender's social context as 'these narratives cannot be understood outside of their social, historical, and structural context . . . Self narratives are developed through social interaction' (Maruna 2000: 8). This belief is echoed by Rex, who argues for the need to look at 'normative processes that support non-offending choices' (Rex 2001). In addition to understanding the impact of social forces on the individual there is an increased recognition of the resources community groups can offer the offender in terms of ongoing support: support that will continue after the end of the offender's contact with the probation service. This is being built into the structure of the probation service's input *via* contracting out services to voluntary bodies. A key challenge to the service will be to devise ways of drawing on the expertise of community groups and specialist services into the core of probation practice. However, statutory bodies and voluntary organisations may have very different aims and underlying philosophies. It will be crucial to ensure that the successes achieved by voluntary bodies are not undermined by having to adopt the stringent requirements necessary to attract probation contracts. There is a danger that 'being tied by the prescriptiveness of contracts (which dictate behaviour and outcomes) many also stifle innovation' (Silvestri 2009).

In order to have credence, interventions need to be evidence-based. Given that empowerment groups are only ever likely to involve small numbers, certain sorts of evidence, especially of the type that demonstrates statistically significant reductions in subsequent offending, will always be difficult to deliver. It is necessary to distinguish between a lack of evidence that has not been provided and that which cannot be provided due to the small numbers involved. More 'realistic' is Pawson and Tilley's (1997) approach, which seeks to clarify 'what works, with who and in what situation'. This type of research is more able to illuminate diversity issues and help offender managers understand the type of intervention that may address the circumstances of specific individuals.

Ultimately, however, we have to ask, how adequate are the current structures within probation to the task of supporting imaginative work with offenders? The picture is mixed. The renewed prioritisation of end-to-end offender management constitutes an acceptance of the import-ance of the relationship between offender manager and offender which, while never denied, has often been neglected in recent years (Rex 2001; Ward and Maruna 2007). Moreover, attention is now being refocused on the content of the one-to-one work. One imaginative piece of training being carried out within the London Probation Area focuses on how attachment theory can contribute to our understanding of how offenders behave and how this can inform OASys assessments. This may shift the focus of attention of assessment interviews toward more relational aspects of people's lives, particularly those with their families.

However, the targets to which the service has to work may pose problems. For example, time limits within which OASys assessments have to be completed are tight, whereas relationships and trust take time to grow. Offenders are more likely to disclose information on which interventions need to be based as their confidence in the worker is built. In cases where the offender manager and the offender are from different ethnic groups there may be anxieties on each side. Some minority ethnic offenders' experiences may have led them to generally mistrust Criminal Justice agencies. Equally, some staff remain unsure about when or whether it is legitimate to raise issues around racism or religious belief or may be unsure of how to do so (Durrance 2008).

Crucially, desistance is seen as a process with the offender manager's role being to support the offender in acquiring the skills that will help them achieve their self-identified goals and 'help the offender maintain motivation in the face of setbacks ... relapses into prior patterns of behaviour are to be expected' (Maguire 2007: 409–10). Again this sits awkwardly with enforcement practice, which focuses on the negatives and allows little space for balancing infringements of rules against progress made. While enforcement practice is driven by the probation service's commitment to protecting the public, it may be necessary to question whether a rigid approach provides the best way of achieving this ultimate aim. Comparing subsequent reconviction rates in areas adopting 'soft' and 'hard' approaches to breaching offenders led Hearnden and Millie (2004: 48) to question whether 'vigorous enforcement is ... necessarily the same as effective enforcement'. The same thinking is true of reconviction, which the probation service understandably equates with failure. Intrinsic to desistance models is the belief that factors outside probation will be far more important than probation interventions and highlights the importance of ensuring that interventions do not get in the way of 'natural healing'. As Ward and Maruna argue, the question 'what helps?' might more accurately reflect the nature and extent of probation impact than 'what works?' (Ward and Maruna 2007). This more humble view sits awkwardly with demands that the probation service should 'protect the public', but may, ultimately, be a more sustainable and effective approach.

Conclusion

This chapter argues for a desistance-focused approach to work with minority ethnic offenders, and highlights some areas of practice in which it is already evident. It is an approach that is necessarily creative as it places a high importance on the recognition of individuality and non-standardised ways of engaging with offenders. Research on foreign national prisoners has shown that identities such as nationality, skin colour and religion entail both vulnerabilities and protective factors in the prison environment that need to be considered if the experiences of prisoners are to be understood (HMI Prisons 2006). In the same way, desistance-focused practice respects the multifaceted identities of minority ethnic offenders and encourages creative ways of reinforcing those which are most positive.

Probation engagement with minority ethnic communities, organisations and, therefore, perspectives, is critical to building relationships with offenders, but this must be underpinned by clear and genuine messages about the aims and objectives of probation work. The role of the social in the creation of identity cannot be overemphasised. At a time when the service is still very much in the process of forging a different identity in a persistently uncertain political context, this is not a straightforward task.

Research on the effectiveness of interventions with minority ethnic groups is underdeveloped. Innovative work has to be accompanied by a willingness to evaluate and a commitment to seeking out research methodologies able to address the demands of particular initiatives. It must also navigate treacherous political and managerialist currents that often demand quick answers that chime with the political mood.

Notes

1 The authors would like to thank Nancy Thorburn and Keith Davies for their help in proofreading this chapter.
2 The use of the term 'race' as an acceptable descriptor for different peoples is relatively recent, much contested and now close to being intellectually redundant. See Smith (2009, chapter 1) for more discussion of terminology.

3 The most recent available statistics show that 71 per cent of Asian prisoners defined themselves as Muslims (Ministry of Justice 2007).
4 In defining extremists it is helpful to differentiate between 'radicalisation' and extremism. The prison service policy statement suggests that radicalisation is a process by which experiences and events in a person's life cause them to support or engage in violent or illegal conduct to resolve perceived grievances. Extremists are those allied to a group that spreads radical views and justifies the use of violence/illegal conduct in pursuit of its objectives. There are other extremists but the government judges this group to be the greatest threat in the UK at this time.

References

Ahmed, S. H., Webster, R. and Cheston, L. (1998) 'Bengali Young Men On Supervision in Tower Hamlets', *Probation Journal*, 45 (2): 78–81.

Attwood, C., Singh, G., Prime, D. and Creasey, R. (2003) *2001 Home Office Citizenship Survey: People, Families and Communities*, Research Development and Statistics Directorate, Research Study 270. London: Home Office.

Bhui, H. S. (2006) 'Anti-racist Practice in NOMS: Reconciling Managerialist and Professional Realities', *Howard Journal*, 45 (2): 171–90.

Bhui, H. S. (2009) 'Prisons and Race Equality', in H. S. Bhui (ed.) *Race and Criminal Justice*. London: Sage.

Calverley, A. (2009) 'An Exploratory Investigation into the Processes of Desistance Amongst Minority Ethnic Offenders', Unpublished PhD thesis, University of Keele.

Calverley, A., Cole, B., Kaur, G., Lewis, S., Raynor, P., Sadeghi, S., Smith, D., Vanstone, M. and Wardak, A. (2004) *Black and Asian Offenders on Probation*, Home Office Research Study 277. London: Home Office.

Campbell, D. and Johnson, G. (2000) 'Anansi and the Offending Behaviour Programme', *Criminal Justice Matters*, 39 (Spring): 17–18.

Carrington, B. and Denney, D. (1981) 'Young Rastafarians & the Probation Service', *Probation Journal*, 28 (1): 111–17.

Cooper, C. (2009) 'Asylum Seekers, Refugees and Criminal Justice', in H. S. Bhui (ed.) *Race and Criminal Justice*. London: Sage.

Davies, K. and Durrance, P. (2009) 'Probation Training: The Experience of Learners and Teachers', *Social Work Education*, 28 (2): 204–21.

Dixon, L. and Okitikpi, T. (1999) 'Working with Racially Motivated Offenders', *Probation Journal*, 46 (3): 157–63.

Durrance, P. (2008) 'Implications of Radicalisation For Community Punishments', unpublished report, London Probation Area.

Durrance, P. and Williams, P. (2003) 'Broadening the Agenda Around What Works for Black and Asian Offenders', *Probation Journal*, 50 (3): 211–24.

Hearnden, I. and Millie, A. (2004) 'Does Tougher Enforcement Lead to Lower Reconviction?', *Probation Journal*, 51 (1): 48–58.

HMIP (2000) *Towards Race Equality: A Thematic Report*. London: HMIP.

HMIP (2004) *Towards Race Equality: Follow-Up Inspection Report*. London: HMIP.

HMI Prisons (2006) *Foreign National Prisoners: A Thematic Review*. London: HMI Prisons.

Home Office (2009) *Pursue, Prevent, Protect, Prepare: The United Kingdom's Strategy for Countering International Terrorism*. London: Home Office.

Jeffers, S. (1995) *Black and Ethnic Minority Offenders' Experience of the Probation Service*. London: ILPS.

Lewis, S. (2009) 'Race Equality and Probation', in H. S. Bhui (ed.) *Race and Criminal Justice*. London: Sage.

Lewis, S., Raynor, P., Smith, D. and Wardak, A. (eds) (2006) *Race and Probation*. Cullompton: Willan Publishing.

Maguire, M. (2007) 'The Resettlement of Ex-prisoners', in L. Gelsthorpe and R. Morgan (eds) *Handbook of Probation*. Cullompton: Willan Publishing.

Maruna, S. (2000) *Making Good: How Ex-Convicts Reform and Rebuild Their Lives*. Washington: American Psychological Association.

McCullough, T. and McNeill, F. (2007) 'Consumer Society, Commodification and Offender Management', in *Criminology & Criminal Justice*, 7 (3): 223–47.

Ministry of Justice (2007) *Statistics on Race and the Criminal Justice System (Section 95 statistics)*. London: Ministry of Justice.

Pawson, R. and Tilley N. (1997) *Realistic Evaluation*. London: Sage.

Powis, B. and Walmsley, R. K. (2002) *Programmes for Black and Asian Offenders on Probation: Lessons for Developing Practice*, Home Office Research Study 250. London: Home Office.

Rex, S. (2001) 'Beyond Cognitive-behaviouralism? Reflections on the Effectiveness Literature', in A. Bottoms, L. Gelsthorpe and S. Rex (eds) *Community Penalties: Change and Challenges*. Cullompton: Willan Publishing.

Sen, A. (2006) *Identity and Violence: The Illusion of Destiny*. New Delhi: Allen Lane.

Shaw, M. and Hannah-Moffat, K. (2000) 'Gender, Diversity and Risk Assessment in Canadian Corrections', in *Probation*, 47 (3): 163–72.

Silvestri, A. (2009) *Partners or Prisoners? Voluntary Sector Independence in the World of Commissioning and Contestability*. London: CCJS.

Smith, D. (2009) 'Key Concepts and Theories about "Race"', in H. S. Bhui (ed.) *Race and Criminal Justice*. London: Sage.

Spalek, B., Lambert, R. and Baker, Abdul Haqq (2009) 'Minority Muslim Communities and Criminal Justice: Stigmatised UK Faith Identities Post 9/11 and 7/7', in H. S. Bhui (ed.) *Race and Criminal Justice*. London: Sage.

Stephens, K., Coombs, J. and Debedin, M. (2004) *Black and Asian Offenders Pathfinder: Implementation Report*, Home Office Development and Practice Report 24. London: Home Office.

Vanstone, M. (2006) 'Room for Improvement: A History of the Probation Service's Response to Race', in S. Lewis, P. Raynor, D. Smith and A. Wardak (eds) *Race and Probation*. Cullompton: Willan Publishing.

Walmsley, R. K. and Stephens, K. (2006) 'What Works with Black and Minority Ethnic Offenders: Solutions in Search of a Problem?', in S. Lewis, P. Raynor, D. Smith and A. Wardak (eds) *Race and Probation*. Cullompton: Willan Publishing.

Ward, T. and Maruna, S. (2007) *Rehabilitation: Beyond the Risk Paradigm*. London: Routledge.

Williams, P. (2006) 'Designing and Delivering Programmes for Minority Ethnic Offenders', in S. Lewis, P. Raynor, D. Smith and A. Wardak (eds) *Race and Probation*. Cullompton: Willan Publishing.

Chapter 8

Asset-based welfare and youth justice: making it local

Mark Drakeford and Lee Gregory

Introduction

In this chapter we set out to argue for a new localism in the way we think and act in relation to young people who get into trouble with the law. We do so partly, at least, in response to the many failures of national policy-making in England and Wales over the past 15 years. The discussion that follows concentrates on three related examples of practical, local contribution that can be made to a refreshed youth justice. In order to place these specific proposals in context, however, it is important to begin with a brief statement of a small number of underlying assumptions and principles upon which they are founded.

As far as youth justice is concerned, our starting point is that success, in relation to young people and the criminal justice system, is achieved when the former have as little as possible to do with the latter. The hallmark of a successful society, and one that is at ease with itself, is that it measures that success by a diminution in the number of young people it locks up, rather than by its increase.

In relation to society more generally, our starting point is that greater equality ought to be the unifying ambition of public policy. More equal societies enjoy better health, are more successful economically, create a greater degree of social mobility and crucially, as far as this chapter is concerned, experience less crime (particularly serious and violent crime) and less fear of crime (see Wilkinson 2005 for an elaboration of all these points).

Measures that assist in narrowing the gap between young people and the rest of the community and by doing so divert them from the formal criminal justice system are therefore doubly welcome. Both the practical examples which form the core of this chapter are rooted in this dual understanding.

Finally, this short ground-clearing section sets out two key advantages that derive from an emphasis on localism. First, we believe that there is evidence to suggest that it is easier, at a local level, to put together coalitions of those who know that the best way to prevent greater criminality in the future is to help create less damaging lives for young people in the here and now (see Haines and Drakeford 1999 for an account of such coalitions during the 1980s and early 1990s). Second, we believe that the weight attached to localism is justified because of the way it recognises the fact that young people drawn into the jaws of the criminal justice system are not recruited at random from across the community. Rather, they live in concentrated areas, characterised, for as long as the system has been in operation, as among the most disadvantaged, relatively least well-off places. New projects that have a locally, geographically concentrated impact are therefore particularly suited to the policy and practice challenge youth justice faces.

None of this, of course, is to deny the downsides localism can also bring – its vulnerability to narrowness and exclusion, to punitiveness and to the distortions of justice-by-geography (see, for example, Youth Justice Board 2003). This chapter argues for a creative alliance between national minimum standards of service, an enforceable set of universal rights for children and an activist youth justice profession, willing to act as a catalyst for local change. It is, equally, an argument against the sort of top-down authoritarianism that has been the watchword of New Labour, stifling local resourcefulness and imagination in the enthusiastic embrace of its popular punitivism.

The theme that links all three of the initiatives with which this chapter is concerned is that of money. Our argument is that youth justice and poverty remain inextricably linked and that a youth justice practice that ignores this dimension of young people's lives places itself at a remove from reality that other initiatives, however valuable in themselves, will always struggle to bridge. Of course, by itself youth justice work cannot reverse the far more powerful social forces that have, for so long, made the criminal justice system align itself along the fault-lines of social class. In our view, however, these conditions cannot allow the search for the perfect to drive out the possible. Not being able to do everything is not a reason for not doing something.

Asset-based welfare

In this chapter we want to concentrate on practical proposals for change. In order to understand the case for the particular actions we advocate, however, it is necessary to set out something of the intellectual underpinning of this approach. Because we seek to direct the attention of youth justice workers to novel or neglected areas it is important to provide the rationale for spending energy and resources in this new way.

It is a well-known and well-rehearsed argument that life chances are determined at a young age (Fabian Society 2006). It is this view of how and what shapes opportunities that is the central concern in asset-based welfare (ABW) theory. Sherraden (1991) suggests that life chances are assigned, fixed and integrated during the early years of an individual's life: and they remain so unless something occurs to break the mould and offer new opportunities. He argues that possession of assets provides such a catalyst, opening up a wider range of possibilities for young people and providing a means to access a wider range of future outcomes. In Sherraden's words (1991: 155), this is 'because assets are concrete and consequential . . . Assets matter and people know it, and therefore, when they have assets they pay attention.'

More generally, as Paxton (2001) has shown, the presence of an asset in a young person's life provides a range of financial, social and psychological benefits: summed up as the 'asset effect'. Psychological benefits include an increased ability to take 'risks' and increase life chances; financially, assets increase in size over time and offer a source of wealth in time of need; socially, assets add improved civic participation, educational benefits and increased personal social influence.

Youth justice workers are in direct contact with young people for whom each of these factors – personal, financial and social – are likely to have been eroded or damaged in some way. If the 'asset effect' can be made to operate in their lives, it offers an opportunity to 'grow back', in their lives, capacities that have both an immediate benefit and a long-term prospect of a better future. This chapter now discusses three separate strands in the overall argument we put for a new set of connections between youth justice practice on the one hand and the financial circumstances of users on the other. Each, in a different way, offers an impact upon the lives of those for whom money is in short supply and where mainstream financial institutions have shown little interest in providing a service, beginning with a discussion of the Child Trust Fund (CTF).

The Child Trust Fund

The CTF is, arguably, the single most radical innovation in the field of poverty policy to have been attempted since the Beveridge reforms of the immediate post-war period. It has its roots in what is known as 'asset-based welfare' theory. This argues that contemporary systems of social security have failed to maintain a link between the lives of those obliged to depend upon it, and the rest of the population. Income maintenance schemes, it is argued, provide a thin (and often grudging) weekly amount, designed to keep recipients out of pauperism, but insufficient to provide an escape from poverty. There is no increment, in such circumstances, to build up any savings, or other assets, on which to draw in times of difficulty. Figures from Wales, for example, suggest that 84 per cent of all women aged between 15 and 29 report having no savings whatsoever (Living in Wales 2006). The effect is to drain the energies of claimants entirely into the fight for weekly survival. Horizons narrow, ambitions shrink as decisions have to be taken on the basis of what matters today, regardless of their impact on the prospects of a better tomorrow.

By contrast, asset-based welfare writers suggest, the majority of the population are very differently placed. Sixty years of economic growth have left most households asset-rich, as well as income-comfortable. Assets include the rapid growth in home ownership; between 1999 and 2003 there was a 23 per cent increase in household wealth in terms of housing assets since the early 1990s (Dorling *et al.* 2007), car ownership and private pensions, to name but three. While income inequality has grown over the last 30 years, continuing to do so (albeit at a much reduced rate) even after the election of a Labour government in 1997, inequality in wealth has grown far more rapidly; as the IPPR found during the decade 1991–2001, the wealthiest tenth of the population increased their wealth holdings from 47 per cent to 56 per cent of total wealth (IPPR (2004), cited by Dorling *et al.* 2007). The result of all this, the argument runs, is to create a gap not simply in ownership, but in expectations and in behaviour. Having an asset changes the way in which individuals are able to think about their futures, making 'investment' decisions designed to make a long-term difference, rather than solve an immediate and pressing crisis.

The CTF is an attempt to turn asset-based welfare theory into practical public policy. It means that every child born in the United Kingdom since September 2002 has been provided with a sum of money in an account that will become available to the recipient on her or his eighteenth birthday. In an example of what has come to be known as 'progressive universalism', every child at birth will receive £250, with a child born into a less well-off family receiving £500. The present Westminster administration is committed to further top-ups to individual funds when a child is aged 7 and 14. In Wales, the Assembly Government has announced a further addition for Welsh children – £50 for every child, £100 for those in less well-off families – as they enter compulsory education. Parents, grandparents and friends are also able to add to the fund.

What does all this mean for youth justice workers and the young people with whom they are in contact? Thus far, it seems clear to us, most debates about the CTF have been conducted on a highly prospective basis. With the first recipients not due to have access to their assets until 2020, the impact of the policy has seemed too remote to make any difference to present-day social welfare practice. That, however, will soon change. The first children to have CTFs will shortly enter secondary school. Some will still be in sixth forms when their funds mature. Others will be the subject of supervision by youth justice workers. In other words, within a few years working with young people who have an asset of their own in prospect will become the norm. Asset-based welfare is about to become a real issue for practitioners, not a distant prospect.

How might it make a difference? The progressive nature of the policy, and the economic circumstances of the vast majority of young people in trouble with the police, means that almost all those in contact with youth justice services will be entitled to the higher amounts of deposit. The Treasury Select Committee (2003) reviewed research evidence about the level of asset needed to make a difference to the decisions an individual might make about their futures. The resulting figure was a modest £660. Knowing that sum of money was available, either as a buffer against the unexpected, or for investment in future success, resulted in a changed approach to life-changing decisions about education, employment or accommodation. At the same time, the Select Committee reviewed a range of economic forecasts, predicting the likely real value of any CTF at the point of maturity. A young person in receipt of maximum government contribution, but with no other deposits of any kind, would, it predicted, have a Fund worth £911[1] (Treasury Select Committee 2003) – well in excess of the amount needed for an 'asset effect'.

What is additionally clear, however, is that this effect will not appear spontaneously, or without substantial preparation. Asset-based welfare depends upon a further investment in financial literacy and awareness-raising, if it is to have its impact. Young people are intended, through new programmes in school, to develop a sense of ownership for their asset, and thus to begin to plan for their futures on that basis. Youth justice workers, we argue, have a particular role to play here. The case for having a social welfare-based service in the criminal justice field rests, we believe, on a set of arguments that have a great deal in common with asset theory. Young people caught up in the criminal justice system will have Child Trust Funds, along with the rest of their generation. Yet they are least likely to be aware of its existence or its possibilities. The bridging role that youth justice workers play, connecting and reconnecting young people to the life of the community around them, will be especially important, we believe, in ensuring that the new life changes that the CTF represents are fully utilised, and realised.

Credit union development and youth justice

A separate, but linked, form of asset-building has been in existence for far longer than the CTF, but has failed to take root in a substantial way within any form of social welfare practice. Credit unions are savings and loans organisations, wholly owned and controlled by their members, and rooted in the advocacy of responsible use of credit, especially in less well-off communities. £100, borrowed from a credit union and returned over a 12-month period, results in repayment of £106. In impoverished communities, where credit has always been hard to obtain, even an organisation such as the Cash Loans Company, the respectable end of money-lending, charges interest rates of 183.2 per cent, in which a £100 loan results in a £168 repayment, while those in the legal but unregulated credit market can charge rates of 140–400 per cent, with illegal lenders offering rates of 1000 per cent or more (Treasury Select Committee 2006). Of course, many families with whom youth justice workers are in contact find themselves at the sharpest end of poverty and disadvantage. Here, illegal money-lenders operate in a murky world of extortion and implicit violence, trading on desperation and an apparent absence of alternatives. This issue has been briefly considered by Homewood (1989) in relation to the work of the probation service and here we take a fresh look at credit union development and draw out specific aspects with relevance to youth justice work.

Over the past ten years, urged on by considerable public investment, the availability of credit unions has widened rapidly. As from October 2008, for example, the whole of Wales is now covered by a network of unions that, between them offer membership to the whole of the population. As a result, membership and assets have also grown strongly. As of 2007, membership to GB credit unions was at 606, 320 while total assets equalled US$1,111,954,005. Nevertheless, in comparison with other countries such as Ireland, Canada or the United States, or even Poland (WOCCU 2007), where credit union membership runs into many millions, unions in the UK remain at the margins of financial services, and have a relatively low (if growing) public profile.

There are two ways in which credit unions have attempted to expand that are of particular interest to youth justice workers. First, they have diversified the range of services provided in order to make membership more relevant to the daily needs of less well-off users and communities. Second, there has been a new focus on developing such service for young people, often based around schools, and designed to improve both financial literacy and the economic circumstances of young members.

As far as diversification is concerned, a wide range of practical ideas are now in operation in many parts of the UK that have as their common core a focus on practical improvement in the financial position of members (for a more extended account of these possibilities see, for example, Drakeford and Gregory 2008a). Many unions are now able to offer instant loans, as a result of the Westminster government's financial inclusion fund. This means that membership is now open to those for whom the previous requirement to establish a savings record had proved a stumbling block. In other places, such as South Wales, a concerted scheme underpinned by the Coalfields Regeneration Trust has been able to provide a 'debt rescue' service for those whose circumstances would otherwise have placed them beyond the help that unions can provide. Debt rescue allows unions to buy out and reschedule an individual's existing debts in a way that, by applying credit union rates of interest instead of the far higher charges incurred elsewhere, both releases cash back into the weekly budgets of individuals and allows for money, now owed to the credit union, to be repaid. In the process, immediate difficulties are resolved while through union membership the longer-term prospects of managing financial pressures are improved.

At a more local level, unions have also developed a wide range of extra services, once again designed to make themselves more accessible and attractive to users. Membership of leisure centres, access to environment-ally friendly nappies, scooter purchase schemes so that young people can access work, sending remittances to countries such as the Philippines, purchase of driving lessons and reliable second-hand cars – all these are just a selection of new reasons for joining credit unions.

The case for youth justice workers taking an active part in connecting users to local credit unions is a simple one. Poverty, and social and financial exclusion are problems faced by youth justice workers on a daily basis. Credit unions can help young people to build up their own financial assets, even in a very modest way, in a fashion that not only provides access to financial services at a time when there is a reduction in mainstream financial services in deprived areas (see Speak and Graham 2000) but, as discussed above, can also offer additional benefits to the young person in the process (see Drakeford and Gregory (2008b) for a wider discussion of this point).

A second set of reasons why credit unions are of interest to youth justice practitioners lies in the special efforts and arrangements unions make to cater for young members. In Wales, the Assembly Government has a commitment, to be delivered within the current Assembly term, to make credit union membership available in every secondary school within its borders. There are a number of different ways in which this policy can be put into practice. At its most basic, the scheme will ensure that every secondary school student will be provided with information about their local credit union, including membership arrangements and any special facilities for junior members. At the other end of the spectrum, there will be schools where a partnership between education authorities and credit unions will result in full-scale junior unions being created within schools themselves, complete with the usual governance arrangements of boards of directors, credit committees and so forth.

Credit unions are savings as well as loans organisations. Indeed, early research established that in least well-off communities it was their provision of a convenient means of savings, rather than as a source of affordable credit, that unions were most highly regarded (Berthoud and Hinton 1989). We now turn to the third of the ways in which youth justice workers might expand their repertoire of interest in the financial field.

Time banks

The final practical example of new developments that can make a difference to the financial circumstances of youth justice users is in a number of aspects the most radical of them all. Time banks are rooted in the underbelly of economic theorising in the UK which can be traced back over 100 years (see Trier 1995 for a fascinating account of this world). These writers shared a belief that the fundamental problem of an industrial economy lay not in production but in ensuring sufficient effective demand for the goods that the machine can provide.[2] In the contemporary era Local Exchange Trading Schemes (LETS) have established themselves on a large scale in many parts of the world (but not, at least as yet, the UK), creating local currencies through which goods and services can be exchanged.

The social and economic circumstances of young people in trouble, and their families, mean that geographically they are most often to be found in those communities where clusters of disadvantage are most acute. The founder of the time bank movement, Edgar Cahn (2000), shared a set of beliefs familiar to most social welfare workers in arguing that such communities are inherently as able, enterprising and committed to the best interests of their members, as any other. Cahn offers two explanations for the failure of such qualities to be realised. First, he suggests that such economies lack sufficient means of exchange – or money, as most people know it – to allow latent abilities to be released. Second, he argues that the design and delivery of social welfare services, intended to remediate the problems of such communities, have become instead part of the problem, trapping people in dependency and treating them always on the basis of their deficits.

The solutions that time banks offer to these difficulties work in the following way. Individuals who are cash-poor are very often time-rich. If time can, therefore, be turned into a currency, it provides a means of exchange through which goods and services can be made to flow. In the time bank system, every hour a person contributes is valued at one time credit, regardless of the use to which that hour is put. Thus, an hour of dog-walking and an hour of help with astrophysics homework each result in one time credit. Once credits have been earned, they can be exchanged with others. Thus, Mary is a mechanic who helps fix John's car. It takes two hours and she therefore earns two time credits, which she uses to pay Simon to dig her garden. Simon uses the two credits he now has to buy two hours of computer training, which John is able to provide.

Turning time into a currency rests on a basic principle of time banking – that each person is an asset, with something to offer. That in turn unlocks a solution to the second of Cahn's problems – the destructive nature of modern social welfare services. In time bank theory, such services fail because they fail to engage the commitment of the user. Instead, they operate on the basis of expert practitioners, applying their trade upon passive recipients. The outcome is alienation and absence of success. Once individuals are regarded as assets, however, then the contribution they have to make becomes valued – and visibly so, through the use of time credits. The relationship between service user and provider becomes remodelled as one of *reciprocity* in which the contribution of both parties is equally valuable.

How does all this make a difference to youth justice work? There are three practical examples already in operation that demonstrate the applicability of time bank techniques to this field. At the level of prevention there are a number of initiatives under way in South Wales that use time bank principles to draw young people on the edge of trouble with the law into mainstream youth service provision. The village of Bettws, for example, shares many of the characteristics of post-coalmining valley communities. It is geographically isolated, distant from the new jobs that have been created in the Welsh economy and among the hundred most deprived communities listed in the Welsh Index of Multiple Deprivation (Welsh Local Government Data Unit 2008). The local youth centre has been the focus of an experiment conducted by local police officers to draw into participation young people thought to be at risk of anti-social behaviour. For every hour that someone spends at the youth centre they receive a time credit. Credits can then be used against a menu of rewards provided by the scheme. In the Bettws example this includes computer classes, driving lessons and events organised through the youth centre.

More generally, however, local authorities are exceptionally well placed to develop a menu of rewards against which earned time credits can be used – at very marginal cost to the local authority itself. This means that any youth justice team with an interest in developing a time bank can do so without having to rely on raising large sums of new money. There are four different ways in which local councils are able to contribute resources at no direct costs. First, almost all local authorities run leisure services – swimming pools, squash courts, gyms, five-a-side football pitches and so on – which are heavily subsidised by council tax payers. At certain times of the day these facilities are underused. Ten hours of time credits, earned through participation in a youth centre, can result in ten hours' free use of leisure facilities that would otherwise be lying idle. Second, local authorities also subsidise cultural activities of many sorts, from concert halls to art galleries, from cinemas to dance studios. Many events in such venues have tickets that remain unsold. At no cost to the council, therefore, ten time credits could be turned into ten tickets to be used at local arts events. Third, local education authorities run extensive programmes of adult education classes many of which can accommodate extra students. From learning Spanish to throwing pots, from computer classes to car mechanics, opportunities exist at no extra cost to the provider. Ten time credits could open the door to ten hours' adult education for those otherwise unable to afford them. Finally, local authorities run heavily subsidised transport services. Buses, especially at out-of-peak periods, are rarely used to capacity. Ten time credits could be traded for ten bus tickets in exactly the same win–win fashion.

Time bank principles do not end at preventative work. In the USA, several states now make use of what are known as Time Dollar Youth Courts (TDYCs), in which young people reported for the sorts of crimes that in England and Wales would attract community penalties are brought instead before a jury of their peers. Volunteer law students from local universities preside over TDYCs, but jurors are made up of young people who have themselves previously appeared before it. At each hearing a jury hears the facts of each case, the charge, the police version of events and the testimony of the young people and his/her parent. After a dialogue and questioning period, jurors deliberate and decide on a sanction. A mandatory part of any outcome is that the young person is required to serve as a youth court juror for a period of ten weeks, including a two-week period of intense juror training. Other disposals available to the TDYC include apologising and making reparation to victims, completing up to 90 hours community service and enrolling on mentoring and drug abuse programmes. Young people who serve as jurors earn time dollars for the hours they put in. Time dollars can then be redeemed against a range of items, such as recycled computers, events at youth projects, participation in an extensive summer programme, savings bonds for college and against the costs of admission and application fees at their local university. The most long-standing TDYC, in Washington's District of Columbia, heard over 850 cases in the year to mid-2008, with 108 different jurors operating in eight different courts on its busiest day (see TDYC 2003, 2004, 2008).

Could any of this be recreated in the youth justice context of England and Wales? We have argued elsewhere (Drakeford and Gregory forthcoming) that the challenge lies not in the difference between the two systems but between attitudes of mind. There is nothing practical, we contend, that prevents a time bank youth court experiment being mounted here. What is required is a conceptual shift from regarding young people in trouble as at best objects of concern, to potential partners in shaping their own futures. Using time as a currency can help unlock the ingenuity, enthusiasm and ambition that lies buried beneath the powerlessness and sense of surrender that is thrust upon so many young people in their experience of the current criminal justice system.

Finally, the third example of practical application of time bank principles returns to the UK and to the city of Gloucester. The Fair Shares time bank is one of the most established in the UK. Among the projects it has developed is a presence at HMP Gloucester, where since 2003 programmes have been developed that allow inmates to earn time credits while serving sentences and to apply these credits to a range of purposes in the community. Within the prison a series of different credit-earning activities have been built up, including a partnership with an existing voluntary group who provide refurbished bicycles for use in developing countries. Bikes are donated in the community and taken to the prison were they are repaired and restored. Up to 200 bicycles are restored to full usability each year. Bikes are in plentiful supply, and volunteers to work on the scheme at the prison have never been in short supply. The only constraint on the further growth of the programme has been funding to pay for the materials and equipment used in the refurbishment.

A number of other projects operate through this scheme while others are still currently in the pipeline; all rely on time credits to make them work. These focus on using the talents and abilities of individuals – tutoring others in literacy and numeracy, mentoring and listening schemes, among others. This work has been possible because of an effective working relationship between Fair Shares and the prison authorities. The success of this relationship is shown through the new ways in which uses for time credits are being created. One recent development has been to train individuals outside the prison to use video cameras, with full sound and editing skills. These can then be accessed by time bank members inside the prison to record letters or read stories for their children, which can be transferred to DVD and sent to their families. This provides a means of maintaining contact when visits are costly and can help overcome literacy problems that deter prisoners from writing home.

To date, some 3,000 hours have been credited through time bank activity at the prison, the majority of which have been sent to the families of prisoners or placed into a 'community pot' at the time bank, which allows individual members and organisations an additional source of credits to draw upon to access time bank services (Fair Shares 2008). The success of the scheme has led to a decision by the Ministry of Justice to roll out time banking at a further ten prisons. Such a move paves the way for time bank activity in custodial settings with the youth justice system, demonstrating that even in the most unpromising circumstances the initiative has a great deal to offer.

Conclusion

The threads that run through this chapter are its focus on assets and the argument that local youth justice activity can release the 'asset effect' in the lives of young people.

Time banks take a commodity in plentiful supply – time – and turn it into an asset that can release a benign cycle of exchange. The CTF provides a major new initiative, rapidly coming into view on the welfare horizon, which aims to release opportunities in the lives of disadvantaged individuals, previously denied to them. Credit unions offer a here-and-now set of benefits that can improve an individual's immediate financial circumstances and offer long-term advantages, through access to affordable and responsible credit.

Each of the ideas explored are linked by a belief in the positive asset that young people themselves represent. Youth justice workers are very well placed to realise such assets, we have argued, because they stand at the confluence where three necessary ingredients come together: they are in direct touch with young people, they operate in specific localities, and they have, by inclination and training, an ability to influence the way in which whole systems operate. This chapter began with the case for a new and reinvigorated localism in youth justice practice. All the live examples discussed here have moved from idea to reality because particular individuals and organisations, operating in particular local contexts, have made things happen. Faced with the monolith that is the criminal justice system, and at the sharp end of those enormous, shaping influences of social class, poverty and disadvantage, it is no wonder that social welfare workers often feel powerless to bring about change. The proposition of this chapter has been to turn away from the rhetoric of empowerment and anti-discriminatory practice in favour of a much more grounded and modest set of ideas that really can make a difference. What is needed now is not more theory, or even more guides to practice, but a simple determination to make that happen.

This discussion of assets started with a focus on the theory behind asset-based welfare. It is argued that in holding an asset, limited and restricted life chances of young people can be replaced with opportunities previously unimagined. In focusing on financial assets we argue that it is not simply having a cash injection at a certain point in one's life that creates this change: it is holding that asset over a lifetime, growing up with it and learning of its potential uses. While at 18 a matured CTF account can provide access to education, training, housing or any other opportunity that, it is important to emphasise, is currently inaccessible to many young people today. Arguments against the universal nature of the CTF tend to focus on how those from more privileged backgrounds will have much larger accounts than those from more deprived backgrounds. This ignores two things. First, that the CTF does not open up as many possibilities for middle-class young people as it does for those from working-class backgrounds. Second, the asset effect is not something that happens when the account matures; it has an impact for every year the asset is held. Youth justice workers must not dismiss this opportunity to engage with the CTF; it needs to be embraced for it offers most to those who are in most need: their clients.

Time banks offer a range of benefits in both the short and the long term. As a form of community currency, time credits offer the possibility of an additional resource to support the opportunity model advocated by Pitts (2005): that excluded young people develop their identities and sense of self-esteem by participating in the same social, recreational and vocational activities as peers, at the same frequency as those peers. It may not be possible for the youth justice worker to increase a client's income, but if they can help them earn time credits, the results are the same. In the long term, time credits offer a means for young people to become integrated into the local communities (Seyfang 2004) and form a central part of local, social networks that show that young people are not hooded hooligans but reciprocal members of the community.

Such creative approaches, combined and individually, impact positively on young people's behaviour. Not only can they become active and respected members of their communities, involved in a range of voluntary and reciprocal exchanges with other community members, they gain an idea of what it means to be a citizen and the rights and responsibilities that come with it. These approaches can help young people realise that their own futures are not as limited as they once believed: by drawing on local organisations like credit unions and time banks, they can take control and create opportunities that lack of income previously prohibited.

Notes

1   This figure is based upon projections that assume a nominal rate of return of 7 per cent and inflation at 2.5 per cent with no top-ups from government or monthly contributions by parents added to the government's original £500. Contributions obviously add to the final sum; for example, using the same projections but with a £5-a-month parental contribution the account after 18 years would equal £2,654.
2   A footnote on the first page of Keynes's greatest work, the *General Theory*, pays tribute to the work of Major C. H. Douglas, inventor of the economic theory, social credit, which tackled the paradox of 'poverty amongst plenty' by proposing a set of 'social dividends', to be distributed as of right to each citizen, in order to provide the purchasing power needed to keep an industrial economy out of recession.

References

Berthoud, R. and Hinton, L. (1989) *Credit Unions in the United Kingdom*. London: Policy Studies Institute.
Cahn, E. (2000) *No More Throw Away People: The Co-production Imperative*. Washington DC: Essential Books.
Drakeford, M. and Gregory, L. (2008a) *Sleeping Giants: Unlocking the Potential of Credit Unions in Wales*, Working Paper 97. Cardiff School of Social Sciences, Cardiff University. Available at www.cf.ac.uk/socsi/research/publications/workingpapers/index.html.

Drakeford, M. and Gregory, L. (2008b) 'Anti-Poverty Practice and the Changing World of Credit Unions: New Tools for Social Workers', *Practice: Social Work in Action*, 20 (3): 141–50.

Drakeford, M. and Gregory, L. (Forthcoming) 'Transforming Time: A New Tool in Youth Justice', *Youth Justice*.

Dorling, D., Rigby, J., Wheeler, B., Ballas, D., Thomas, B., Fahmy, E., Gordon, D. and Lupton, R. (2007) *Poverty, wealth and place in Britain, 1968 to 2005*. Bristol: Polity Press.

Fabian Society (2006) *Narrowing the Gap: The Fabian Commission on Life Chances and Child Poverty*. Bell and Bain: Glasgow.

Fair Shares (2008) *Fair Shares: Gloucestershire Prisoners and Families Project Final Report for the Lankelly Chase Foundation*. Gloucestershire: Fair Shares.

Haines, K. and Drakeford, M. (1999) *Young People and Youth Justice*. Basingstoke: Macmillan.

Homewood, R. (1989) 'Must the Poor Pay More? Wigan's Community Credit Union', *Probation Journal*, 36 (4): 159–64.

Living in Wales (2006) *The Economy of Households*. Cardiff: Local Government Data Unit.

Paxton, W. (2001) 'The Asset-effect: An Overview', in J. Bynner and W. Paxton (eds) *The Asset-Effect*. London: IPPR.

Pitts, J. (2005) 'Election 2005 Putting Social Care in the Picture Campaign Briefing: Youth Crime', *Community Care*, 1562 (3) March.

Seyfang, G. (2004) 'Working Outside the Box: Community Currencies, Time Banks and Social Inclusion', *Journal of Social Policy*, 33 (1): 49–71.

Sherraden, M. (1991) *Assets and the Poor: A New American Welfare Policy*. New York: Armonk.

Speak, S. and Graham, S. (2000) *Service Not Included: Social Implications of Private Sector Restructuring in Marginalized Neighbourhoods*. Bristol: Polity Press.

Time Dollar Youth Court (2003) *Annual Report 2003*. Washington: Time Banks USA.

Time Dollar Youth Court (2004) *Annual Report 2004*. Washington: Time Banks USA.

Time Dollar Youth Court (2008) *Annual Report 2007*. Washington: Time Banks USA.

Treasury Select Committee (2003) *Child Trust Funds: Second Report of Session 2003–4*. London: The Stationery Office.

Treasury Select Committee (2006) *Financial Inclusion: Credit, Savings, Advice and Insurance*, HC 848–1. London: The Stationery Office.

Trier, W. V. (1995) *Every One A King*. Leuven: Katholieke Universiteit Leuven.

Welsh Local Government Data Unit (2008) *Welsh Index of Multiple Deprivation*. Cardiff: Welsh Local Government Association.

Wilkinson, R. G. (2005) *The Impact of Inequality: How to Make Sick Societies Healthier*. London: Routledge.

WOCCU (World Organisation of Community Credit Unions) (2007) *2007 Statistical Report*. Available at: www.wocco.org/publications (accessed 6 November 2008).

Youth Justice Board (2003) 'Youth Justice Board Renews Calls for Consistent Sentencing', YJB Press Release, 3 November.

Chapter 9

Dancing through gaps: a Welsh approach to personal support in custody for young people

Jo Brayford and Duncan Holtom

Introduction

This chapter focuses attention on the Personal Support for Developing Learning Pathways in Custody (PSIC) pilot project. The project was an initiative developed by the Welsh Assembly Government (WAG) and was set up as one creative way in which to work with socially excluded young people. Although its focus upon supporting the transition from custody to the community and a focus upon helping young offenders access education and training is aligned with current orthodoxy (Pitts 2001), the project diverges in its methodology and as such fits well with this book's focus on creative work with offenders.

The chapter first provides the backdrop to the PSIC project, which is rooted in the Welsh Assembly Government's commitment to rights and entitlements for all children and young people in Wales (WAG 2004). After a brief summary of the project, some of the main impacts and outcomes for young people returning from custody to the community are discussed. The chapter then changes tack and presents some qualitative data to highlight how the project has been able to help some of the young people involved. However, being given access to support mechanisms by themselves is not enough, and statistically the chances of making the transition from crime to a stable home life and employment are poor. The challenge is to engage and develop a relationship with young people if there is to be any chance of reconnecting them with their communities. The chapter then focuses more specifically on where the project has helped before considering some 'fateful moments' (Giddens 1991) where young people express a desire to change but the problem arises in the need to sustain change. Evidence from the project indicates that support for young people in terms of helping them to develop social and emotional skills was necessary to sustain their desire to change and therefore ways in which the project helped in this respect are discussed. The chapter finally puts forward an argument that simply being tough upon crime, without also addressing its causes, is likely to be ineffective and that although approaches such as PSIC may initially seem to be costly in monetary terms, if one looks at the human cost to victims and the monetary cost of dealing with offending and re-offending behaviour the costs are minimal.

The Welsh context

Over the last five years (since 2004) the number of young people sentenced to custody in the UK has remained relatively stable, although it still remains high at around 2,700 to 3,000 (YJB 2009; Controller and Auditor General 2004). This has placed considerable pressure upon the secure estate, which has had limited spare capacity, leading to frequent transfers, often to make room for new arrivals. The pressure on services has meant that targets for delivering education and other programmes are sometimes missed (Controller and Auditor General 2004). The costs of detentions in custody are very high and accounted for over two-thirds of the Youth Justice Board's 2003–04 £394 million budget (Controller and Auditor General 2004). This, coupled with the social costs to both victims and perpetrators of crime and rising public concern about youth crime, has created strong political pressures to reduce re-offending (Margo and Dixon 2006).

In order to reduce re-offending, the current orthodoxy emphasises the importance of support to help young offenders make the transition from custody to the community and then to engage in purposeful activity (SEU 2002; Pitts 2001; YJB 2001). Custodial sentences are seen as offering an opportunity for young people to lead more structured lifestyles, and providing support and learning opportunities to help prepare them for education, training or employment. However, weaknesses remain in the way young offenders, in particular those released from custody, are supervised in the community. For example, only 6 per cent of youth offending teams reported that young people were able after release to continue education started in custody. This is mainly down to logistical problems in finding young offenders suitable courses, sometimes due to a reluctance of young people to attend, and difficulties in persuading schools to accept young people that might have previously been excluded (Controller and Auditor General 2004).

Partly because of the above weaknesses in resettlement and because of high re-offending rates (Ministry of Justice 2009), one of the YJB's key aims is to reduce the numbers of young people in custody. Reconviction rates among those on higher tariff community sentences (excluding the Intensive Supervision and Surveillance Programme) have remained stubbornly high at around 60 per cent (Controller and Auditor General 2004), while analysis of the 2004 cohort found that in England and Wales, four out of five male juveniles aged 15–17 sentenced to custodial sentences had re-offended within a year (Whitting and Cuppleditch 2006). Improving the credibility and effectiveness of higher tariff community sentences will need to be a key element of any strategy to reduce re-offending.

Strategies for reducing re-offending among Welsh young offenders are complicated by political devolution. Although the Youth Justice Board, established under the Crime and Disorder Act 1998, still has responsibility for monitoring the youth justice system across England and Wales, many of the members of the 18 youth offending teams in Wales are drawn from statutory services such as education or social work: services that the Assembly has responsibility for (Dingwell 2009). A further complication is added by the shortage of places in the secure estate in Wales. There has been some increase in provision within Wales, and there is the Parc Young Offender Institution in Bridgend, South Wales, but there is no provision in North Wales or specifically for females in Wales. As a consequence, many young people from Wales serving a custodial sentence are detained some distance from their home community and over half of them are detained in England, creating additional challenges for the support and resettlement of Welsh young people in the youth justice system (Thomas 2008). The number of young people from Wales in custody at any one time remains high, although relatively stable, at around 180–190 (Thomas 2008).

In 2004, the Welsh Assembly Government adopted the United Nations Convention on the Rights of the Child (UNCRC)[1] as the basis of all its policy affecting children and young people. *Children and Young People: Rights to Action*, the Assembly Government's strategy for children and young people, translates the Convention into seven Core Aims for children and young people in Wales (WAG 2004). Every child and young person in Wales should:

- Have a flying start in life.

- Have a comprehensive range of education and learning opportunities.

- Enjoy the best possible health and be free from abuse, victimisation and exploitation.

- Have access to play, leisure, sporting and cultural activities.

- Be listened to, treated with respect, and have their race and cultural identity recognised.

- Have a safe home and community which supports physical and emotional well-being.

- Not be disadvantaged by poverty.

The adoption of the seven Core Aims complemented earlier work outlining ten Universal Entitlements for young people, which were also informed by the UNCRC (WAG 2002). Every young person in Wales has an entitlement to:

- Education, training and work experience – tailored to their needs.

- Basic skills which open doors to a full life and promote social inclusion.

- A wide and varied range of opportunities to participate in volunteering and active citizenship.

- High-quality, responsive, accessible services and facilities.

- Independent, specialist careers advice and guidance and student support and counselling services.

- Personal support and advice – where and when needed and in appropriate formats – with clear ground rules on confidentiality.

- Advice on health, housing benefits and other issues provided in accessible and welcoming settings.

- Recreational and social opportunities in a safe and accessible environment.

- Sporting, artistic, musical and outdoor experiences to develop talents, broaden horizons, and promote rounded perspectives including both national and international contexts.

- The right to be consulted, to participate in decision-making, and to be heard on all matters that concern them or have an impact on their lives.

In this spirit, the All Wales Youth Offending Strategy stipulates that 'Young people should be treated as children first and offenders second' (WAG 2004: 3). Its focus is upon identifying those children and young people at risk of offending and then intervening, providing support to re-engage them in purposeful activity, such as education, training and employment, and diverting them away from their offending behaviour. This has led some to argue that Wales has placed greater emphasis than England upon tackling the 'causes of crime', as opposed to being 'tough on crime' (Drakeford 2008; Smith 2007; Pitts 2001). The PSIC project was rooted in the Welsh Assembly Governments's commitment to rights and entitlements for all children and young people in Wales (WAG 2004). It is to the PSIC project that we now turn.

The project

The backdrop to this project are re-offending rates for young people. As outlined in the previous section, re-offending rates for young people are very high. In response to this, the Youth Justice Board for England and Wales has focused upon eliminating or mitigating the 'risk factors' that are linked to re-offending. These risk factors (from YJB, no date) include:

- Returning to unsuitable or unstable accommodation.

- Becoming or being NEET (not in education, employment or training).

- Poor mental and physical health, including substance misuse.

- A lack of support from the family, friends and community.

In many ways, the Welsh Assembly Government PSIC project, with its strong focus upon resettlement and partnership working to enable a holistic response to the needs of young people, was closely aligned to this orthodox policy response.

However, in other important ways, the project diverged from the current orthodoxy. It was rooted in the Welsh Assembly Government's commitment to rights and entitlements for all children and young people in Wales (WAG 2004) and was an innovative approach for the simple reason that it adopted and stressed the importance of a youth work methodology. Trained youth workers who worked as support workers established a voluntary relationship with young people. The support workers were 'non-aligned' to other criminal justice workers, but worked closely with young offender institutions (YOIs) and the local youth offending team (YOT). They remained, however, independent of the YOIs and YOTs, and were employed by the local youth service. These support workers aimed to straddle the divide between the YOI and the YOT, by beginning to work with young people in custody and continuing to support them after their return to their home community. They worked with smaller numbers of young people (typically between five to ten at any one time) than many other workers within the youth justice system, and hence were able to offer more intensive support.

As outlined in the introduction, the majority of young people from Wales serving a custodial sentence do so in England. The All Wales Youth Offending Strategy includes a commitment to ensuring that Welsh children and young people entering custodial facilities in England are 'given the same rights as their English counterparts and as other children and young people in Wales' (YJB/WAG 2004: 2). The strategy also stipulates that 'Young people should be treated as children first and offenders second' (2004: 3). In response, the Personal Support for Developing Learning Pathways in Custody (PSIC) pilot project was

developed to help ensure that Welsh young people in two English YOIs
– HM YOI Ashfield and HM YOI Stoke Heath – serving relatively short
sentences could access their entitlements both in custody and upon their
return to their communities in Bridgend and Denbighshire.

Two personal support workers were appointed in 2005. They were each
employed by their local youth service, Bridgend and Denbighshire, and
one of their first tasks was to establish working relationships with their
key partners: Stoke Heath with Conwy and Denbighshire YOT, and
Ashfield with Bridgend YOT.

Both workers faced the daunting challenge of establishing a new role
for youth work in a custodial environment. This involved working with
challenging young people in an environment considered beyond the pale
for some sections of the youth work profession, who felt that it risked
compromising the voluntary ethos at the heart of youth work.

An external evaluation of the project was commissioned by the Welsh
Assembly Government in 2005 and was undertaken by the People and
Work Unit, a voluntary sector organisation based in South Wales. It is this
evaluation that provides the basis for this chapter. The evaluation
included interviews with 16 of the 23 young people on the project (four
of whom were interviewed on a number of different occasions) and
discussions with 38 professionals over the lifetime of the evaluation
(October 2005–February 2007). These interviews and discussions were
informed by a review of the literature on offending behaviour and of
approaches to working with juvenile and young offenders. Wherever
possible, data generated through interviews and discussions were compared, or triangulated, with that from other sources. So, for example, the
accounts of the young people on the project were compared with the
accounts and assessments of the professionals working with them and the
wider literature on young people's thinking and behaviour including the
work of Farrington (1995, 1997); Jones (2002, 2005), Rutter *et al.* (1998) and
Williamson (2001, 2004).

Given the relatively small number of young people involved, data on
outcomes for young people serving sentences in HM YOI Ashfield and
HM YOI Stoke Heath and returning to Neath Port Talbot and Conwy,
respectively, without the additional support provided by personal support workers, was sought. This was used to provide 'proxy comparators'
to provide a richer picture of the likely impact of the project upon the
young people involved.

The impact of the project

The evaluation found that both young people and the professionals
working with them judged that the project was very effective at helping
young people access housing, diversionary activities, and other services

such as healthcare, following their release and return to their communities. The project helped ensure that young people did not lose focus in the first two weeks following release, and 19 of the 21 young people on the project who were released by March 2007 made it through their first two weeks in the community without serious incident.

Overall, as Table 9.1 illustrates, the project enabled just under half of the young people it supported following their return to the community to access education, training and employment (ETE); one-third had not re-offended by the end of the project.

There were marked differences, though, in outcomes for young people from Bridgend compared with outcomes for young people in Denbighshire. The evaluation concluded that this reflected differences in the worker's relationships with young people, given differences in their experience and interests like multi-media and sports that helped them find shared interests with young people; the ease with which workers could broker access to diversionary activities and to education, training and employment, given differences in the social, economic and geographical contexts in which the projects worked (and in particular the rural nature of Denbighshire, which meant that this was easier in Bridgend); and the extent to which the work was integrated with the local YOT, Young People's Partnership and YOI, given the stronger integration of the work in Bridgend with both the Bridgend YOT and HM YOI Ashfield.

Outcomes for young people from Bridgend were also markedly better than outcomes in Neath Port Talbot, a quasi control group of young people who were not supported by the project. In order to check that this was not because young people from Neath Port Talbot were more serious or persistent offenders, their criminal records were compared with those of young people from Denbighshire. They were broadly comparable in terms of the age of the onset of offending. However, there were differences in the types of offences and young people in Neath Port Talbot were on average more prolific offenders. In contrast, outcomes for young people returning to Denbighshire who were supported by the project appear worse than outcomes for young people returning to Conwy who were not supported. However, given the very small numbers, considerable care needs to be taken in drawing conclusions from these data.

Overall, the data on outcomes is limited. However, the evidence gathered by the evaluation does give some indication that the approach of the project was not itself a 'magic bullet'. When the evaluation ended, almost two-thirds of the young people released to the community were known to have re-offended, and rates of re-offending for young people returning to Denbighshire in particular were disappointing. However, there was encouraging evidence that for some young people, around a third of the total (and around half of those in Bridgend) the approach was extremely effective. Moreover, the project established a new youth work approach with young offenders in a custodial setting. Having been

Table 9.1 Outcomes for young people returning from custody to Bridgend, Neath Port Talbot, Denbighshire and Conwy (outcomes as of February 2007)

Type of outcome	Number of young people returning from custody . . .			
	To Bridgend and supported by the project over the period October 2005–March 2007	To Neath Port Talbot over the period October 2005–February 2007	To Denbighshire and supported by the project over the period October 2005–September 2006	To Conwy over the period October 2005–September 2006
Entered ETE and not re-offended	6	1	0	0
Not entered ETE, but not re-offended	1	0	0	1
Entered ETE and re-offended	1	5	2	2
Not entered ETE and re-offended	4	5	6	3
Unknown	0	0	1	0
Total	**12**	**11**	**9**	**6**

established, this new approach can be a model that could be used by other youth workers and refined and developed further. Some things work with some people sometimes, and the remainder of this chapter explores why the approach was so 'successful' with some young people yet appeared to 'fail' with others. We present Gavin's[2] story (all the names used in this report are fictional to protect the identity of the young people involved in the project) and then consider the reasons why the project has been able to help young people like Gavin.

Gavin's story

Gavin was serving a lengthy sentence in a YOI. He was convicted for a serious assault in which he came close to killing his victim. When interviewed in the course of the evaluation, he described what happened:

> I was drunk, like every day, heavy on weekends ... Friday night, walking home with my girlfriend, drunk again ... with my mates, [this] bloke pushed one of the boys away, [saying] like, 'Mind where you're going', I'm like, 'Get him, boys!' One thing leads to another, like I punched him, kicking him on the floor. I thought he was dead like, [he ended up] on life support for two days, on intensive care for 14 days ... not good like.

At the time of the assault, Gavin explained that he was on bail for another assault, 'wasn't even bothering with school ... pointless – not doing no GCSEs', and taking and selling drugs. As he put it, he 'just wanted to be someone, [so I was] showing off, getting into trouble'. When put to him, he agreed that at that time his life was 'getting out of control'; he explained: 'It was, like, something coming in here [the YOI]. It was, like, God telling me "sort it out", you'll end up dead like. Might sound a bit crazy, but if I'd not come in here, I'd be dead like.'

It was clear that the shock of almost killing someone followed by a lengthy sentence had had a huge effect on Gavin. However, as he explained, this wasn't the first time he'd tried to turn his life around:

> Like when I was eleven in year 7, always causing trouble, showing off, brought to the police every week ... it made me think. I woke up once [thinking] 'I've got to sort my head out. My mum was crying, worrying about me, [I was] driving her mad. [I] just woke [thinking], 'What am I doing?!'

Unfortunately, as he explained: 'I'd be good for about six months, then did something stupid ... then be good again ...' and so the cycle continued. During this time a range of different agencies including a school counsellor, a child psychologist, youth offending team (YOT) workers and Social Services all tried to help but, as Gavin put it, during this time, he 'Never even thought of going for help . . . I could have spoken to Mum, but couldn't talk about the drugs . . . she'd be disappointed.'

Gavin's story may differ in the seriousness of his crime but the themes – failure at school, limited support, delinquent peer groups, boredom, alcohol and drug abuse – were shared by almost all of the young people interviewed in the course of the evaluation of the project. Like them all, Gavin expressed the desire to turn his life round and like them all, statistically his chances of making the transition from crime to a stable home life and employment were poor.

Where the project did help

There are many reasons why the prospects for the young people like Gavin were so poor. Many discussed their past experiences of custody and its aftermath, of being exposed to the risk of post-release depression, as the hopes and excitement of 'freedom' gave way to the cold reality of unemployment, fractured families, stigmatisation, low incomes, limited opportunities and life in often poor housing sometimes surrounded by peers abusing drugs and alcohol. For example, as Richard, another of the young people supported by the project, explained:

> I've been released a couple of times before. Get your clothes, taken to the gate and go to the house, have something tidy to eat like McDonald's, friends are excited to see you. Just chill out. Then the excitement starts going. There's nothing. Friends coming along, saying lets do a robbing and [I] end up back here.

The young people in the project faced multiple and complex problems, including low levels of basic skills, weak social and emotional skills, negative prior experiences of education, and drug and alcohol misuse, making full participation in social and economic life extremely challenging. Moreover, their past history of offending meant that the risks or costs of offending to them were great: because they were still on licence any relapse could carry a heavy penalty and could knock them off course. During the final round of interviews in January 2006, one of the young people who was reported to be making good progress was re-arrested for stealing a car, raising the prospect of a return to custody. During another interview, Tony, then on licence in the community and working hard to find a job, explained how difficult he found it to change:

> Problems come to me. Two minutes before you got here, two little boys saying call [name omitted] [he] wants to have a fight . . . my

name comes first, it has to, I don't want to be known as a poof, [I] know it's more of a man to walk away [*sic*], but this has to be sorted out ... like kids come to my house thinking I'm [still] dealing ... [I] don't need this shit coming to me ... apart from that, my life's been doing good ... to be honest, [I] really need to sort my head out, but this isn't right ... you don't send kids round.

Tony's experiences provide a vivid illustration of the challenging circumstances that these young people's previous choices and behaviour have created for them. As he summed it up: 'Everything's going to hell ... when you're young [you] don't have so many problems, now I'm trying to move on from it, but it keeps coming back and back.'

Yet in trying to turn their lives around, without the project's helping hand these young people had little assistance. In the past they had returned from YOIs to fractured and often difficult family environments. While parents wanted to help, their limited knowledge and resources limited the efficacy of the support they were able to offer. In some cases there was also evidence that the young people's parents were themselves having to cope with extremely challenging environments and circumstances, including serious physical and mental ill health, which meant that in effect the young people were supporting *them*. Moreover, young people's knowledge of, and ability to use effectively, other support services such as Job Centre Plus, Careers Wales, health and housing services was limited. All had weakness in their emotional intelligence. This was reflected in the lack of confidence many felt in dealing with some situations, the difficulty some had in focusing on and sustaining a specific task, and in communicating, working and empathising with others. Most struggled to control and master their desires and impulses and some struggled to control their moods and temper. There was considerable variation, though, and while some of the young people had weakness in areas, like their ability to master their emotions, they also had strengths in other areas and could be reflective, articulate and sometimes highly self-motivated.

In order to address their weaknesses, the young people on the project were offered broadly the same level of support; but, as outlined previously, the outcomes differed markedly. Crucially, not only did some have better access to opportunities, some chose and some were able to make better use of the support they were offered to help them exploit these opportunities. We consider why this was in the following section.

'Fateful moments'

Some young people were facing their first period of detention, for others it was their third or even fourth time in a YOI. Although there was often a degree of bravado, with descriptions of their YOI as a 'holiday camp', none of the young people interviewed in the course of the evaluation was enjoying their time in custody and all those who were interviewed expressed a desire to stop offending.

For some young people, particularly those serving longer sentences, their detention had shaken them up. For others, their detention had given them time to reflect upon lives that many felt had 'got out of control', with escalating criminality fuelled by alcohol and drug abuse. They experienced what Professor Howard Williamson has described as 'wake up time' (Williamson 2001; Giddens 1991), a process of reflection and reassessment in the wake of a shock. However, it was striking that for some this was a clearly, unambiguously expressed desire, that appeared to carry real force and determination. In crude terms, they had got to a point in their lives where they felt they had to change. For example, as Richard explained, the initial catalyst was an encounter with a policeman:

> This copper goes to me, 'You'll never change'. He was taking the piss, but he made me think. [The copper pointed to a drug dealer] ... trampy clothes, scruffy like, 'You're going to be like that one day', and I thought about it, thought I will be ... when you're young, like, it's cool, [but now I] know I don't want to be known as a criminal, want to be like known as a builder ... like I don't want to go back. Not scared of prison like, but I'm scared of failing ... never thought this before, hell of a dickhead [before] wish I could slap that person: 'Sort your head out'.

In contrast, for others, the sentiment was expressed much more weakly, with much less confidence that it could be realised. As Phil, currently serving his sentence in a YOI, put it: 'It'll look well different when I get out. I'll get a job [*laughs*] always says this, but I do something stupid ... get a job, then start messing about ... [and without a job] I just walk about with my mates doing stupid stuff.'

Sustaining the desire to change

What was striking in the accounts of many of the young people interviewed was that this was not the first time they had experienced 'wake up time'. A number talked about times when they had decided they had to change and had successfully stopped offending for months at a time. In each case, though, they had not been supported and lacked the social and emotional skills necessary to sustain the change alone.

The sorts of changes required in young people's lives included resisting the temptation to engage in criminal activity to ward off boredom and secure status and recognition; the moderation of drug and alcohol abuse;

confronting and overcoming negative experiences of school to return to education or training; and moving from often chaotic lives to the discipline of getting up and getting to work or college on time.

We used the five 'domains of emotional intelligence' identified by Daniel Goleman (1995) – self-awareness, mood-management, empathy, handling relationships and self-motivation – as the basis for thinking about the social and emotional skills that, together with support, young people would need to turn their lives around. Goleman explains these domains as follows:

- **Self-awareness** – understanding of your self, your abilities (leading to self-confidence and self-efficacy) and your emotions and feelings – the key to 'self-mastery', feeling in control of yourself and your passions and emotions.

- **Mood-management** – the capacity to control your emotions (e.g. calm yourself down, shake off anxiety) and to respond appropriately to others (e.g. not getting angry/irritated with them).

- **Empathy** – understanding of others, recognising their emotions and responding appropriately (e.g. offering support).

- **Handling relationships** – 'social competence' – ability to work, communicate and socialise with others, negotiate, persuade and achieve consensus.

- **Self-motivation** – the ability to focus upon a task, show interest, put in effort, not to get distracted, to defer gratification.

Helping to develop strong social and emotional skills in turn did enable some young people to change. Self-motivation was needed to sustain the hard work and difficult choices required. The support workers were crucial here. Deciding to change is a difficult choice. It is even more difficult to sustain change. Empathy and the ability to handle relationships effectively helped them successfully negotiate interviews for employment and training opportunities and make friends, so that they felt less isolated and more supported. Self-awareness and empathy helped them make sense of their lives and the impact of their criminal behaviour upon their victims, which in turn helped some to sustain changes in their behaviour and lifestyle. The problem the project addressed was that those young people who wanted to turn their lives around, who wanted to change, were held back by weakness in some or many of their social and emotional skills. What the project was able to do was provide the support through a voluntary arrangement (between the support worker and the young offender) to help them make the transition from custody to their communities. In other words, to resettle in the 'real world'. Because the relationship was voluntary, the work was focused upon the young person's interests and wishes and negotiated between the young person and the worker. The workers' challenge was to maintain this voluntary relationship, while where appropriate challenging the young person's thinking and behaviour.

Weak social and emotional skills may also be a consequence of depression, in that the symptoms, such as anxiety, irritability, anger, low self-esteem and lack of self-confidence, problems forming relationships and a lack of motivation, are all characteristic of those with weak emotional intelligence. Young people leaving custody may be particularly vulnerable to depression as their hopes and dreams fade in the cold hard light of day. The project may have made an important contribution here too, because there is some evidence that those suffering from depression are more likely to be motivated to try to change their thinking and behaviour if they know they will be supported in this (Paul Saunders, personal communication). Moreover, the personal support worker model, which is focused upon increasing motivation, challenging negative thinking, fostering self-belief and self-esteem, and encouraging social contact, is in line with approaches such as cognitive behavioural therapy, designed to treat depression (Gilbert 1997).

Crucially, the project offered young people like Gavin not only more support but support that was qualitatively different from that they would have received from other professionals, such as YOT workers. This appears to be due to a number of reasons, including the voluntary nature of the relationship that personal support workers had with young people; differences in their role and remit (for example, the PSIC workers were not required to hold young people to account for breaching conditions of their licence and their focus is purely upon support rather than risk management); the time they can spend building a relationship that starts in custody and continues in the community; and their skills and training as professional youth workers. The workers' relationship enabled them to provide two distinct, but complementary types of support:

- Pastoral support that enhances and develops young people's emotional intelligence and shapes their attitudes and aspirations.

- Direct practical support that helps or enables young people to exploit or access opportunities and services, such as college courses, housing and healthcare more effectively.

In other words, it was helping some to develop social and cultural capital; the project provided a change-focused approach. This support, together with young people's skills and their motivation and desire to change, shaped the way young people responded to opportunities and risks (such as the temptation to re-offend). To some extent, the project was able to create and broker access to new opportunities, by, for example, developing links with local services, employers and learning providers. However, there were limits on what the project could do, and the range of opportunities in Denbighshire was more limited than those in Bridgend, because of the rural nature of much of the county and the inaccessibility of diversionary activities and ETE opportunities. This is an important point. There will be different issues facing young people and those who work with young people, be they support workers or people working in the youth justice system, in rural and urban areas. There will also be different issues in socially deprived and more affluent areas. It is important to think about the geographical make-up of an area before piloting or implementing projects of this nature.

Conclusion

This was a small-scale, but pioneering project, with encouraging results, particularly in Bridgend. It suggests that for some young people this type of approach, when introduced at the right time and in a conducive context, can be extremely effective. In crude terms, the personal support workers can, within limits, broker access to new opportunities, provide encouragement and challenges and help equip young people with the skills they need to access and sustain their participation in these. However, they can only make it a little easier for these young people. They can encourage, reinforce and applaud change (Howard Williamson, personal communication) but the hard work, turning up at college or work every day, moderating drug and alcohol use and exchanging the 'highs and lows . . . of the chaotic lifestyle' for the 'less exciting rewards of stability [and] reliability', can only come from the young people themselves (Sam Jones, personal communication). Moreover, variations in local labour markets, education, training, sports and leisure provision mean that there are differences in young people's access to opportunities and the diversionary activities that can help them sustain changes in their lives.

The project demonstrates that in order to change, young people need more than punishment; they need the *motivation* to change – including a desire to change, which may flow from their incarceration – and a vision of what they will gain, plus the self-belief in their ability to change; they also need the *capacity* to change, which is likely to include access to opportunities and services, support and personal capabilities, such as literacy and numeracy and social and emotional skills. The PSIC approach works when a young person has the motivation to change; that is, they have reached a point in their lives when they are ready to change and are ready to develop their capacity to change. In this context, the approach works by providing the resources necessary to make effective use of opportunities and to enable the changes in behaviour required to sustain the decision to change.

What makes the PSIC project innovative is the focus upon a youth work methodology. The project support workers are distinctly youth workers rather than youth justice workers, although their role goes far beyond the boundaries of traditional youth work. They work through a voluntary relationship with a young person that enables them to inform, support and challenge in a way that is meaningful and relevant to the young person. They can help catalyse change and they can help broker access to opportunities for those young people who want to and are ready to change, by advising and advocating on young people's behalf and brokering access to opportunities, and also by developing young people's capacity and motivation to exploit these opportunities, while avoiding risks.

The PSIC approach may initially appear to be a costly one (estimated at between £4,000 and £6,000 per young person over the course of a year). However, the costs of the current system are also substantial. The human cost to the victims can, in cases such as Gavin's, be extremely severe. Moreover, these costs fall upon some of the most vulnerable in society. Although the young people have done great damage to other people's lives, they themselves have also suffered, and without support are likely to continue to suffer from exclusion from society.

The financial costs of not intervening are also substantial. The Audit Commission (2009) calculated that a young person who starts showing behavioural problems at the age of five, and is dealt with through the criminal justice system, will cost the taxpayer around £207, 000 by the age of 16. Alternative interventions to support changes in behaviour would cost around £47, 000. Over £113 million a year would be saved if just one in ten young offenders was diverted towards effective support.

The costs to society and the state rapidly accumulate if offending continues and escalates. The average non-criminal justice costs to society of crime per offence have been calculated at £4,700 for vehicle theft and £2,300 for burglary. These costs rise to £19,000 in cases of violence against the person. In addition, the Home Office estimates that each offence leading to reconviction costs the criminal justice system on average £13,000, because before they are reconvicted each offender is likely to be responsible for multiple recorded offences, and these costs multiply to tens of thousands of pounds per offender. If sentenced to a custodial sentence, a year's detention in a YOI costs around a further £50,000. The costs are likely to continue after their release. Even if the young person does not re-offend (and almost half will within the first year, while over 80 per cent will do so over two years (SEU 2002)), they face a significantly higher risk of unemployment, which will cost the state over £9,000 per year in terms of benefit payments and foregone taxes (SEU 2002; Brand and Price 2000).

What is perhaps most challenging about the project is the implication that the type of support it offers should be targeted at those judged ready and able to change. This raises practical challenges about the reliability of assessing a young person's capacity and readiness to change, and also ethical questions about offering some young people support while denying it to others. The choice may not be quite so stark; there may be, for example, value in providing a lower level of support to those judged unready or unable to change at that point in their lives, so that when they *are* ready and able, the support is there. What this chapter has highlighted is a need for a more dynamic understanding of motivation, and engagement with young people can help with this. A creative practice is necessary – one that recognises the fluid and dynamic nature of motivation.

Further information

The final report for the external evaluation of the project (D. Holtom, *Dancing Through the Gaps: The External Evaluation of the Welsh Assembly Government Personal Support in Custody Pilot Project*), together with a series of supporting papers, is available from Nick Keating, Senior Manager for the Children and Young People within the Criminal Justice System Learning Initiative (email: nick.keating@wales.gsi.gov.uk).

Acknowledgements

The authors would like to thank all the young people and professionals who gave up their time to be interviewed as part of the research. The help of the two personal support workers, Cari-Sioux Hodgkinson and Sam Jones, the Denbighshire Emotional Health and Well-being worker Samantha Challis, and the staff at both Stoke Heath and Ashfield YOIs, was particularly important in facilitating interviews with the young people on the project. Thanks also go to the staff at Bridgend, Conwy and Denbighshire and Neath Port Talbot YOTs, who took part in discussions about the project, helped facilitate additional interviews with young people and provided important additional information and data on outcomes for young people.

Thanks also go to the other members of the evaluation team, Dr Sarah Lloyd-Jones and Rhodri Bowen for their help with the fieldwork and for their comments on evaluation reports, and to Suzanne Chisholm, Nick Keating and Professor Howard Williamson and the other members of the project steering group for their insights and feedback through the course of the evaluation.

Notes

1   www.unicef.org/crc
2   Typically over 90 per cent of young people in custody in England and Wales are male.

References

Audit Commission (2009) *Tired of Hanging Around: Using Sport and Leisure Activities to Prevent Anti-social Behaviour by Young People*. London: Audit Commission.

Brand, S. and Price, R. (2000) *The Economic and Social Costs of Crime*. Home Office Research Study 217. London: Home Office.

Controller and Auditor General (2004) *Youth Offending: The Delivery of Community and Custodial Sentences*. London: National Audit Office.

Dingwell, G. (2009) 'Resolution Through Devolution? Policing, Youth Justice and Imprisonment in Wales', *Crimes and Misdemeanours* 3 (1).

Drakeford, M. (2008) 'The Welsh Assembly Government', in B. Goldson (ed.) *The Dictionary of Youth Justice*. Cullompton: Willan Publishing.

Farrington, D. P. (1995) 'The Development of Offending and Antisocial Behavior from Childhood: Key Findings from the Cambridge Study in Delinquent Development', *Journal of Child Psychology and Psychiatry*, 36: 929–64.

Farrington, D. (1997) 'Human Development And Criminal Careers', in M. Maguire, R. Morgan and R. Reiner (eds) *The Oxford Handbook Of Criminology*. Oxford: Clarendon Press.

Giddens, A. (1991) *Modernity and Self-Identity*. Cambridge: Polity

Gilbert, P. (1997) *Overcoming Depression: A Self-help Guide Using Cognitive Behavioural Techniques*. London: BCA.

Goleman, D. (1995) *Emotional Intelligence: Why It Can Matter More Than IQ*. New York: Bantam.

Jones, G. (2002) *The Youth Divide: Diverging Paths To Adulthood*. York: Joseph Rowntree Foundation.

Jones, G. (2005) *The Thinking and Behaviour of Young Adults: Literature Review for the Social Exclusion Unit*. London: ODPM.

Margo, J. and Dixon, M. (2006) *Freedom's Orphans: Raising Youth in a Changing World*. London: Institute for Public Policy Research.

Ministry of Justice (2009) *Reoffending of Juveniles: Results from the 2007 Cohort*, England and Wales Ministry of Justice Statistics Bulletin (published 21 May). Available at: www.justice.gov.uk/publications/docs/reoffending-juveniles-2007.pdf (accessed 20 June 2009).

Pitts, J. (2001) 'The New Correctionalism: Young People, Youth Justice and New Labour', in R. Matthews and J. Pitts (eds) *Crime, Disorder and Community Safety*. London: Routledge.

Rutter, M., Giller, H. and Hagell, A. (1998) *Antisocial Behaviour by Young People*. Cambridge: Cambridge University Press.

Smith, R. (2007) *Youth Justice: Ideas, Policy, Practice*, 2nd edn. Cullompton: Willan Publishing.

Social Exclusion Unit (SEU) (2002) *Reducing Re-Offending by Ex-Prisoners*. London: ODPM. Available at: www.Socialexclusion.Gov.Uk/Downloaddoc.Asp?Id=64 (accessed 9 August 2005).

Thomas, S. (2008) 'Juvenile Justice', in R. Croke and A. Crowley (eds) *Stop Look and Listen: The Road to Realising Children's Rights in Wales*. Cardiff: Save the Children.

Welsh Assembly Government (2002) *Extending Entitlement: Direction and Guidance*. Cardiff: Welsh Assembly Government.

Welsh Assembly Government (WAG) (2004) *Children and Young People: Rights to Action*. Cardiff: WAG.

Whitting, E. and Cuppleditch, L. (2006) *Re-offending of Juveniles: Results from the 2004 Cohort*, Home Office Statistical Bulletin 10/06. Available at: www.homeoffice.gov.uk/rds/pdfs06/hosb1006.pdf (accessed 2 February 2007).

Williamson, H. (2001) *The Milltown Boys*. Leicester: National Youth Agency.

Williamson, H. (2004) *The Milltown Boys Revisited*. Oxford: Berg.

YJB (no date) *Youth Resettlement: A Framework For Action*. London: Youth Justice Board. Available at: www.yjb.gov.uk/Publications/Resources/Downloads/Youth%20Resettlement%20Framework%20for%20Action.pdf (accessed 12 April 2009).

YJB (2001) *Risk and Protective Factors Associated with Youth Crime and Effective Interventions to Prevent It*. Research Note No. 5, Chapter 4: Reducing Levels of Risk – What Works. London: Youth Justice Board.

YJB (2009) *Youth Justice – Annual Workload Data 2007/08*. London: Youth Justice Board.

YJB/Welsh Assembly Government (WAG) (2004) *The All Wales Youth Offending Strategy*. London: Youth Justice Board. Available at: www.new.wales.gov.uk/docrepos/40382/sjr/crime/youthoffendingstrategye?lang=en (accessed 20 February 2007).

Chapter 10

Contemporary sex offender treatment: incorporating circles of support and the good lives model

Mark S. Carich, Chris Wilson, Peter A. Carich and Martin C. Calder

Introduction

Sexual aggression is a complicated and socially emotionally charged phenomenon given the extensive impact on society, rendering many sex offenders as 'outcasts'. Yet, society and offenders have to cope with human and social agencies, humanity, laws, and the risk of re-offence. It is imperative therefore that we accurately identify and intervene with this population to enhance treatment focus, engagement and outcomes. Furby *et al.* (1989) have formally questioned the effectiveness of sex offender treatment, although evidence does suggest that cognitive behavioural therapy (CBT) does reduce recidivism. This doesn't mean that we should be complacent and dampen other innovative treatment options that have the potential to challenge or complement long-standing treatment approaches. Fortunately there are a number of encouraging innovative conceptual approaches to offer new paths to enhance treatment effectiveness and we will draw upon the Good Lives Model (GLM) and Circles of Support as two such examples in this chapter.

Contemporary sex offender treatment

Inevitably there is a wide range of different treatment approaches, although we will outline just the most recognised and widely used here. Cognitive interventions primarily involve thinking covert behaviours.

These interventions range from simple thought-stopping techniques to problem-solving tactics. Several primary interventions include thought-stopping, cognitive restructuring, problem-solving, word-storming, and catching self. Behavioural interventions involve using the principles of conditioning and overt activities. Covert (internally oriented) interventions are considered behaviourally based upon the conditioning procedures of instrumental or operant conditioning, classical conditioning and their variations (that is, modelling). Operant conditioning procedures involve learning through reinforcement or the consequences of behaviour. Offenders can learn to set up behavioural modification schedules, thus reinforcing positive behaviours, while reducing negative behaviour. Classical conditioning is the learning through the pairing of two or more stimuli and/or stimuli with responses. Thus, deviant responses are reduced, while appropriate behaviours are enhanced. It is learning through association. Some of the variations include self-aversive conditioning techniques, covert sensitisation, stimulus control, escape and avoidance. Cognitive behavioural interventions encompass a variety of techniques that involve both primarily thinking and behavioural (activity) experiential domains. There are several tactics that offenders can use as relapse interventions. These include writing techniques such as journals/logs, or tracking systems, lists, letters, repetitive listing, reminder cards and notes, crashing fantasies, and reprogramming formats. The most dominant treatment approach is cognitive behavioural (Carich and Calder 2003; Carich and Mussack 2001).

A cognitive behavioural approach seems to have some different interpretations, thus showing large degrees of flexibility – such as the addition of dynamic (Carich 2009) and 'emotional' (Marshall 2007) to the title of cognitive-behavioural, reflecting the incorporation of dynamic processes within treatment. It also seems to have expanded to embrace a more holistic view, addressing a variety of issues along multiple experiential domains (see Longo 2008). This reflects the reality that there is much more to treatment than targeting cognitive distortions and arousal control. Most recently Ward (2002) and Ward *et al.* (2007) have emphasised the importance of GLM, reflecting a shift in attitude towards the offender from professionals.

Underlining philosophical/theoretical themes: setting the tone

The general philosophical themes of treatment involve three points: learn to live offence-free; reduce harm; and enhance the offender's quality of life. These themes simultaneously both reflect society's concerns of future victim impact and also attend to the offender's (frequently unmet) needs. Historically the emphasis was on reducing harm to society, maintaining abstinence from offending and attaining 'recovery' without cure (Carich and Calder 2003). However, this approach doesn't sit comfortably in the real world. An imbalanced approach to risk assessment and treatment is one premised on an exclusive focus on risks or deficits and a belief that should they be eradicated, then safety could be achieved. Such thinking supported a punitive confrontational approach to sex offenders, who often retreated from any intervention feeling persecuted, and which arguably supported or potentially aggravated the risks. More realistically, however, is a view that risk is part of life – risks must be managed and a more balanced approach emerged that aimed to balance risks with assets (Calder 2008) and so a more motivational, holistic and engaging approach emerged that has been referred to as 'wellness planning' (Longo 2001). Theoretical themes here centre on self-determinism: social interest, inter-personal contextual dimensions, responsibility, teleology and holism (see Adler 1941, 1956; Dreikurs 1950, 1967; Carich and Calder 2003 for a fuller discussion on these points). What is clear is that much sex offending is not driven by sexual needs but by a vast range of unmet needs in offenders' early years (Ryan *et al.* 1999). Behaviour is goal-oriented or purposeful within any given living system and humans seek primary goods (needs) appropriately or inappropriately. Offenders meet needs and/or secure goods through offending.

All treatment work entails the concept of change, as the offender moves from offending to a non-offending state. Typically, change is viewed from a content perspective of treatment targets (Carich *et al.* 2008), often ignoring the dynamic aspects (Carich and Dobkowski 2007).

Therapeutic change

Generally, change has been defined as creating difference within the human condition, typically in terms of functioning, and ranging from dysfunctional to functional (Carich and Dobkowski 2007). Change involves different experimental domains including cognitive, affective, behavioural, biological, physiological, spiritual, contextual, interpersonal or social, sensory modes, all connecting and interacting at what has been referred to as the mind-body perceptual control core process (Carich and Dobkowski 2007; Carich, Williamson and Dobkowski 2008). Each domain mutually interacts with the other with differing influences. Change occurs in levels and degrees vs a dichotomous view.

Watzlawick *et al.* (1974) outlined two levels of change: the first order of change refers to superficial change, change within the system, while second order change involves a systemic transformation. A higher level of change was proposed, reflecting the complexities of life, as well as multiple levels of change (Carich 1998, 2000). The third meta-level refers to ongoing deeper levels of change. This helps eliminate the 'mystery' of therapeutic change.

Applied to sex offenders, at a minimal level, change occurs when an offender moves from an offending to a non-offending state. The deeper levels of change encompass changes in core schemas or implicit theories (ITs). ITs are the basic templates or blueprints guiding one's activities (Ward 2000). Dysfunctional ITs are involved in offending states and decisions. Therefore, the deepest levels of change require a dramatic shift in the offender's core perceptual system, thus replacing them with functional ITs. At this level of change, the offender enters a transformational process.

Key elements of treatment

There are a number of treatment targets and elements involved in the treatment process, summarised by Carich *et al.* (2008). In surveying the literature, essential critical elements of treatment for most sex offenders are outlined as follows.

Essential elements of treatment comprise:

- Responsibility and cognitive restructuring

- Empathy
  - Victim specific
  - Global

- Regulation (coping) skills
  - Sexual arousal
  - Mood management
  - General intervention regulation skills

- Change maintenance strategies (RP related)
  - Offence/dysfunctional patterns/processes and regulation (coping) skills

- Interpersonal (skills, issues, attachments)

- Needs and issues
  - Esteem/worth
  - Related motivational issues
  - Primary human goals

Key process variables in treatment

Along with the advancing conceptualisation of therapeutic change has been an acknowledgement of the centrality of evaluating process variables, such as the therapy sessions, group and therapist style (Drapeau

2005; Fernandez 2006; Marshall 2005, Marshall and Serran 2000; Marshall *et al.* 2003). The four critical process variables involving the therapist style: include the need for rapport, with empathy, respect and warmth; encouragement/reward (reinforcing positive responses); being directive to a degree; and encouraging hope. Ward *et al.* (2007) concurred with the need for such a therapeutic alliance and framed GLM through a desire to help the offender; and by eliciting cooperation through collaboration. Emphasis is placed on the therapeutic style, in terms of delivery and responsibility to the offender's needs in a non-punitive context.

Introducing and applying the Good Lives Model (GLM)

As outlined earlier, the primary goal of the risk management approach is to *enhance public safety* by reducing the risk that apprehended offenders will engage in future sexually abusive behaviour (Andrews and Bonta 2003; Gendreau 1996). Risk management theory is based on the premise that by identifying and reducing risk factors predictive of sexual offending, offending rates will be reduced. While historical (static) risk factors are unchangeable and have their value in helping predict the likelihood of recidivism over time, dynamic risk factors (that is, criminogenic needs) are potentially modifiable and become the clinical problems to target in treatment. In essence, dynamic risk factors are treated as the cause of future offending and hence the appropriate clinical targets for intervention.

From a risk management perspective, treatment aims to identify deficits or problems with offenders' psychological and behavioural functioning that are associated with sexual offending (for example offence-supportive beliefs, deviant sexual arousal). Treatment is designed to eliminate, reduce, or manage the extent of these problems (risk factors) so the likelihood of future sexual offending is lessened. The ultimate goal of treatment is to increase public safety by reducing future sexual offences in those offenders who remain living, or return to live, in the community.

The risk management approach to rehabilitation is enunciated by a core set of risk–need principles (Andrews and Bonta 2003). The *risk principle* states the assessed risk level should determine the need for treatment (higher-risk offenders should receive more intensive and longer-term treatment). The *need principle* states that treatment should aim to modify dynamic risk factors (criminogenic needs). Non-criminogenic needs (those presenting problems that are not dynamic risk factors) can become the legitimate focus of intervention if they interfere with individuals' ability to engage in a risk reduction programme. Otherwise such problems are not appropriate treatment targets; their amelioration will not contribute to reduced risk of recidivism and therefore will not contribute to the overarching goal of enhancing public safety. The *responsivity principle* states interventions should be matched to individuals' learning styles.

The major form that risk management rehabilitation takes is *relapse prevention programmes*. Relapse prevention is a form of cognitive behaviour treatment that teaches offenders to (a) recognise the psychological and situational dynamic risk factors associated with past sexual offending, and (b) how best to avoid or respond to these risk factors in the future to support desistance from sexual offending (Ward and Hudson 2000). Alternatively, the GLM integrates etiological assumptions about the causes of sexual offending and incorporates risk management principles into a much more holistic, strengths-based approach to sex offender rehabilitation. The GLM of rehabilitation has the overarching goal of *enhancing* individuals' capacity to live meaningful, constructive, and ultimately satisfying lives so they can desist from further offending (Ward *et al.* 2005). The central premise is that rehabilitation should seek to equip individuals with the necessary psychological (internal) and social (external) conditions to meet their *inherent human needs* in socially acceptable and personally satisfying ways. The GLM is a comprehensive rehabilitation theory that provides (a) a set of overarching principles, assumptions and values that underpins rehabilitation and guides clinicians decision-making; (b) a set of etiological assumptions that explain the causes of sexual offending, and (c) treatment guidelines that anchor existing therapeutic practices with sexual offenders in a more meaningful structure (Collie *et al.* 2007).

The GLM of rehabilitation is a strengths-based approach (Rapp 1998) with a dual focus on risk management and psychological well-being. The GLM proposes that rehabilitation will be most effective when offenders learn to manage their risk of re-offending within the broader goal of learning to lead a better kind of life. A better kind of life is one in which an individual meets his or her basic human needs in socially acceptable and personally satisfying ways.

From a GLM perspective, it is not sufficient simply to teach skills to reduce or manage risk factors. Instead, the task of achieving and maintaining behaviour change needs to be meaningfully embedded within the notions of personal well-being, personal identity and a positive lifestyle. Attention to individuals' internal capacity (for example knowledge, skills, attitudes and values) and ecological contexts (such as social supports and opportunities) are critical for understanding the development of sexual offending and the interventions necessary to achieve psychological well-being and desistance from offending.

The GLM views humans (including sexual offenders!) as active, goal-seeking beings whose actions reflect attempts to meet inherent human needs or primary human goods (Emmons 1999; Ward 2002). Primary human goods are states of affairs, states of mind, activities or experiences that are inherently beneficial to humans and are sought for their own sake rather than as a means to some other end (Arnhart 1998; Deci and Ryan 2000; Emmons 1999; Schmuck and Sheldon 2001).

Examples of primary human goods are autonomy, relatedness and competence (Deci and Ryan 2000). To secure primary human goods individuals engage in a range of activities, strategies, relationships, and experiences (referred to as secondary goods). For example, the primary human good of intimacy (a sub-class of relatedness) can be sought through a romantic relationship or friendship (types of secondary goods).

The main categories of primary human goods sought are: *life* (healthy living, optimal physical functioning, sexual satisfaction), *knowledge* (wisdom and information), *excellence in work and play* (mastery experiences), *excellence in agency* (autonomy, self-directedness); *inner peace* (freedom from emotional turmoil and stress), *friendship* (intimate, family, romantic); *spirituality* (finding meaning and purpose to life); *community, happiness,* and *creativity*.

The pursuit and achievement of primary human goods is integral to individuals' sense of meaning and purpose in life and, in turn, psychological well-being. No one primary human good is 'better' to attain than others. Instead, when individuals secure the full range of primary human goods (meet their inherent human needs), psychological functioning and well-being flourish. In contrast, inability to secure a number of primary human goods frustrates and compromises the ability to construct meaningful and purposeful lives and achieve optimal psychological well-being (Ward 2002; Ward and Stewart 2003a, 2003b). To attain the full range of goods in socially acceptable and personally satisfying ways, individuals require both the *internal* capacity (such as knowledge, skills, attitudes and values) and *external* conditions (social support and opportunities) to do so.

From a GLM perspective individuals offend due to problems in one or more dimensions of their good lives plans: individuals may use inappropriate means to secure goods (for example seeking intimacy through child sexual abuse); lack scope in the goods sought (devaluing relatedness resulting in a lack of socially acceptable means to achieve sexual satisfaction); have conflict among the goods sought (wanting both autonomy of sexual freedom and intimacy within the same relationship); lack the skills or the internal capacity to achieve goods (poor self-regulation skills and impulsive decision-making); or lack the opportunity, support or ecological context to achieve the goods sought (being geographically and socially isolated or dislocated). The presence of dynamic risk factors, such as social skills deficits and emotional congruence with children, simply alerts clinicians to problems in the way offenders are seeking to achieve primary human goods (Ward and Stewart 2003a, 2003b). For example, hostile and anti-social attitudes are understood as an internal obstacle to establishing the trust necessary to meet the basic human need of intimacy in relationships.

The aim of treatment, therefore, is not to remove risk factors *per se* but to equip individuals with the necessary psychological (internal) and social (external) conditions to meet their inherent human needs through socially acceptable and personally satisfying means.

Applications of GLM

GLM is considered a rehabilitation model, and is applied to sex offender treatment by including both meeting needs appropriately as part of the client's life plan and clinical guidelines, within the treatment setting. The clinical setting needs to be positive, non-punitive and non-shaming. Group cohesion is emphasised, along with an appropriate therapist style of intervention. The responsivity principle matching treatment integrity with client needs and resources is emphasised as well. McMurran and Ward (2004) provide a list of clinical guidelines with a strengths-based approach:

- Seek positive life plan
- Focus on goal orientation and features
  - Sense of purpose and meaning
  - Setting goals and goal achievement
  - Structuring life
  - Short, intermediate, long term
  - Developing essential skills in fulfilling life
  - Build on strengths
  - Good life plan
  - Capabilities/potential
  - Positive language

Ward *et al.* (2007) summarise contemporary treatment by denoting six modules:

1. Understanding offence patterns and cognitive restructuring

2. Deviant sexual arousal

3. Victim impact/empathy training

4. Affective regulation

5. Social skills training

6. Safety planning or maintenance strategies

The first module is designed to help them understand the offence process, contributing factors and related dynamics including needs or goals being met. Patterns are identified, along with cognitive distortions and ITs (implicit theories). For moderate and high-risk chronic/serial offenders, core schemas need to be restructured. Thus, cognitive restructuring is the key. Restructuring involves changing one's rules of varying types of judgements (such as cognitive, values, practical (how to act), and acquisition of skills (Ward *et al.* 2007). Lastly, one's personal sense of worth is targeted. Responsibility or internal locus of control is emphasised.

Deviant sexual arousal (2) is only addressed in treatment *via* conditioning related techniques if the offender has these issues. When sexually deviant preferences are entrenched, conditioning tactics are recommended (see Carich and Calder 2003 for a review).

Empathy training (3) is conducted in a non-shaming based context. Both global (if needed) and victim-specific empathy are targeted. The goal of this module helps the offender understand the perspective of the survivor and impact of the offence (Ward *et al.* 2007). Advocated tactics include review of survivors' accounts, making connections to offenders' own victims, full recognition of consequences of offending, and role-plays. The therapist must model empathy, which involves imagination, perspective-taking and imaging outcomes of others' situations. The primary goods associated with empathy include knowledge and emotional regulation, resulting in inner peace.

Affective regulation (4) encompasses both affective recognition and management. This includes stress management with the primary good of inner peace (Ward *et al.* 2007). Offenders identify affective states precipitating offences. They learn to deal with emotional states. Ward *et al.* (2007) outline eight sets of affective regulation skills, based on GLM, and these are as follows.

- Awareness of emotional states
  - identify and detect emotional states
  - requiring orientation and interest in others *via* social skills

- Use cult-bound emotional vocabulary
  - requiring socialisation and community connectedness; emotional knowledge, intimacy skills

- Capacity to respond empathetically connected to others
  - see things from others' perspectives (suppressing own inappropriate emotions)

- Ability to adjust one's emotional presentation depending on circumstances
  - acquiring problem-solving skills and increased relatedness to others

- Capability to manage aversive emotions *via* range of adaptive strategies
  - use of stress management, problem-solving and communication skills
  - understanding emotions plays a critical role in establishing and maintaining intimate relationships, acquiring intimacy skills, social supports, knowledge, sense of agency (independence, individuality)

- Capacity for emotional self-efficacy, develop confidence in coping ability and resilience (agency issues)

- Client understands why they receive treatment and how it relates to offenders and good lives plans.

The social skills training module (5) involves addressing difficulties in relationships and social competency. Ward *et al.* (2007) emphasise the overarching goods associated with social competency are relatedness, community connectedness and agency (autonomy). Offenders learn to meet their needs through a mastering of interpersonal relationships. A variety of skills are emphasised, ranging from conversational skills to assertiveness and including intimacy skills. Ward *et al.* (2007) emphasise that external conditions are necessary for offenders to practise skills and connect with the community. This is a direct connection to the circle of support system that enhances skills and allows the offender to connect with the community.

The last stage of treatment (6) is a safety plan. Emphasis is placed on life plans reflecting appropriate strategies to receive to secure goods (Ward *et al.* 2007). Classical RP (relapse prevention) places emphasis on the following in a high-risk situation: develop safety plan; strengthen awareness of personal risk factors with management; and develop external support. Criticisms include: a narrow focus on offence pathways; emphasis on avoidance strategies; negative orientation; and insufficient opportunity to practise skills (Ward *et al.* 2007). With the GLM approach, they emphasise an approach-oriented intervention strategy; a positive approach; plans reflect promoting goods and risk management and help equip the offender to live a rewarding life. The approach orientation emphasises that offenders can only avoid few risk factors, and therefore needs to have an active set of interventions. Both approach and avoidant strategies are considered important skill set orientations (Carich 1991; Carich and Stone 1996, 2001; Carich *et al.* 2001; Carich and Calder 2003; Ward *et al.* 2007). Interventions are coping skills or responses: they are keys to the process (Cortoni and Carich 2007). Emphasis is placed on identifying offender-related and including dysfunctional patterns and interventions (Carich, Dobkowski and Delehanty 2008). As a result of treatment, the offender learns to meet his needs or secure goods appropriately and develop maintenance strategies to continue a non-offending lifestyle.

The life plan must include social support, given offenders live in a social context. Thus, the circle of support is a useful system, promoting the GLM and traditional approach.

Circles of support and accountability

The Circles of Support started off as a completely unrelated treatment option but the approach sits well with the changing face of sex offender treatment globally.

Circles of Support and Accountability (Circles) originated in Canada as a response to public fear and outrage at the release from prison into the community of a high-profile child sex offender. The Mennonite community, worried by the demonising of this particular individual and the moral panic that existed around the subject of child sexual abuse, responded with a restorative based concept and established the first Circle. A Circle of Support and Accountability (a Circle) is a group of trained volunteers who meet on a regular basis both as a group and as individuals with a high-risk sex offender (core member) living in their community. They hold him or her accountable for past offending behaviour through a relationship of care and support. This relationship seeks to enhance any treatment plan the core member may have prepared and helps to formulate personal goals that will hopefully result in the acquisition of a more satisfying and meaningful life.

The Correctional Service of Canada had made its own efforts to educate the public about the management of sex offenders living in the community and had tried to alleviate fear while lessening the public's expectation of the statutory agencies' ability to protect. Therefore, when in 1996 the Mennonite Central Committee in Ontario produced a manual for the delivery of Circles and entered into a contract with Correctional Services Canada, an opportunity was provided for communities to play a positive role in enhancing their own protection. What was becoming clear was that professional staff within the Canadian criminal justice system had accepted that Circles were not in any way at odds with the work of community-based treatment programmes, but was likely to enhance them. Likewise those police officers who had experience of Circles also began to realise that Circles could be seen as a part-solution to the scarce resources available to them and enhance their ability to effectively manage high-risk sex offenders. The vital component evident in the Canadian experience, which was later replicated in England and Wales, was the strength that was offered through their independence from statutory agencies. However, success for any Circle project can only be achieved if it is supported by those agencies with confidence and respect. Partnership is crucial and while statutory agencies need to perceive themselves as stakeholders in their relationship with Circles, it is members of the community who must perceive themselves as the primary stakeholders of a local Circles project.

Exporting Circles: the UK experience

Since it was the Mennonite Church that established the first Circle in Canada in 1994, it was consistent that the most successful Circles project in England, based in the Thames Valley, was originally managed by Quaker Peace and Social Witness. This project is now an independent charity known as HTV Circles. The Thames Valley area was identified by the government to pilot Circles because of its excellent record in restorative practice. Two other pilot schemes were established at the same time as the Thames Valley pilot in 2002, both of which were managed by non-faith-based organisations.

While there are many similarities between the Canadian and English models, there are some key differences also: namely legally, structurally and culturally. For example, in Canada those offenders statistically assessed as high-risk would serve the whole of their sentence and be released without parole or supervision. In England there had been over a decade of excessive legislation related to sexual offending, designed not only to enhance the effective management of high-risk offenders being released from custody but also, in truth, to assuage public anxiety. The development of Circles in Canada remained rooted within the community and grew organically, while in England, Circles was government-funded and developed systemically, with targets set and development controlled.

It was a courageous act by the British government to fund three pilot sites for a politically contentious project such as Circles, particularly at a time when the media was creating public hysteria and moral panic over child sex offenders. However, the philosophy of community responsibility that is intrinsic to Circles sat firmly within the government's criminal justice and civil renewal agendas. At the same time, the government was creating a new organisation called the National Offender Management Service (NOMS), whose remit was to bring together the prison and probation services into one organisation. This new policy and practice framework for managing sex offenders in the community was wholly consistent with the core values of Circles. This model of offender management had at its heart a desire to ensure that all practice was based upon a personal relationship rather than a bureaucratic one, a relationship in which the offender takes an active part. One of the core values of NOMS is 'involvement of local community in offender management through improving communication with local people, fostering greater organisational awareness of public concerns and encouraging active participation of the community in local projects' (Home Office, www.noms.homeoffice.gov.uk). This is a value that could result in Circles becoming an integral part of offender management specific to sexual offenders.

The development of sex offender treatment and sex offender legislation in England and Wales over the past 20 years highlights some interesting parallels as well as some contradictions. These developments give a context and understanding as to how and why Circles was so successful and its growing importance to the statutory agencies of police and probation.

- Throughout the late 1980s and 1990s, sex offender treatment pro-grammes were becoming increasingly evidence-based, with practice informing research and research informing the theoretical models that underpinned practice. Sex offender legislation throughout the 1990s and into the next decade began to reflect the concept of punishment based on a perceived likelihood of re-offending. The influence of knowledge accrued from sex offender research on this legal concept was significant with the development of a succession of risk assessment tools that helped to influence sentencing. This new legislation contained actuarial elements and was becoming increasingly punitive.

- It is important to recognise that the culmination of such legislation, based on a perceived likelihood of re-offending, moves the sentencing and subsequent management of sexual offenders into a different context where punishment of sex offenders is based on belonging to a particular category of risk. While legislators continued to justify their actions as in the public interest and state that their intention is to enhance public protection through risk management, punishment based on the perceived likelihood of re-offending is at odds with the notion fundamental to the concept of retributive justice; that is, that there should be some degree of proportionality between the crime and the punishment.

- Despite the increasingly punitive nature of new and developing legislation, the proliferation of sex offender treatment programmes was facilitating a deeper understanding through research in identifying the factors that contributed to sexually deviant behaviour (Marshall *et al.* 1998) and what was effective in reducing those factors (Bates *et al.* 2004).

- As in Canada, one of the criteria for an offender's inclusion in a Circle was an assessment of high risk. The core member would initially inform and share with the volunteers in his or her Circle the work they had undertaken in treatment and the strategies he or she had developed to avoid future re-offending. This was considered vital in order for the Circle to identify dynamic factors and therefore address the principle of need. Recruitment and selection of volunteers for a Circle was done with diversity in mind. The more diverse the Circle, the more it would be responsive to the personal needs of the core member.

- It is testimony to the growing theoretical knowledge base and its influence in the implementation within treatment programmes that the Good Lives Model (GLM), developed by Ward, has now been adapted as the Better Lives programme (Fisher 2008) and included in the accredited treatment programmes delivered in England and Wales.

- It is also important to recognise that both the legislation and the system in which it is delivered (multi-agency work), is by definition restrictive and negative towards the individual offender. It is essential that restrictive measures designed to enhance public protection are also weighted with positive influences; offenders with employment and stable social relationships have lower recidivism than those without jobs or significant others (Andrews and Bonta 2003). This recognition should not be lost upon those responsible for public protection through risk management. As Ward observes, 'measures which legislate intensive monitoring and control of sex offenders can result in individuals being unable to relocate into social networks and to establish adaptive ways of meeting their needs. Paradoxically the combination of social stigma and an exaggerated notion of risk can increase the chances of re-offending' (Ward and Maruna 2007).

It was timely that the development of Circles in England and Wales coincided with the implementation of the European Social Charter. Formally adopted in December 2000, the Charter contained the principles derived from case law of the Court of Justice and the European Court of Human Rights. By making fundamental rights clearer and more visible, the Charter helped to develop the concept of citizenship of the European Union, enhancing legal certainty as regards the protection of fundamental rights. The initial impact of this resulted in a number of challenges through the courts by individual sex offenders against restrictions placed upon them by MAPPA. Although the courts always ensured that the rights of the individual were superseded by the right of a community to be protected (Henham 2001), this new European dimension required MAPPA to take into account the rights of the individual offender and ensure that any restrictions and control placed upon him or her were proportionate in relation to the risk they continued to pose.

As had the Correctional Services in Canada previously recognised the value of Circles in complementing their work, MAPPA also began to perceive Circles as enhancing their ability to effectively manage sex offenders living in the community. It became increasingly understood by individual members of MAPPA that effective resettlement is more likely to occur if the offender is released into a community of care and support rather than one of hatred and fear. Indeed, Brown suggested that within a human rights framework, it is the responsibility of government to counter public anxiety, fear and hostility towards sex offenders by promoting a socially inclusive approach to the management of sex offenders in the community (Brown *et al.* 2008). This responsibility was taken seriously when in June 2006 the then Home Secretary John Reid commissioned the *Review of the Protection of Children from Sex Offenders* (Home Office 2007: 14). It was testimony to the success and impact Circles had made both in the four years it had been operational in Britain and the decade in Canada that it was recommended as a positive intervention.

The legal and cultural context in which Circles in England was to develop required a theoretical framework that would address all the constituent parts. Therefore the framework was based on three key principles (see Figure 10.1). The principles of support, monitor and

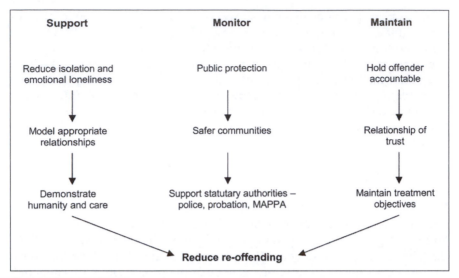

Figure 10.1   Theoretical framework: the three key principles

maintenance (Saunders and Wilson 2003) were intended to address those issues that were significant to the recidivism of sexually aggressive behaviour. The reduction of isolation and emotional loneliness had been proved to be an imperative as was confirmed by research where the psychometric score relating to emotional loneliness was the only one that was statistically significant in differentiating recidivists from non-recidivists (Bates *et al.* 2004). It was also widely known that perceptions of intimacy and the significance of attachment deficits demonstrated the need for appropriate modelling, a central feature of the volunteer's role. Any relationship is only meaningful if it is based on honesty and trust. As in treatment when the collaboration between the therapist and the offender in developing goals results in a stronger therapeutic alliance (Mann and Shingler 2006) the Circle too needs to continue modelling those alliances and working collaboratively with the core member. This is essential in building upon those strategies to avoid re-offending previously identified through treatment. It is in this way that the core member can acquire the components needed to achieve a positive life. It is only through a relationship that defines itself within a context of humanity and care that the core member is likely to accept the relationship of being held accountable by the Circle as anything other than positive.

It is this context that exemplifies Circles as embodying the Good Lives Model. The Good Lives Model (GLM) adopts an overt humanist notion of human development and social interaction. Human beings are seen as essentially social creatures with an objective to find meaning in their lives through communication, social interaction and individual achievement. The Circle aims to provide the offender with the ability necessary to implement a Better Life Plan on the values inherent within a strengths-based approach to offender management and rehabilitation.

The second principle, monitoring, is related to the ability of Circles to place itself within the existing structure of interagency cooperation. MAPPA is the statutory structure that has a strategic responsibility for the oversight of agencies charged with the management of sexual and violent offenders living in the community. MAPPA brings these agencies together on a regular basis to review, discuss and formulate action plans. By definition MAPPA's process and actions tend to be reactive methods of control, such as registration, sex offender prevention orders and community notification. Circles facilitates the ability to gain intelligence, for the purposes of public protection, through a creative and community-based initiative. This line of communication between the Circle and MAPPA works because graduates of treatment programmes, who have truly internalised the values of safety and responsibility, recognise the need for a model of openness and honesty between the Circle and/or the statutory agencies of police and probation. This is also the case with Circles in Canada. Representatives of these two agencies are invited, when appropriate, to attend the Circle so that the core member (the offender) is overtly aware of the communication that takes place between his Circle and these agencies (Wilson *et al.* 2008). This model of communication does not seem to inhibit the relationship between the core member and his or her volunteers, particularly if volunteers are clear in articulating the need to keep all concerned informed. Core members have consistently shared problematic behaviours with their Circle volunteers, knowing that the information may be shared through the MAPPA process. Indeed, the fact that they are prepared to disclose information to the volunteers is testimony to the viability of positive community involvement relating to public protection. As such, monitoring becomes a positive and community-based activity.

The initial evaluation of the original Hampshire and Thames Valley projects (Bates *et al.* 2007) showed that Circles not only provided 'a unique insight into the details of core members behaviours and lifestyles' (Bates 2005) but is also well positioned to identify and contain potential risk, providing a valuable source of information and support to partnership agencies. The majority of statistical evidence as to the effectiveness of Circles still relies on the Canadian evaluation (Wilson *et al.* 2005, 2007). However, the evaluation of the Hampshire and Thames Valley Circles' first four years of operational activity recorded that, from a total of sixteen Circles, nine core members who had displayed high-risk behaviours were reported to the police by their Circle volunteers. Of that nine, four of the core members were recalled to prison on licence, while the remaining five were managed through MAPPA, in the community by police, probation and the Circle. For those recalled to prison their volunteers continued to have contact with them and when released the core member returned to the Circle. For these core members the experience of being held to account but not abandoned was a profound experience and society is witness to this powerful model of change. The core member's experience is best understood when viewed within the context of Ward's Good Life Model, in that to reduce risk the core member must acquire a sense of who they are and what really matters to both themselves and to others. Essential to this process is the appropriate acquisition of what is referred to as 'primary goods' (Lindsay *et al.* 2007), achieved through meaningful relationships with other people resulting in a sense of belonging.

The third key principle, maintaining, relates specifically to the link between treatment and Circles and their combined role in the prevention of re-offending. Many high-risk sexual offenders are, by definition, socially isolated and without a support network, other than that provided by key professional persons paid to be in their lives. A Better Lives/New Life Plan, detailing re-offending prevention strategies, is a dynamic document that needs to be shared with significant others. The purpose of a Circle, in its purest form, is to provide the core member with a support network, so that his or her efforts to prevent re-offending become meaningful in their attempt to sustain a balanced, self-determined lifestyle. Through that all-important relationship of trust and honesty, the Circle can help to hold the core member accountable, maintaining treatment objectives and community expectations.

Volunteers are members of the community who act as representatives for that community and are the essential ingredient to the success of any Circle project. It is vital that volunteers are supported, monitored and held accountable for the work they are undertaking. Supervision needs to be undertaken by a Circle coordinator who understands not only the issues related to risk management, but also the needs of the volunteers. The challenge is to find a balance whereby the volunteers feel supported, but are not wholly dependent on that professional support to work effectively. It is important to understand that when undertaking something new, this something new is approached from a point of naivety. Both advice and guidance are needed until experience consolidates into sound judgement. The Circle coordinator provides this guidance and advice both formally and informally. The personal well-being of volunteers is paramount and, as such, they are invited to attend quarterly reviews in which they can explore their experience of Circle work. The coordinator will also ensure that the Circle as a whole is regularly reviewed.

Like the original Canadian model, the experience of volunteers working in Circles is built upon a foundation of training. Volunteering for Circles is far more demanding than other types of volunteer work. After an initial interview, designed to elicit motivation, attitudes and beliefs, the prospective volunteers are invited to an introductory training programme lasting 16 hours. They are screened and assessed for their suitability. After training, it is hoped that volunteers are familiar enough with the model and expectations that they are able to be functional, effective volunteers. The aim is to ensure that each Circle has a balance of gender, age, experience and skills, reflecting a true representation of community. This healthy robustness to the Circle ensures that the needs of the core member can be addressed and managed by the volunteers. A series of further training events are made available to the volunteers throughout the year, which include housing and employment issues, substance misuse, questioning styles and listening skills. The Circle meets on a regular weekly basis where the core member will share the work he or she has undertaken in treatment. Not only will the Circle volunteers learn to recognise when the core member is falling into old patterns of behaviour, they will understand the coping strategies that the core member has developed. When the Circle and the coordinator feel all are ready, the volunteers will start to meet individually with the core member, engaging in safe activities that are likely to enhance the core member's life. This allows the Circle to facilitate the Better Life/New Life/relapse prevention plan to become truly dynamic. The Circle becomes the quintessence of the GLM, capitalising on the core member's interests and preferences, providing them with the skills and abilities they need to attain both their primary and their secondary goals. Circles act as a control against the 'constraints relating to the individual's abilities, their resources and the degree of support moderate the nature of treatment plans' (Ward and Maruna 2007). While it would be easy to argue that such a statement is self evident and that the support of Circles facilitates against such constraints, the Canadian evaluation evidences this as a truth, (Wilson *et al.* 2005, 2007) as does the emerging evidence from England and Wales (Bates *et al.* 2007).

The growth of Circles emanates from a strengths-based approach and is wholly complementary with the GLM. Ward states that 'emerging out of the science of positive psychology, the strengths based approaches shift the focus away from criminogenic needs and other deficits and instead asks what the individual can contribute to his or her family, community and society. How can their life become useful and purposeful?' (Ward and Maruna 2007). It is, of course, obvious that the ability of the individual to find purpose cannot be achieved without the support of family, community and society. The growth of Circles in England and Wales since 2002 has been so significant that the government saw the need to support and fund a new charitable organisation known as Circles UK to ensure that the best practice developed during the pilot period was disseminated and adhered to. The organisation has been charged to ensure the development and delivery of Circles:

- To ensure the quality and consistency of practices through training and assessment processes.

- To coordinate a national perspective for the evaluation and research of Circles.

- To promote an awareness and provide consistent, accurate information about Circles, while maintaining the profile of Circles activity with strategic partners at national and regional level.

- To ensure the sustainability of local Circles projects and to support their expansion into mainstream activity by adopting a coordinated and high level approach to funding negotiations.

The creation of such an organisation proved timely in that a number of European governments, specifically Holland and Belgium, are now also implementing Circles.

Although Circles needs to be adapted to ensure it is relevant to the legal and cultural context of the country adopting the system, it continues to operate within a value base that remains essentially restorative. As observed by Newell:

> Circles of Support and Accountability are grounded in a commitment to the principles of restorative justice. All those involved in Circles seek to take seriously the needs and concerns of the victims and community as well as the offender. The safety of the community and potential victims is imperative if there is to be restoration in the community. A restoration of peace must be realised for true community safety to be enhanced. This is the key motivating factor for Circles of Support and Accountability. (Newell 2000)

Understandably, face-to-face victim–offender restorative mediation rarely happens in offences of a sexual nature; however, the restorative nature of Circles work was summarised by a volunteer when she described Circles as 'restorative justice by proxy' (QPSW 2003). As McAlinden observes, 'Circles of support present an opportunity to move away from the further enactment of situational legislative and policy responses to sex offender management, which are often implemented after specific cases occur' (McAlinden 2007). She asserts that instead of reaction, restorative justice offers the opportunity of changing multi-agency procedures to become more effective risk management strategies that are not simply reactive responses to sexual offending but are also resolute in their ability to prevent further victimisation. The question is, how do you turn a concept like restorative justice into a practice known for its effective risk management with a resolve to prevent further offending? Sounds remarkably like Circles of Support and Accountability.

Conclusion

The managing and treatment of sexual offenders is a complex process and highly controversial. Contemporary cognitive behavioural treatment has proven to be effective in the treatment of sexual offenders. The majority of professionals in the field of sexual offender treatment agree that treatment is effective even though there is no cure. A constant follow-up plan of management must be in place to avoid or reduce recidivism.

The emergence of new dynamic models of intervention is essential if we are to work effectively with offenders to understand the causes and consequences of their behaviour and effect changes to enhance the quality of their lives linked to risk reduction for others. The Good Lives Model and Circles of Support are excellent models for illustrating how theory development can inform creative practice. The early signs are optimistic but the challenge for the future is to mould these models further through case application and subsequent modification and to encourage the continuation of evidence-based frameworks drawn from a wide range of subject areas. The key to progress is to be clear about those cases that appear on the radar screen and so they can be monitored and tracked to avoid unnecessary danger occurring.

References

Adler, A. (1941) *Understanding Human Nature*. New York: Tower Books.
Adler, A. (1956) *The Individual Psychology of Alfred Adler*. H. L. Ansbacher.
Andrews, D. A. and Bonta, J. (2003) *The Psychology of Criminal Conduct*, 3rd edn. Cincinnati, OH: Anderson.
Arnhart, L. (1998) *Darwinian Natural Right: The Biological Ethics of Human Nature*. Albany: State University of New York Press.
Bates, A. (2005) *Circles of Support and Accountability in the Thames Valley: The First Three Years*. London: Quaker Communications.
Bates, A., Falshaw, L., Corbett, C., Patel, V. and Friendship, C. (2004) 'A Follow-up Study of Sex Offenders Treated by the Thames Valley Sex Offender Group Work Programme 1995–1999', *Journal of Sexual Aggression*, 29.
Bates, A., Saunders, R. and Wilson, C. (2007) 'Doing Something About it: A Follow Up Study of Sex Offenders Participating in the Thames Valley Circles of Support and Accountability', *British Journal of Community Justice*, 5 (1).
Brown, S., Deakin, J. and Spencer, J. (2008) 'What People Think About the Management of Sex Offenders in the Community', *Howard Journal*, 47.
Calder, M. C. (2008) 'Risk and Child Protection', in M. C. Calder (ed.) *Contemporary Risk Assessment in Safeguarding Children*. Dorset: Russell House Publishing.
Carich, M. S. (1991) *The Recovery of Sex Offenders: Some Basic Elements*.
Carich, M. S. (1998) 'The Third Alternative: A Meta-recursive View', *The Milton Erickson Foundation Newsletter*, 18 (3, 2).

Carich, M. S. (2000) 'The Directions of Contemporary Sex Offender Treatment: An Issue of Social reconstruction vs. Logical Positivism', *The Forum*, 12 (3): 4–5.

Carich, M. S. (2009) 'The Essentials of Sex Offender Treatment', unpublished handout.

Carich, M. S. and Adkerson, D. (2003) *Adult Sexual Offender Report*. Brandon, VT: Safer Society Press.

Carich, M. S. and Calder, M. C. (2003) *Contemporary Treatment of Adult Male Sex Offenders*. Dorset: Russell House Publishers.

Carich, M. S. and Dobkowski, G. (2007) 'Utilizing Interpersonal Influence in Working Through Resistance', *ATSA Forum*, 19.

Carich, M. S., Dobkowski, M. A. and Delehanty, B. S. (2008) 'Should Relapse Prevention be Abandoned?', *Forum* (Summer). Beaverton, OR: Association for the Treatment of Sexual Abusers.

Carich, M. S. and Mussack, S. E. (eds) (2001) *A Handbook for Sexual Abuser Assessment and Treatment*. Brandon, VT: Safer Society Press.

Carich, M. S. and Stone, M. (1996) *Sex Offender Relapse Intervention Workbook*. Chicago, IL: Adler School.

Carich, M. S. and Stone, M. (2001) 'Using Relapse Intervention Strategies to Treat Offenders', *Journal of Individual Psychology*, 57: 26–36.

Carich, M. S., Grey, A., Stone, M. and Pithers, W. D. (2001) 'Relapse Prevention and the Sexual Assault Cycle', in M. S. Carich and S. E. Mussack (eds) *A Handbook for Sexual Offender Assessment and Treatment*. Brandon, VT: Safer Society Press.

Carich, M. S., Spilman, K. and Stanislaus, A. (2008) 'Evaluating Treatment Process', in B. K. Schwartz (ed.) *The Sex Offender: Offender Evaluation and Program Strategies*, Vol. VI. Kingston, NJ: Civic Research Institute.

Carich, M. S., Williamson, S. and Dobkowski, G. (2008) 'Treating Resistance in Sex Offenders: Enhancing Motivation', in M. Calder (ed.) *The Carrot or the Stick? Promoting Effectiveness Practice with Involuntary Clients*. Dorset: Russell House Publishing.

Collie, R. M., Ward T., Huffum, L. and West, B. (2007) 'The Good Lives Model of Rehabilitation: Reducing Risks and Promoting Strengths with Adolescent Sexual Offenders', in M. C. Calder (ed.) *Working with Children and Young People Who Sexually Abuse: Taking the Field Forward*. Dorset: Russell House Publishing.

Cortoni, F. and Carich, M. S. (2007) 'The Why and How of Building Coping Skills in Treatment', in D. Prescott (ed.) *Knowledge and Practice: Challenges in the Treatment and Supervision of Sexual Abusers*. Brandon, VT: Safer Society Press.

Deci, E. L. and Ryan, R. M. (2000) 'The "What" and "Why" of Goal Pursuits: Human Needs and the Self-Determination of Behavior', *Psychological Inquiry*, 11: 227–68.

Drapeau, M. (2005) 'Research on the Process Involved in Treating Sexual Offenders', *Sexual Abuse: A Journal of Research and Treatment*, 17 (2): 117–27.

Dreikurs, R. (1950) *Fundaments of Adlerian Psychology*. Chicago, IL: Alfred Adler Institute.

Dreikurs, R. (ed.) (1967) *Psychodynamics, Psychotherapy and Counseling: The Collected Papers* Chicago, IL: Alfred Adler Institute.

Emmons, R. A. (1999) *The Psychology of Ultimate Concerns*. New York: Guilford Press.

Fernandez, Y. (2006) 'Focusing on the Positive and Avoiding the Negative in Sexual Offender Treatment', in W. Marshall, Y. Fernandez, L. E. Marshall and

G. A. Serran (eds) *Sexual Offender Treatment: Controversial Issues*. Chichester: John Wiley.

Fisher, D. (2008) *Better Lives – Thames Valley Sex Offender Group Work Programme*. London: Ministry of Justice.

Furby, L. Weinrott, M. R. and Blackshaw, L. (1989) 'Sexual Recidivism: A Review', *Psychological Bulletin*, 105 (1): 3–30.

Gendreau, P. (1996) 'Offender Rehabilitation: What We Know and What Needs to be Done', *Criminal Justice and Behavior*, 23: 144–61.

Henham, R. (2001) 'Sentencing Dangerous Offenders: Policy and Practice in the Crown Court', *Criminal Law Review*, 693.

Home Office (2007) *Review of the Protection of Children from Sex Offenders*, Ref. 280124. London: Home Office.

Lindsay, W. R., Ward, T., Morgan, T. and Wilson, I. (2007) 'Self-regulation of Sex Offending Future Pathways and the Good Lives Model: Applications and Problems', *Journal of Sexual Aggression*, 13 (1).

Longo, R. E. (2001) *Paths to Wellness: A Holistic Approach and Guide for Personal Recovery*. Holyoke, MA: NEARI Press.

Longo R. E. (2008) 'Risk in Treatment: From Relapse Prevention to Wellness Planning', in M. C. Calder (ed.) *Contemporary Risk Assessment in Safeguarding Children*. Dorset: Russell House Publishing.

Mann, R. and Shingler, J. (2006) 'Collaboration in Clinical Work with Sex Offenders: Treatment and Risk Assessment', in W. L. Marshall, Y. E. Fernandez, L. E. Marshall and G. A. Serran (eds) *Sexual Offender Treatment: Controversial Issues*. Chichester: John Wiley.

Marshall, W. (2005) 'Therapist Style in Sexual Offender Treatment: Influences on Indices of Change', *Journal of Research and Treatment*, 17: 109–17.

Marshall, W. L. (2007) Interview with M. S. Carich and S. Smith, unpublished.

Marshall, W. L. and Serran, G. A. (2000) 'Improving the Effectiveness of Sex Offender Treatment', *Journal of Trauma and Violence*, 1 (3): 203–22.

Marshall, W. L., Fernandez, Y. M., Hudson, S. M. and Ward, T. (1998) *Sourcebook of Treatment Programs for Sexual Offenders*. New York: Plenum Press.

Marshall, W., Serran, G. A., Fernandez, Y. M., Mulloy, R., Mann, R. E. and Thornton, D. (2003) 'Therapist Characteristics in the Treatment of Sexual Offenders: Tentative Data on Their Relationship with Indices of Behaviour Change', *Journal of Sexual Aggression*, 9: 25–30.

McAlinden, A. (2007) *The Shaming of Sexual Offenders: Risk, Retribution and Reintegration*. Oxford/Portland, OR: Hart Publishing.

McMurran, M. and Ward, T. (2004) 'Motivating Offenders to Change in Therapy: An Organizing Framework', *Legal and Criminologinic Psychology*, 9: 295–311.

Newell, T. (2000) *Forgiving Justice: A Quaker Vision of Criminal Justice*. London: Quaker Communications.

Rapp, C. A. (1998) *The Strengths Model: Case Management with People Suffering from Severe and Persistent Mental Illness*. New York: Oxford University Press.

Ryan, G. and Associates (1999) *Web of Meaning: A Developmental-contextual Approach in Sexual Abuser Treatment*. Brandon, VT: Safer Society Press.

Saunders, R. and Wilson, C. (2003) *The Three Key Principles: A Theoretical Framework. Circles of Support and Accountability in the Thames Valley: An Interim Report*. London: Quaker Communications.

Schmuck, P. and Sheldon, K. M. (2001) (eds) *Life Goals and Well-being*. Toronto: Hogrefe & Huber.

Ward, T. (2000) Sexual Offenders' Cognitive Distortions as Implicit Theories, *Aggression and Violent Behavior*, 5, pp. 491–507.

Ward, T. (2002) 'Good Lives and the Rehabilitation of Offenders: Promises and Problems', *Aggression and Violent Behaviour*, 7: 513–28; *Behavior*, 12: 87–107.

Ward, T. and Hudson, S. M. (2000) 'A Self-regulation Model of Relapse Prevention', in D. Laws, S. M. Hudson and T. Ward (eds) *Remaking Relapse Pprevention with Sex Offenders: A Sourcebook*. Thousand Oaks, CA: Sage.

Ward, T. and Maruna, S. (2007) *Rehabilitation: Beyond the Risk Paradigm*. London: Routledge.

Ward, T. and Stewart, C. A. (2003a) 'Criminogenic Needs or Human Needs: A Theoretical Critique, *Psychology, Crime and Law*, 9: 125–43.

Ward, T. and Stewart, C. A. (2003b) 'Good Lives and the Rehabilitation of Sexual Offenders', in T. Ward, D. R. Laws and S. M. Hudson (eds) *Sexual Deviance: Issues and Controversies*. Thousand Oaks, CA: Sage.

Ward, T., Mann, R. E. and Gannon, T. A. (2007) 'The Good Lives Model of Offender Rehabilitation: Clinical Implications', *Aggression and Violent Behavior*, 12: 87–107.

Ward, T., Polaschek, D. L. and Beech, A. R. (2005) *Theories of Sexual Offending*. Chichester: John Wiley.

Watzlawick, P., Weakland, J. and Fisch, R. (1974) *Change: The Principles of Problem Formation and Problem Resolution*. New York: Garland Press.

Wilson, R. J., McWhinnie, A. J. and Wilson, C. (2008) 'Circles of Support and Accountability: An International Partnership in Reducing Sexual Offender Recidivism', *Prison Service Journal*, 178.

Wilson, R. J., Picheca, J. E. and Prinzo, M. (2005) *Circles of Support and Accountability: An Evaluation of the Pilot Project in South-Central Ontario*, Research Report R – 168. Ottawa, ON: Correctional Services of Canada.

Wilson, R. J., Picheca, J. E., Prinzo, M. and Cortoni, F. (2007) 'Circles of Support and Accountability: Engaging Community Volunteers in the Management of High Risk Sex Offenders', *Howard Journal of Criminal Justice*, 46 (1): 1–15.

Chapter 11

Getting out: offenders in forestry and conservation work settings

Claudia Carter and Aaron Pycroft

Introduction

This chapter highlights how contact with nature and working with people in forest and conservation management can be critical elements in helping some prisoners and probationers find a future away from crime. One case in point are Offenders and Nature (O&N) schemes run by the Forestry Commission in partnership with various prison and probation services across England. By examining their context and existing evidence about the schemes, we look for lessons to be learned and how these fit with and inform existing concepts of reducing crime. Our research on evaluating the schemes has so far focused on projects operating with prisons. However, in terms of developing a model of desistance, we discuss implications for the overarching offender management model, thus including probation practice.

We first define and outline the different types of O&N schemes and observed outcomes from our research. The existing criminal justice and environmental sector policy contexts form part of the rationale for starting these work placement schemes and are briefly outlined. We then review in some depth the theoretical context for O&N schemes, focusing on the 'meaningful work' literature and the concepts of desistance and identity shift. Insights from a range of O&N schemes, the highlighted concepts and other work from several disciplines (including sociology, criminology, geography and psychology) have informed our conceptual framework for these schemes to explain their role and significance in helping people desist from crime and find a place in mainstream society. We identify key criteria for and links between (1) the individual, (2) societal structures and social relationships, and (3) connections with nature in facilitating positive changes in offenders' lives and their experience of and contribution to society. We conclude with some insights gained from these schemes and how these findings fit into existing debates about policies for offender management.

Addressing desistance through O&N schemes

O&N schemes are designed to allow individuals who are sentenced *via* the criminal courts to work in green space (which can be forested or non-forested areas) to gain experience and skills (and in some cases accredited qualifications) in forest and conservation management (see Carter 2007). This can be a significant step in assisting sentenced individuals to gain employment or start a business, especially in forestry or other land-based industries. These schemes are of interest because they appear to operationalise a model of desistance (see Maruna 2001: 7). The desistance paradigm is covered in detail by Weaver and McNeil (Chapter 3, this book), and so we simply need to state that for our purposes desistance, is defined by Farrall and Calverley (2006: 2) as 'the end of a period of involvement in offending' and involves primary and secondary desistance with the latter being permanent. An analysis of the aims, practices and impacts of O&N schemes in providing meaningful work may help us to be more sophisticated in our theorising about desistance and in the application of that theory to a range of psychosocial interventions.

Structure and characteristics of O&N schemes

O&N schemes involve sentenced individuals working alongside Forestry Commission (FC) staff or a probation supervisor on woodland sites, carrying out tasks such as creating and maintaining footpaths, coppicing, fencing sites, brashing, tree planting, small-scale felling and opening up dense vegetation to create more diverse habitats. The FC is one of a number of nature provider organisations running O&N schemes.[1] This conservation and forest management work would otherwise largely remain undone due to resource constraints, but is highly beneficial to the public (giving improved access and amenity) and for biodiversity.

Those entering the FC O&N schemes during a community sentence are often working for one or two days per week, whereas those serving a custodial sentence usually participate full-time during the last five to nine months of their prison sentence, after having been granted release on temporary licence. By 2009, over 1,500 probationers and over 100 prisoners have participated in various FC O&N schemes, both male and female, ranging in age from 12 to late fifties.[2]

Carter (2007) found that all schemes provide a range of benefits for the sentenced individuals, such as experience of teamwork, life and skills training, and at the same time are able to boost participants' confidence and outlook through the worthwhile and visible tasks and outcomes. There are also many concrete and potential positive impacts of the schemes for the other involved parties, society and the environment (see Table 11.1).

Partnership approach

O&N schemes are partnership-based initiatives with shared responsibilities, costs and benefits. Each scheme involves an offender-management organisation and a natural environment organisation, sometimes also including public sector and non-governmental organisations. There are often links with land-based training colleges or organisations and individuals that can provide expertise. For example, the FC Dartmoor Rehabilitation Scheme uses Stroud College to oversee the training at HMP Dartmoor; previously the scheme had used local instructors who provided an effective service but were more costly. Successful partnerships between organisations require some understanding of each other's priorities, drivers and the policy context in which they operate. Despite partnership working being a defining feature of contemporary public service provision it is a contentious area in theoretical, policy and practical terms (see Pycroft 2005; Pycroft and Gough 2010).

O&N schemes offer placements in line with the aims of the Home Office's Reducing Reoffending Alliances, the Community Payback drive and the cross-government Green Paper *Reducing Reoffending through Skills and Employment* (Home Office 2005). The FC's remit includes managing forests in a way that enables the public to experience, enjoy and benefit from wooded landscapes. Environmental voluntary work has been an important element in local probation and youth-offender programmes for many years; now the synergies and benefits of extending these schemes to paid placements are being recognised and developed.

From volunteering to paid employment

In most O&N schemes, offenders are unpaid 'volunteers'. A possible criticism of volunteer work schemes is that they exploit a pool of cheap labour to the benefit of the prison and 'employers'. However, by utilising Wilson and Wahidin's definition of meaningful work (see next section) we argue that employment schemes that offer the acquisition of skills, qualifications, experience and job references provide an important contribution to offenders desisting from crime; even if they are not being paid wages.

There is also scope to develop transitions from unpaid to paid schemes. For example, the FC district in the south-west of England (FC Peninsula), in partnership with Dartmoor Prison, is delivering a particularly successful scheme where O&N participants have the option of paid employment

Table 11.1 Observed impacts and benefits of Offender and Nature schemes

Offender/volunteers	Prison/probation service	Nature provider/environment	Community
Opportunity to test structured approach to working	Deliver effective rehabilitation and opportunities for reintegration into society	Able to carry out work that is desirable but not done due to lack of resources	Areas are 'opened up' (improved feeling of security)
Improved physical fitness and general feeling of well-being	Provide commercial work experience in a supportive environment	Provide access to forests and forestry activities for disadvantaged people	Improved aesthetics of woodlands and other landscapes (looking 'tidier')
Improved mental well-being and emotional stability	Build partnerships with potential employers and other services	Nurture a potential future workforce and volunteer base	Improved local recreation and amenity provision
Experience restorative effects of woodlands and green spaces	Facilitate reparative work that benefits society	Create more diverse woodlands and habitats	Increased sightings of birds, butterflies and other attractive fauna and flora due to active conservation-management practices
Develop interpersonal and communication skills (with supervisor, fellow workers, site visitors)	Build trust (e.g. between participants and supervisors)	Restoration of neglected habitats	Experience positive outcomes of 'punishment' system; form of reparation and reconciliation

Develop teamworking skills, awareness of health and safety issues and safe approach to working in potentially hazardous environments	Offer personal skills development opportunities outside the classroom	Encourage respect for nature and people; stimulate positive human-nature interactions	Experience offenders as 'working people' and 'fellow human beings' (de-stigmatisation of offenders)
Opportunity to develop decision-making skills while also having to receive and follow through instructions from others	Improved morale and respect in prison wing through meaningful and successful work placements	Increase public awareness of investment in social forestry, nature conservation and access to green space	Move towards more environmentally, socially and economically sustainable outcomes
Learn new (transferable, technical) skills and possibly gain certificate/qualification through training	Reduce re-offending		
Feel satisfaction and encourage positive thinking through meaningful work	Sense of support and achievement		

Source: Adapted from Carter 2007; Carter and West 2008; original concept developed by Ben Phelan based on the FC South-East England/Winchester Prison O&N scheme.

after successfully completing a 30-day voluntary work placement. Of the 17 prisoners who participated in the Dartmoor Rehabilitation Project by September 2008, most found employment or a training position within the first six months of release and 11 are now in full-time employment (Carter and West 2008). The success of this scheme in gaining employment on release from prison is well above average (65 per cent compared to 30 per cent). One of the key factors for its success appears to be the experience and training gained during the sentence in carrying out real and meaningful work. These concepts and the use of work as punishment, occupation and/or rehabilitation are considered in some detail next.

Meaningful work

It is only recently within the criminal justice system that the significance of 'meaningful' or 'real' work has been recognised. In their report, *'Real Work' in Prison*, Wilson and Wahidin (no date) argue that despite the emphasis by government on the importance of employing ex-prisoners, there is an absence of meaningful and rewarding work in prison; what work there is tends to be mundane, repetitive and boring. Government identified that almost 70 per cent of prisoners are not in employment, training or education prior to imprisonment, and that 70 per cent of people leaving prison do not have a job, training or education lined up (Niven and Stewart 2005). Evidence exists that the social and welfare needs of individuals contribute to triggering criminal activity and reinforce re-offending with the added problem of prison sentences amplifying those problems (see SEU 2002). Prison itself is therefore a criminogenic factor (Maruna 2007); for example, one-third of prisoners lose their homes while in prison, two-thirds of those who had employment lose their jobs, over one-fifth face increased financial problems, and over two-fifths lose contact with their families (SEU 2002).

The Social Exclusion Unit (SEU) identified (2002: 6) nine key factors that they saw as contributing to re-offending: education, employment, drug and alcohol misuse, mental and physical health, attitudes and self-control, institutionalisation and life-skills, housing, financial support and debt, and family networks. In particular, the SEU argues that being in employment reduces the risk of re-offending by between a third and a half, and having stable accommodation by a fifth (2002: 6).

The social and financial costs of crime are well documented (see SEU 2002) and concern about it and responses to it have formed a defining feature of the state over the last 30 years (see Simon 2007); effects of punishment, and particularly imprisonment, are also well documented (Liebling and Maruna 2005). A theoretical and practical problem for the agencies of state and society is that offenders (at least those who are convicted of crimes) are disproportionately drawn from communities who are socially and materially disadvantaged, and thus tend to be 'consumers' of welfare services. A key strand of neo-liberal thinking has been a 'welfare to work approach' whereby individuals are able to work themselves out of poverty.

Punishment, occupation and rehabilitation

Within the criminal justice system, and specifically in relation to providing occupation for and dealing with prisoners or probationers, 'work' still occupies an ambiguous and contested position concerning its punitive or rehabilitative purposes. This is evidenced by a system that provides punishment in the form of high visibility community payback schemes (Casey 2008) while also giving the opportunity for rehabilitation *via* 'pathway projects' intended to help offenders get jobs. There are also still significant obstacles (for example, fitting into prison routine) for external employers who want to become involved in employing prisoners and people with past convictions (Haslewood-Pócsik *et al.* 2007).

In seeking to understand the contemporary use of prison Liebling (2004) argues that prison has been a key project of modernity arising from the industrial revolution, and she utilises Rutherford's (1993) typology of three working credos to inform her analysis of the penal system. The first credo is concerned with punishment, moral condemnation and the degradation of prisoners; the second credo of efficiency is pragmatic, management-based, essentially utilitarian and lacking in correctional ideology; the third credo of care is liberal and humanitarian, is optimistic and inclusive, believes in constructive work and has links with social policy agendas. These credos are not mutually exclusive and often are found alongside each other within the penal system as a whole and within its component parts. Similarly, all three credos can be applied to the type of work that is to be found in prison and probation work schemes. With reference to prisons, the SEU (2002: 54) identifies three main types of work:

- Work to maintain and service the prison, carrying out cleaning, laundry and grounds maintenance.

- Mundane and repetitive work for external contractors involving bagging items, stuffing envelopes, and simple assembly-line activity.

- Work that forms part of complex production tasks either for external contractors or more often for internal consumption; this might include light engineering projects and furniture-making.

Within broader social policy debates work is very much bound up with discussions about conditional citizenship (Johanssen and Hvinden 2005) and the 'something for something' society (see Halpern 2005). The so-called Third Way of the Blair/Brown administrations combining elements of neo-liberalism with communitarian thinking has in effect conflated the aims of punishment with the principles of rehabilitation.

A review of the literature on interventions that seek to change human behaviour appears to show that punishment is not any more effective in bringing about lasting change than voluntaristic approaches (see McSweeney *et al.* 2007). Increasingly, within the literature on behavioural change and in practice, there has been a focus on motivational working, which stands as an antithesis to punishment and coercion (see Miller and Rollnick 1991, 2002). Despite these approaches being seen as antithetical (see particularly Miller 2006), they are also informing practices within the criminal justice system, where professionals (for example probation officers, drug workers) have to straddle this divide between punishment and rehabilitation.

Defining 'meaningful' and 'real' work

Wilson and Wahidin (undated) point to a range of national and local initiatives that exist to promote 'real work' for prisoners but also noted the lack of definition as to what this actually means in practice. They develop the concept of 'real work' in the following way: first, it has to be more than the provision of a 'real wage' in that it should be work undertaken for an external employer rather than working for the prison; second that it is about developing a relationship with the employer who provides an environment in which training and appropriate equipment are provided in return for producing a quality product. Here Wilson and Wahidin argue that training should come with the job and that it is the job that is important rather than training for future work. Work should be meaningful, not mundane, and make a profit. If mundane work is available and necessary, it should not be used as a punishment but assist in motivating people to achieve tangible positive outcomes.

Wilson and Wahidin importantly argue that work needs to be connected to the legitimate world of work through the payment of taxes as opposed to operating in the black economy. Earning a wage allows people

Table 11.2 Average weekly earnings for male prisoners

Weekly earnings	More than £10	Between £5 and £10	More than £2.50, less than £5	£2.50 or less
Percentage of prisoners earning*	15	55	8	23

Note: *Figures are rounded up.
Source: (SEU 2002: 54).

to open bank accounts and save money to provide for self and family and affordable accommodation. Prisoners are not entitled to the national minimum wage, and the levels of wages and the type of work undertaken vary between prisons (SEU 2002). The SEU report shows that the weekly earnings for the majority of male prisoners as being less than £10 (see Table 11.2). Wage levels for prisoners have remained the same for about ten years, with Gordon Brown reversing the decision of the Prison Board to raise the weekly pay from £4 to £5.50 (*Guardian News* 2008). Prisoners do not handle cash and money is used *via* a credit system. The wage system is intended to act as an incentive, with prisoners being paid £2.50 per week if they wish to work but are unable to do so. Saving some money can be regarded as necessary and positive, even if the amounts are small. For those serving a prison sentence, working with an outside employer may also be a crucial step for reintegration into society, paving the way to mainstream employment in the open market. Having a meaningful job and earning a decent wage is also important for self-esteem and self-worth, and has a large impact on a person's life and how they feel about themselves and interact with others. The next section further develops the link between meaningful work and desistance by elaborating how work placement and employment contexts can help shape pro-social identity and build social capital.

Desistance and identity

Studies of desistance from crime suggest that the frequency of offending depends upon the individual propensity for committing crime, the environmental opportunity to do so as well as cognitive decision-making processes (Farrington 2007). Building upon the work of Bottoms and McWilliams (1979, cited in McNeill 2006) who argued for a 'non-treatment paradigm' for probation practice, McNeill (2006) has argued that there are important questions to be addressed not only in our understanding of desistance, but also the role that probation professionals might play in supporting this process. Within the National Offender Management Service (NOMS) framework and the intended merger of the prison and probation services this is relevant to all 'correctional' workers. Insights from the desistance literature should influence any evaluation of the efficacy of psychosocial interventions generally and their explanatory and predictive potential.

Within a psychosocial approach to desistance it is argued that personality tends to be consistent over the life-course, leading to the relative stability of anti-social behaviour. However, there is a paradox here because while most adult offenders were once juvenile offenders, the majority of juvenile offenders do not become adult offenders (Maruna 2007). Maruna (2001: 7) argues that desistance is brought about by ex-offenders developing 'a coherent pro-social identity for themselves'. By drawing upon the work of Maruna and others we can examine the importance of identity shift in building 'good lives' and desisting from crime.

The factors associated with desistance are reviewed by Farrall (2002), with existing literature demonstrating the importance of employment leading to stable and reliable work patterns, and the acquisition of social and economic resources. Being in full-time work leaves little time and reduces financial need for criminal activity. Other important factors include the formation of significant life partnerships, the possibility of becoming a parent and personal motivation to avoid offending. The emphasis of this paradigm is clearly upon the mutually affirming relationship between one's self and others, and the ways in which this relationship confers 'normality', legitimacy and ultimately citizenship. In research carried out by Mercier and Alarie (2002), regaining social status was a key pathway out of crime and indicative of a changing relationship with society. This notion of citizenship is developed by Stenner and Taylor (2008) who argue that it is based upon inclusion through public participation of the individual with the aim of securing social outcomes in the form of the acquisition of social capital (see below). Stenner and Taylor (2008: 418) found a clear link between social welfare and the social well-being of the individual; thus securing 'the viability of the social order through the regulation of the well-being of welfare subjects and recipro-cally, the individual well-being of its subjects is regulated through the social order'.

Giving offenders the opportunity to develop and access resources outside the criminal justice infrastructure can help in desistance from crime and fits within an emerging framework of psychosocial welfare (Stenner and Taylor 2008) and social capital. This approach to psychosocial welfare (which builds on individual's strengths and capacities rather than dwelling on their shortcomings) allows for core psychological constructs involved with a sense of personal identity to be explored and developed, particularly self-efficacy (the belief of a person in their ability to succeed in a particular situation; see Bandura 1977) and self-esteem (see Mruk 1999).

In line with Bandura's approach to self-efficacy, cognitive behavioural therapy (CBT) programmes, with the aim of helping prisoners to change behaviour, have focused on situational confidence as opposed to self-esteem. Within the criminal justice system the current emphasis on CBT programmes as part of sentences has, however, been criticised for a lack of emphasis on the social context of crime (Vanstone 2000). Furthermore, with reference to drug addiction, the evidence shows that existing psychological interventions are not working or are at best equivocal in their outcomes (see Orford 2008).

Bandura (1977) argues that we do not have to feel good about ourselves to make necessary changes to problematic behaviour; change can be achieved despite negative feelings of self-worth. Another issue is that self-esteem is seen to stabilise in late adolescence, and remain the same, whereas self-efficacy is situationally determined. Emler (2001) finds little evidence to suggest that raising self-esteem is effective in changing problematic behaviour. However, Mruk (1999) argues that there are a number of differing definitions of self-esteem, emphasising different elements such as worthiness, stability, confidence, cognition, feelings and openness. He also indicates that positive self-esteem correlates with positive mental health and psychological well-being, whereas low self-esteem is linked with mental health problems and a lack of personal and social functioning. Mruk (1999) proposes a definition of self-esteem that incorporates cognitions and feelings, openness and stability, competence and worthiness. A key question for this research is the extent to which O&N schemes build self-efficacy, self-esteem and a sense of well-being, and enable individuals to engage in pro-social networks.

Social capital has become an increasingly important concept within social policy (see Portes 1998) and also within criminal justice (see McSweeney and Hough 2006) where it is evident in the NOMS alliances with Civil Society, the Corporate Sector and the Faith, Voluntary and Community Sectors (www.noms.justice.gov.uk/about-us/working-with-partners/a lliances/). Using the concept of social capital, defined as 'people's access to resources in their networks' (Finsveen and Van Oorschott 2008: 295), implies that a lack of social structure (in an empirical sense) can mean that individuals are unable to achieve their goals. The intention of O&N schemes is to provide some of that structure through meaningful work that is sustainable and transferable by gaining experience, receiving training, obtaining work references and the possibility of ongoing employment. In the next section we capture the observed impacts of and related theoretical concepts underlying O&N schemes to explain their role in building social capital and helping people desist from crime.

Conceptual framework

The conceptual framework presented here was predominantly informed by research observations and insights gained from FC's O&N schemes, but also builds on models and insights gleaned from the literature on social exclusion, offender rehabilitation and desistance, ecotherapy, and health and well-being. The framework consists of three interlinking and interdependent components: (1) the individual sphere; (2) the social environment (subdivided into social relationships and societal structures); and (3) the natural environment (see Figure 11.1). Each component has several sub-components that we view as significant factors relating to and helping to explain how people find a way out of crime, as detailed in the following sections.

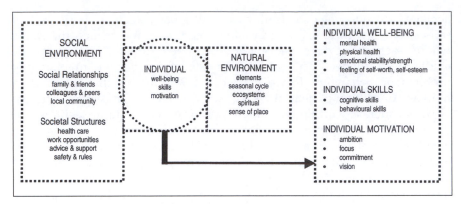

Figure 11.1 The context of desistance

The individual sphere

We identify three key components in the individual sphere: well-being, skills, and motivation. Each component in turn features several aspects and, as for the overall framework, there are also interdependencies and interlinkages between these sub-components. Well-being has become a primary social policy focus (see Department of Health 2009) and increasingly the importance of mental health alongside physical health, engagement in meaningful relationships, purpose in life and rewarding employment is being recognised (for example Steuer and Marks 2008). In April 2009 the National Mental Health Development Unit was launched, funded by the Department of Health and the National Health Service, to provide support for implementing mental health policy and improving mental health services. The prison population has a significantly larger percentage of physical and particularly mental ill-health compared with the national average. The SEU report (2002: 20–21) lists statistics for sentenced adult prisoners (male and female) showing that they were anything from 2 to 40 times more likely to experience a range of mental and physical diseases/problems; the situation is even worse for remand and young prisoners. In addition, the National Treatment Outcome Research Study (NTORS) (Gossop *et al.* 2001) and the Drug Treatment Outcome Research Study (DTORS) (www.dtors.org.uk/) clearly demonstrates the range of multiple needs experienced by drug users accessing treatment, including within the criminal justice system.

Emotional stability and strength is another important aspect of well-being, especially when faced with life changes, such as imprisonment or reintegrating into society with all its demands and pressures. There are links with mental and possibly also physical health, but it is also seen as an important issue in its own right: how we perceive and deal with situations day to day and when under pressure. Receiving a sentence, especially a prison sentence, will for most individuals affect their emotional state and significantly impact on their feeling of self-worth (Liebling and Maruna 2005). The prison sentence and routine mean that there is little scope for personal freedom, choice, development or privacy.

In terms of skills, most sentenced individuals have fewer/lower cognitive and behavioural abilities and achievements than the average population (see for example SEU 2002: 6, 53). This is evident in poor reading, writing, communication and arithmetic skills across most of the prison population and reflected in poor employment histories and low prospects of finding employment on release (Home Office 2005).

Individual motivation is crucial in personal development but as a concept it is complex and nuanced. When considering the work of Miller (2006) and Miller and Rollnick (1991, 2002) it is clear that psychology needs to be considered within the context of a biopsychosocial paradigm (see Pycroft 2007, 2010 forthcoming). The importance of this is that there may be powerful interacting factors that affect an individual's ability to assume responsibility over certain behaviours, even though they would like to do so. The obvious example of this is relapsing to drug or alcohol use, despite efforts to the contrary. A key aspect of developing personal motivation is to build upon existing strengths and attitudes (see below), which may include one's ambitions to change life away from crime, being focused, showing commitment, and having a vision for the future. Sometimes new situations or events can trigger all these processes. For many the prison environment is not an inspiring or nurturing place to stay out of crime, thus links with the outside community and employers become crucial. Positive experiences are more motivating and conducive to developing skills than negative ones. In prison the offender identity tends to dominate, whereas outside work placements offer the chance of 'normality' and being a 'person'; being appreciated and treated as such will also make a difference to that person's thinking, well-being and behaviour.

Social relationships

For some, family and friends can act as lifelines to the outside world; for others, family bonds can be weak or damaging and thus being away from them and starting afresh in a different location and community is a necessary step to move away from crime. Good friendships and trust are rare in prisons. In the words of one focus group participant in our research: 'Being in a prison environment, having a lot of criminals locked together . . . there is not really a great deal of trust in there' (male prisoner, 42, three weeks into an O&N scheme, having served several prison sentences). This makes links with 'ordinary' and well-meaning people outside prison so important, be it with colleagues at work placements or other contact with members of the public and local communities. People with a natural capacity (or assigned role) for mentoring and/or as role models potentially have a huge influence on encouraging and facilitating change in offenders' lives. Especially for young offenders, finding the 'right' peer group to help them stay out of trouble is significant (Farrington 2007). However, new opportunities and change do not only depend on individuals and groups but also require societal structures of support, clear and fair rules, and access to resources and employment.

Societal structures

Most individuals entering prison have a drug and/or alcohol misuse problem; of the 70 per cent with a drug problem, the SEU reports that 80 per cent have not had any contact with drug treatment services (SEU 2002: 7, 61). Since the implementation of the National Drugs Strategy in 1998 Reuter and Stevens (2008) have estimated that as many as 58 per cent of problematic Class A drug users in the UK have been assessed for their drug problem, but with very little impact upon overall crime rates. DTORS data shows that 71 per cent of the 1,796 drug users who were followed through treatment had previously utilised either community or residentially based structured drug treatment. Of the criminal justice referrals, 73 per cent had previously received structured treatment. Research by Stewart (2009) shows that 51 per cent of the 1,457 prisoners interviewed had previous treatment and 17 per cent had drug treatment during a previous prison term. Considering that it is estimated by government that one-third of crime is linked to drug offences or the influence of substance misuse (Home Office 2002), and existing high levels of mental and physical illnesses, this emphasises the importance of good healthcare in prison and of the planned transition to the community health system and therapy provisions. Alongside conventional replacement and prescribed drug treatment for those with addiction and mental health issues, there are now also alternative therapies such as 'ecotherapy' (Burls 2005, 2007), which take a more holistic approach and use being and working in nature to enable social inclusion, rehabilitation and cure.

Advice and support is often needed to secure and afford accommodation, and gain employment or set up a business. It is important to find out about what services and support exist to aid integration into mainstream society and how they can be accessed. The more information that is made available and relevant links made early on, then the easier transition may be and the temptation to commit further crimes lowered.

Safety regulations and other rules are important for the protection of all, including those on the wrong side of the law. Respect for and adherence to safety practices and rules are important in prison as much as outside prison; but often their purpose and origin may be unclear. Experience of working in forestry can help develop a better sense of safety through the need for basic rules and measures to ensure one's own safety as well as that of others. Thus rules and regulations are not experienced as tools of power but as meaningful safety measures; and thus foster respect and trust.

Natural environment

Socio-economic deprivation has been found to correlate strongly with poor environmental quality, including lack of access to natural green space (see for example ESRC 2001). This matters for individual and community quality of life and well-being. At the same time, an increasing body of research is confirming the extent to which contact with natural places supports both physical and mental health (see Seymour 2003; Cohen 2005; Pretty *et al*. 2005; O'Brien 2004, 2005; Health Council of the Netherlands 2004). Spending time in natural environments/outdoors also aids social and psychological development by providing outlets for risk-taking and physical energy, which is important in child development as well as for personal development and dealing with change throughout one's life (see Kaplan and Talbot 1983; Davis-Berman and Berman 1994). Other observed impacts include reduction of stress (see Ulrich 1984), recovery from attention fatigue (see Wells 2000; Faber Taylor *et al*. 2001), reduction in anti-social behaviour (Kuo 2003) and facilitating positive social interactions, teamwork and social inclusion (Sempik *et al*. 2005).

In addition to the many instrumental aspects of nature, there are significant fundamental concepts. Attachment to and meaning of place has received much attention, especially within geography, environmental and social psychology, sociology and anthropology. Of particular importance here is the role of place in contributing to the definition of self within the natural and social environment (see for example Ingold 2000), and how attributes of the natural environment and activities with other people in natural settings form identities (see Low and Altman 1993; Stedman 2003; Manzo 2005). Gustafson (2001), for example, found that meanings attributed to places related to self, others and place, reflecting the different physical characteristics as well as the individual and social construction, perceived values and actual activities associated with place; and meaning is not just attached to 'special' places but also to everyday/familiar surroundings. The physical setting and the experiential, interactive and relational components of places are important (Relph 1976, 1985; Gieryn 2000).

For some offenders, being outside in green space reminds them of positive times in their childhood; for others being and working in nature is largely a new experience and some discover enjoyment in this. Being in a natural environment, observing and working with specific habitats and ecosystems, noticing seasonal changes and experiencing different elements can create an emotional connectedness and an environment that for some aids reflection, learning, visioning and change. There are physical elements, but also spiritual and metaphysical aspects associated with many landscapes, and especially mountains, ancient trees and old woodlands (see Lane 1998; Hagender 2000; Lewis and Sheppard 2005). Of those involved in O&N schemes, many observe or experience a distinct spiritual component to spending time in natural environments, with many complex facets. Averill (1998), for example, characterises spiritual experiences as showing vitality, connectedness and meaningfulness (1998: 104–5) and thus can be significant to aid change (of seeing, doing and feeling about things) and emotional well-being. Feeling part of a larger 'picture' can facilitate healing, forgiveness, a sense of meaning and belonging – a coming back to fundamental aspects and values of life and being.

Desistance as a process

Our conceptual framework views desisting from crime as an embedded process rather than a distinct state, event or method. The path into crime is usually a complex interplay of predisposing factors, surrounding context and immediate triggers. Similarly, for the path out of crime, there is no generic formula that works for all although the process can be aided and supported. The specific circumstances for each case are a combination of individual experiences, dispositions and skills (natural or acquired/learned); social relationships, networks and openings; and the influences and opportunities of the immediate and wider environment (see Figure 11.2).

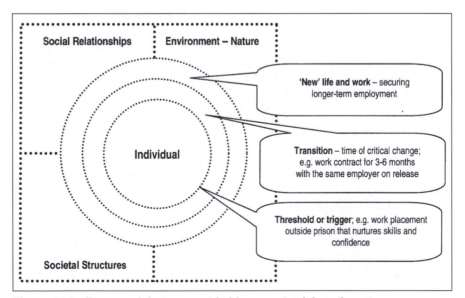

Figure 11.2 Process of desistance aided by meaningful work setting

Changes in life can be gradual or quite sudden and often there may be specific triggers or a 'threshold' reached where a change in perspective and/or circumstances marks a turning point. There may be a period of transition, where old patterns are being gradually replaced with new ones. This critical phase is likely to require much emotional, and maybe financial and other support. The desired long-term outcome may be a more positive, stable and socially accepted/integrated way of life and work. Based on observed impacts of O&N schemes (Carter 2007), we argue that spending time in natural environments can for some help trigger and facilitate the transition to a life without committing crimes through a combination of factors: connectedness (with nature, other people, self); creative and meaningful activity; and, ideally, sufficient income to afford suitable accommodation and a healthy lifestyle.

Discussion

In this section we draw together some of the specific evidence that illustrates the scope of O&N schemes for improving self-esteem and developing self-efficacy alongside providing opportunities for positive engagement with mainstream society. We frame the discussion along three axes: the importance of relationships and trust; the availability of resources and networks; and the provision of reflective space. This structure of argument reflects the basic framework (social relationships, societal structures, and natural environment respectively) and shows how the components tend to work in combination.

Importance of relationships and trust

For those serving a prison sentence of several years, qualifying for work outside of prison towards the end of their sentence is a major step. There are challenges and important opportunities to being trusted to leave prison and come back, being able to interact with 'ordinary' citizens, and engaging in a normal full-time work routine. Depending on the prison and locality, a limited number of placements and paid employment opportunities are on offer; typical examples include painting/decorating, construction, catering and administration. FC O&N schemes stand out, as they provide work opportunities in wooded landscapes, and offer becoming part of a small local team. For example, in a recent focus group we undertook we heard that one participant had requested a transfer to another prison to be able to join that particular O&N scheme, even though it meant being based in a 'worse' prison. Another did not apply for parole in order to be able to continue working on the O&N scheme. The FC Dartmoor scheme is particularly attractive, as after a 30-day unpaid work placement there is the option to continue with a programme of paid structured work, mentoring and skills training.

Being outside and doing physical work develops stamina and fitness; getting involved in forest management planning and decisions also helps build confidence. Participants often observe that they feel tired but happy at the end of a working day and sleep much better. More importantly, they begin to feel more positive about themselves, about their abilities and contribution and more confident about work; this affects their morale, general work ethic and views for their future. This positive change about how participants feel about themselves, work and people/society around them can be highly significant in triggering or persevering with other changes.

Working in forest management also poses potential danger, and requires the skilled and safe use of hand and motor tools and general compliance with health and safety instructions. Tasks require working safely both alone and as part of a team. This reliance on each other helps develop a positive work ethos and trusting relationships with co-workers and supervisor. As Wilson and Wahidin (undated) argue, training that comes with the job rather than taken in isolation seems to be more effective.

It would be naive to assume that any placement of this kind can provide a range of impressive benefits. One factor that seems to stand out is that the attitude and personality of the supervisor, manager and also fellow workers matters a great deal. Being with a motivated peer group and working alongside well-meaning and capable/qualified people sets a new tone after the negativity of most prison landings. O&N scheme participants are treated like any other volunteer or employee and this really matters. As one supervisor put it: 'the guys are part of the squad ... I just don't think of these guys as prisoners ... We see a side of them that probably no one else ever does ... they are just glad to be out' (FC beat manager who has been involved in O&N schemes for over four years). Similarly, members of the public who sometimes show initial hesitation and apprehension end up chatting to the work squad and in several instances bring round chocolates or other treats towards the end of a prisoner's work placement.

Working in forest management and conservation increases personal health and well-being but also leaves a visible legacy. After release from prison, several scheme participants have taken family members to the forest to show them the work. This can be a step towards healing or improving relationships and gaining recognition within their family, especially parents. Thus the meaningful work carried out seems to improve motivation, instils confidence and a sense of self-worth (Mruk 1999) and provides a chance to develop self-efficacy. At the same time, going out to work helps develop positive relationships, trust and transferable skills and knowledge. Once aspects of a 'good life' start to emerge, motivation and confidence tend to be self-reinforcing factors of positive change. Meaningful work placements in the community seem to fit with a biopsychosocial approach to desistance and symbolise a big step from feeling and being seen as offender or ex-offender to feeling and taking one's place as a citizen. This in turn can facilitate access to a range of resources and networks.

Resources and networks

Prison is the initial main hub for enabling offenders to get employment and improve their qualifications and skills in order to gain a proper job. Considering the average reading, writing and arithmetic skills of offenders, receiving support for up-skilling is important to gain suitable qualifications for employment on release. This is often carried out in classroom conditions but learning in applied environments can be easier. Furthermore, based on experience with forest schools (see O'Brien and Murray 2007) a natural environment can assist in focusing on and facilitating learning. Thus, work placements outside prison in natural environments can have some added value not only for those with attention deficit disorder, emotional or behavioural issues, but more generally. Choosing and obtaining a good work placement and gaining worthwhile qualifications and experiences plus some income are thus a strategic way towards desistance. The more constrained the environment and options available for the individual, the more difficult may be the realisation of positive change.

There are a range of barriers for both prisons and employers (see Carter and West 2008). For example, working with limited financial and staff resources, a strongly regulated system within a highly charged political climate, and with the prison population exceeding prison capacity affects what 'rehabilitation' measures a prison can offer. From an employer's perspective (Haslewood-Pócsik et al. 2007) many barriers exist, including a seemingly complex administrative and legal criminal justice system, resource implications especially if training and mentoring is required, tight security, and somewhat inflexible regulatory criteria. For example, the set period of when prisoners are allowed out and the need to specify the exact place of work is not always convenient for landscape conservation work where workload can vary with different seasons/tasks and parcels of land to be worked may be spread out.

Reflective space

Space to reflect, think afresh and plan one's future can be difficult to find in a prison environment. Many experience woodlands and other natural spaces as calming, beautiful, refreshing, changing but long-standing, life-giving, nurturing and inspiring. In combination with constructive social contact and support, working and spending time in woodlands/green space can act as a catalyst of personal change, motivation and strength. For many O&N participants, working outdoors and in woodlands is a 'new' space and experience. In the words of a female prisoner in her twenties, who was 11 weeks into an O&N scheme at the time of the interview: 'I have realised that I enjoy working outside, whereas before I had never worked outside properly ... I just feel healthier in myself; so it has been good ... I am not scared of hard work and it helps me sleep at night.' She enjoyed the work so much that she started to look out for ranger and similar kinds of jobs, though she was aware that actually securing a position may be difficult for her due to her limited experience and criminal history.

Directions for offender management

Irrespective of the rights or wrongs in terms of ethics or effectiveness, the use of imprisonment is set to continue and has been reflected in the growth in prisons and prisoner numbers; there does not appear to be any political appetite on the part of either voters or legislators to stop this trend. In this chapter we have highlighted the context in which prison schemes operate, and in particular some of the negative impacts that prison causes which Maruna (2007: 660) describes as 'desistance-impeding interventions'. How, then, do criminal justice workers and offenders work with the realities of the criminal justice system to create 'desistance-enhancing interventions' (2007: 662)? Maruna makes the point that just allowing people to 'grow out' of crime is not an option, because it takes too long, creates victims, and amplifies a wide range of social problems.

There is evidence to show that psychosocial interventions, such as O&N schemes, can be effective and there are obvious links here with the resettlement agenda and the importance of a joined-up approach between the prison and probation services. This has formed a part of the rationale for the 'seamless services' envisaged by the creation of NOMS (Carter 2003) and it was hoped that its agenda would support a more effective resettlement strategy (Pycroft 2005; Pycroft and Gough 2010). Maruna (2007) points to the promising theoretical developments in linking desistance with resettlement practice, and argues that this approach has increased the emphasis on highlighting and working with the strengths and contributions (human and social capital) that the offender has and does make to themselves, their families and communities. As indicated above, this also fits with an approach that seeks to build motivation and the acquisition of resources for behavioural and lifestyle change. However, a practical and conceptual difficulty is that current correctional practice is very much based upon a deficit model that highlights criminogenic factors and may effectively serve to reinforce negativity and a sense of failure on the part of the offender.

In discussing the implications of a desistance paradigm for offender management McNeill (2006) argues for a new paradigm that focuses on processes of change rather than on modes of intervention. This approach would be more individualised and 'accommodate interventions to meet needs, reduce risks and (especially) to develop and exploit strengths' (2006: 56). The role of the offender manager then becomes one of being a conduit to resources for building human and social capital, and also helping the offender to navigate the 'system' (see Pycroft 2010 forthcoming). Within the offender management model, which incorporates a range of different agencies providing rehabilitative services to the offender, the working relationships are key to successful outcomes. In research conducted for the Home Office (Partridge 2004) looking at case management models, it was found that offenders did not object to having to attend a range of different agencies as long as they had one central point of contact to relate to. A combination of individual contacts, personal support and availability of meaningful and appropriate employment options are important in the desistance process. Work placements experienced while still serving a sentence can play a crucial role to build those contacts and facilitate significant positive changes, as observed in many participants of O&N schemes.

Acknowledgements

This research has been supported by the Forestry Commission and a grant from the Crime Solutions Partnership between the universities of Central Lancashire and Portsmouth.

Notes

1 Other nature provider organisations are engaged in similar schemes, for example Natural England, the Royal Parks and Small Woods Association.
2 The figures are based on an internal FC/FR survey.

References

Averill, J. R. (1998) 'Spirituality: From the Mundane to the Meaningful – and Back', *Journal of Theoretical and Philosophical Psychology*, 18 (2): 101–25.
Bandura, A. (1977) 'Self-Efficacy: Towards a Unifying Theory of Behavior Change', *Psychological Review*, 84: 191–215.
Burls, A. (2005) 'New Landscapes for Mental Health', *Mental Health Review*, 10 (1): 26–9.
Burls, A. (2007) 'People and Green Spaces: Promoting Public Health and Mental Well-being Through Ecotherapy', *Journal of Public Mental Health*, 6 (3): 24–39.
Carter, C. (2007) *Offenders and Nature: Helping People – Helping Nature*. Farnham: Forest Research.

Carter, C. and West, D. (2008) *Policy into Practice – Employment for Ex-offenders: An Innovative Approach*. Farnham: Forest Research.

Carter, P. (2003) *Managing Offenders, Changing Lives: A New Approach*, Report of the Correctional Services Review. London: Strategy Unit.

Casey, L. (2008) *Engaging Communities in Fighting Crime*. London: HMSO, Cabinet Office.

Cohen, M. J. (2005) 'Counselling and Nature: The Greening of Psychotherapy', *Interpsych Newsletter* 2(4) [Online]. Available at: www.userpage.fu-berlin.de/~expert/psychnews/ix.htm (accessed 15 January 2009).

Davis-Berman, J. and Berman, D. S. (1994) *Wilderness Therapy: Foundations, Theory and Research*. Dubuque, IA: Kendall/Hunt Publishing Company.

Department of Health (2009) *Be Active, Be Healthy: A Plan for Getting the Nation Moving*. London: HMSO. Available at: www.dh.gov.uk/en/Publicationsand statistics/Publications/PublicationsPolicyAndGuidance/DH_094358.

Emler, N. (2001) *Self-Esteem: The Costs and Causes of Low Self-Worth*. York: Joseph Rowntree Trust.

ESRC Global Environmental Change Programme (2001) *Environmental Justice: Rights and Means to a Healthy Environment for All*, Special Briefing No. 7. Brighton: University of Sussex.

Faber Taylor, A., Kuo, F. E. and Sullivan, W. C. (2001) 'Coping with ADD. The Surprising Connection to Green Play Settings', *Environment and Behavior*, 33 (1): 54–77.

Farrall, S. (2002) *Rethinking What Works with Offenders: Probation, Social Context and Desistance from Crime*. Cullompton: Willan Publishing.

Farrall, S. and Calverley, A. (2006) *Understanding Desistance from Crime*. Maidenhead: Open University Press.

Farrington, D. (2007) 'Advancing Knowledge About Desistance', *Journal of Contemporary Criminal Justice*, 23 (1): 125–34.

Finsveen, E. and Van Oorschott, W. (2008) 'Access to Resources in Networks: A Theoretical and Empirical Critique of Networks as a Proxy for Social Capital', *Acta Sociologica*, 51 (4): 293–307.

Gieryn, T. F. (2000) 'A Space for Place in Sociology', *Annual Review of Sociology*, 26: 463–96.

Gossop, M., Marsden, J. and Stewart, D. (2001) *NTORS after Five Years (National Treatment Outcome Research Study): Changes in Substance Use, Health and Criminal Behaviour in the Five Years after Intake*. London: Department of Health.

Guardian News (2008) 'Inside job', *The Guardian*, 1 May. Available at: www.guardian.co.uk/commentisfree/2008/may/01/insidejob/ (accessed 21 April 2009).

Gustafson, P. (2001) 'Meanings of Place: Everyday Experience and Theoretical Conceptualisations', *Journal of Environmental Psychology*, 21 (1): 5–16.

Hagender, F. (2000) *The Spirit of Trees: Science, symbiosis and inspiration*. Edinburgh: Floris Books.

Halpern, D. (2005) 'Something for Something: Personal Responsibility meets Behavioural Economics', *Public Policy Research*, 12 (1): 22–9.

Haslewood-Pócsik, I., Brown, S. and Spencer, J. (2007) 'A Not So Well-lit Path: Employers' Perspectives on Employing Ex-offenders', *Howard Journal*, 47 (1): 18–30.

Health Council of the Netherlands and Dutch Advisory Council for Research on Spatial Planning, Nature and the Environment (2004) *Nature and Health: The*

Influence of Nature on Social, Psychological and Physical Well-being. The Hague: Health Council of the Netherlands and RMNO.

Home Office (2002) *Updated Drug Strategy.* London: Home Office Drug Strategy Directorate.

Home Office (2005) *Reducing Reoffending Through Skills and Employment.* Cm 6702. London: The Stationery Office.

Ingold, T. (2000) *The Perception of the Environment: Essays in Livelihood, Dwelling and Skill.* London/New York: Routledge.

Johansson, H. and Hvinden, B. (2005) 'Welfare Governance and the Remaking of Citizenship', in J. Newman (ed.) *Remaking Governance, Peoples, Politics and the Public Sphere.* Bristol: Policy Press.

Kaplan, S. and Talbot, J. F. (1983) 'Psychological Benefits of a Wilderness Experience', in I. Altman and J. F. Wohlwill (eds) *Human Behavior and Environment: Advances in Theory and Research.* New York: Plenum Press.

Kuo, F. E. (2003) 'The Role of Arboriculture in a Healthy Social Ecology', *Journal of Arboriculture*, 29 (3): 148–55.

Lane, B. C. (1998) *The Solace of Fierce Landscapes: Exploring Desert and Mountain Spirituality.* New York/Oxford: Oxford University Press.

Lewis, J. L. and Sheppard, S. R. J. (2005) 'Ancient Values, New Challenges: Indigenous Spiritual Perceptions of Landscapes and Forest Management', *Society and Natural Resources*, 18: 907–20.

Liebling, A. (2004) *Prisons and Their Moral Performance: A Study of Values, Quality and Prison Life.* Oxford: Oxford University Press.

Liebling, A. and Maruna, S. (eds) (2005) *The Effects of Imprisonment.* Cullompton: Willan Publishing.

Low, S. M. and Altman, I. (1993) 'Place Attachment: A Conceptual Inquiry', in I. Altmand and S. M. Low (eds) *Place Attachment.* New York and London: Plenum Press.

Manzo, L. C. (2005) 'For Better or Worse: Exploring multiple Dimensions of Place Meaning', *Journal of Environmental Psychology*, 25 (1): 67–86.

Maruna, S. (2001) *Making Good: How Ex-convicts Reform and Rebuild their Lives.* Washington, DC: American Psychological Association.

Maruna, S. (2007) 'After Prison What? The Ex-prisoners Struggle to Desist from Crime', in Y. Jewkes (ed.) *The Handbook on Prisons.* Cullompton: Willan Publishing.

McNeill, F. (2006) 'A Desistance Paradigm for Offender Management', *Criminology and Criminal Justice*, 6 (1): 39–62.

McSweeney, T. and Hough, M. (2006) 'Supporting Offenders with Multiple Needs: Lessons for the "Mixed Economy" Model of Service Provision', *Criminology and Criminal Justice*, 6 (1): 107–25.

McSweeney, T., Stevens, A., Hunt, N. and Turnbull, P. (2007) 'Twisting Arms or Helping Hand? Assessing the Impact of "Coerced" and Comparable "Voluntary" Drug Treatment Options', *British Journal of Criminology*, 47: 470–91.

Mercier, C. and Alarie, S. (2002) 'Pathways out of Deviance: Implications for Programme Evaluation', in S. Brochu, C. Da Agra and M.-M. Cousineau (eds) *Drugs and Crime Deviant Pathways.* Aldershot: Ashgate.

Miller, W. (2006) 'Motivational Factors in Addictive Behaviors', in W. Miller and K. Carroll (eds) *Rethinking Substance Abuse: What the Science Shows and What we Should Do About It.* New York: Guilford Press.

Miller, W. and Rollnick, S. (1991) *Motivational Interviewing: Preparing People to Change Addictive Behavior*. New York: Guilford Press.

Miller, W. and Rollnick, S. (2002) *Motivational Interviewing: Preparing People for Change*. New York: Guilford Press.

Mruk, C. (1999) *Self-esteem, Research, Theory and Practice*. London: Free Association Books.

Niven, S. and Stewart, D. (2005) *Resettlement Outcomes on Release from Prison*, Home Office Findings 248. London: Home Office.

O'Brien, E. (2004) *A Sort of Magical Place: People's Experiences of Woodlands in Northwest and Southeast England*. Farnham: Forest Research.

O'Brien, E. (2005) *Trees and Woodlands: Nature's Health Service*. Farnham: Forest Research.

O'Brien, L. and Murray, R. (2007) 'Forest School and its Impacts on Young Children: Case Studies in Britain', *Urban Forestry and Urban Greening*, 6: 249–65.

Orford, J. (2008) 'Asking the Right Questions in the Right Way: The Need for a Shift in Research on Psychological Treatment for Addiction', *Addiction*, 103 (6): 875–85.

Partridge, S. (2004) *Examining Case Management Models for Community Sentences*, Home Office Online Report 17/04.

Portes, A. (1998) 'Social Capital: Its Origins and Applications in Modern Sociology', *Annual Review of Sociology*, 24: 1–24.

Pretty, J., Peacock, J., Sellens, M. and Griffin, M. (2005) 'The Mental and Physical Health Outcomes of Green Exercise', *International Journal of Environmental Health Research*, 15 (5): 319–37.

Pycroft, A. (2005) 'A New Chance for Rehabilitation: Multi Agency Provision and Potential under NOMS', in J. Winstone and F. Pakes (eds) *Community Justice: Issues for Probation and Criminal Justice*. Cullompton: Willan Publishing.

Pycroft, A. (2007) 'The Psychology of Addiction – Are There More Questions than Answers?', in F. Pakes and J. Winstone (eds) *Psychology and Crime: Understanding and Tackling Offending Behaviour*. Cullompton: Willan Publishing.

Pycroft, A. (2010 forthcoming) *Complex Realities: Understanding and Working with Substance Misusers*. London: Sage.

Pycroft, A. and Gough, D. (2010 in press) *Multi-Agency Working in Criminal Justice: Control and Care in Contemporary Correctional Practice*. Bristol: Policy Press.

Relph, E. (1976) *Place and Placelessness*. London: Pion.

Relph, E. (1985) 'Geographical Experiences and Being-in-the-world: The Phenomenological Origins of Geography', in D. Seamon and R. Mugerauer (eds) *Dwelling, Place and Environment*. New York: Columbia University.

Reuter, P. and Stevens, A. (2008) 'Assessing UK Drug Policy from a Crime Control Perspective', *Criminology and Criminal Justice*, 8 (4): 461–82.

Rutherford, A. (1993) *Criminal Justice and the Pursuit of Decency*. Oxford and New York: Oxford University Press.

Sempik, J., Alridge, J. and Becker, S. (2005) *Health, Well-being and Social Inclusion: Therapeutic Horticulture in the UK*. Bristol: Policy Press.

Seymour, L. (2003) *Nature and Psychological Well-being*, English Nature Research Reports 533. Peterborough: English Nature.

Simon, J. (2007) *Governing Through Crime: How the War on Crime Transformed American Democracy and Created a Culture of Fear*. Oxford: Oxford University Press.

Social Exclusion Unit (SEU) (2002) *Reducing Re-Offending by Ex-Prisoners*. London: Office of the Deputy Prime Minister. Available at: www.socialexclusionunit.gov.uk/downloaddoc.asp?id=64.

Stedman, R. C. (2003) 'Is it Really Just a Social Construction? The Contribution of the Physical Environment to Sense of Place', *Society & Natural Resources*, 16 (8): 671–85.

Stenner, P. and Taylor, D. (2008) 'Psychosocial Welfare: Reflections on an Emerging Field, *Critical Social Policy*, 28 (4): 415–37.

Steuer, N. and Marks, N. (2008) *Local Well-being: Can We Measure It?* London: New Economics Foundation.

Stewart, D. (2009) 'Drug Use and Perceived Treatment Need Among Newly Sentenced Prisoners in England and Wales', *Addiction*, 104 (2): 243–7.

Ulrich, R. S. (1984) 'View Through a Window May Influence Recovery from Surgery', *Science*, 224: 420–1.

Vanstone, M. (2000) 'Cognitive-behavioural Work with Offenders in the UK: A History of Influential Endeavour', *Howard Journal*, 39 (2): 171–83.

Wells, N. M. (2000) 'At Home with Nature: Effects of "Greenness" on Children's Cognitive Functioning', *Environment and Behavior*, 32: 775–95.

Wilson, D. and Wahidin, A. (no date). *'Real Work' in Prison: Absences, Obstacles and Opportunities*. Birmingham: University of Central England. Available at: www.lhds.bcu.ac.uk/criminaljustice/docs/Real_Work_Report.pdf

Chapter 12

Putting the OM into NOMS: problems and possibilities for offender management

Mike Maguire and Peter Raynor

The background: Carter and after

Four years ago, in July 2005, we were invited to take part in a symposium organised by members of the School of Law at King's College, London, on the subject of what was then the proposed National Offender Management Service (NOMS). Our contribution focused particularly on the emerging National Offender Management Model (NOMM), and was subsequently published (Raynor and Maguire 2006), together with other contributions to the symposium. At that time the final shape of NOMS was unclear (though perhaps nobody expected it would remain unclear for so long); the relevant legislation was struggling through parliament and was withdrawn to make room for a General Election, then reintroduced afterwards with some changes. The Carter Report, published at the end of 2003 and immediately welcomed by government after only the most perfunctory consultation, proposed a system of 'end-to-end offender management' to overcome what was seen as a dysfunctional separation between prisons and probation, and a new body, NOMS, to oversee the correctional system as a whole (Carter 2003). Offenders would be subject to a single sentence management process whether in custody or under supervision in the community, and this developed in due course into the NOMM. However, alongside these integrative proposals in the Carter Report ran another set of proposals which tended more towards the fragmentation and splitting of services in order to achieve 'contestability' and to allow the market testing and possible privatisation of elements of community sentences in imitation of the private sector prisons. Most importantly, these proposals resulted in a fundamental split between 'offender management' and 'interventions', the latter being commissioned (internally or externally) as discrete services or activities that offenders can be directed to attend by their offender managers. In our paper we reviewed a variety of evidence that supported the idea of greater continuity in offender management, but questioned whether contestability and continuity could easily be pursued together. We also pointed to an important distinction, not always clearly made in the plans, between continuity of contact with people ('relational continuity'), which research tends to support, and continuity understood simply as an administrative responsibility – continuity in the case record rather than in the offender's lived experience.

Since then we have seen many changes in the design and structure of NOMS, and an implementation process which at times seemed to have been diverted into a squabble with staff unions about privatisation rather than an attempt to deliver evidence-based improvements (Raynor 2006). In the meantime what was in 2005 an early blueprint for the NOMM has been refined and developed largely through the work of Tony Grapes, and the process of rolling it out to successive groups of offenders has been described by Christine Knott, who as National Offender Manager had a lead role in implementation of the model (Knott 2008). The role of National Offender Manager no longer exists (a casualty of yet another reorganisation) and implementation of the NOMM has been slowed by resource constraints, but it is now established as the system for managing all the higher risk groups of offenders. The purpose of this chapter, four years into the implementation process, is to revisit some of our concerns from 2005, to review progress in the light of experience and research, and to consider whether or not the model shows signs of fulfilling its earlier potential.

Essential elements of the NOMM

First, it is necessary to outline briefly the key features of the NOMM in its developed version. These are set out in a helpful document on the Ministry of Justice website (NOMS 2006) which not only describes the organisational components of the model, but articulates some laudable – if ambitious – aspirations for the quality and tone of its delivery. It argues that the NOMM should be experienced positively by offenders in terms of the '4 Cs': Consistency, Commitment, Consolidation and Continuity. It also emphasises that the model is 'offender focused' and has a 'human service approach, because the main impact of the correctional services is considered to arise from the personal relationships developed with an offender'. The model itself is described as, in essence, 'A single, universal, core, end-to-end process which transcends the separate contributions of the main providers', based on a 'one offender, one manager structure' and 'a single sentence plan' (NOMS 2006: 12). This notion of 'end-to-end' offender management, the need for which was a key plank of Carter's argument for the creation of a 'joined-up' NOMS, permeates this and most other government publications about the NOMM. In brief, it means that every effort should be made to ensure that the same person oversees every aspect of the progress of an offender through the criminal justice and penal systems, from the preparation of pre-sentence reports to the end of the order or licence – hence making the 'rehabilitative process' as coherent and personalised as possible from the offender's point of view.

Core roles

The key roles in the delivery of the model are played by:

1. The *offender manager*, who acts as the 'Responsible Officer', as defined under the Criminal Justice Act 2003 (s.5.3–5.6). He or she carries out an assessment of the offender for the court, and following conviction develops a sentence plan in consultation with other key staff (including prison service staff, if a custodial sentence is passed), which takes into account both the offender's needs and any requirements of the court. The offender manager has the authority to direct the sequence of interventions in the plan and provides a consistent reference point for the offender.

2. The *offender supervisor*, who is tasked with motivating and supporting the offender to maintain constructive engagement with the sentence. This role may be carried out by the offender manager or by a separate nominated person. In custodial sentences, this is normally a member of staff in the establishment where the offender is held, to whom the offender manager delegates responsibility to undertake specific work and broker interventions designated in the sentence plan. In the case of community sentences, PSOs (probation service officers) often take on the role of offender supervisor under the direction of a more experienced offender manager.

3. The *case administrator*, who is responsible for scheduling, organising and tracking the delivery of all the elements of the sentence plan. In prisons, again, this role is undertaken by someone within the establishment.

4. *Key workers*, who are tasked with delivering the required interventions, and reporting on progress or outcomes to the offender manager. They may be probation or prison officers, or members of other statutory, private or voluntary agencies. Although they do not make decisions about what will happen to offenders during their sentence, they are formally members of the 'Offender Management Team' and should have an input into sentence planning reviews.

Tiering

A core principle of the NOMM is that 'resources follow risk'. This is reflected in the Tiering Framework (Probation Circular 65/2005), which sets out criteria by which offenders are to be allocated to one of four tiers, based primarily upon their risk of re-offending and/or risk of harm. The tier selected has important consequences, both for the appointment of offender managers (the higher risk offenders placed in tiers 3 and 4 must be managed by probation officers, while those in the lower tiers may be managed by a PSO) and for the type and intensity of interventions the offender receives. In theory, the aim in selecting interventions for tier 1 offenders should be simply to 'punish', for tier 2 it should be to 'punish and help' (for example offer them employment or accommodation services), for tier 3 to 'punish, help and change' and for tier 4 to 'punish, help, change and control'. This is not always rigidly applied, but means that, for example, accredited programmes (most of which are lengthy and expensive interventions aimed at bringing about fundamental change in thinking and attitudes) will normally be delivered only to tier 3 and 4 offenders.

Whole system approach

Finally, the NOMM postulates a 'whole system approach', by which all the component parts and functions of NOMS – leadership, policy forums, partnerships, quality assurance, research, HR and IT systems, and so on – are designed to work in unison to support the 'core business' of offender management.

Recent developments: the skills agenda and holistic offender management

Now that the NOMM is more developed and more widely implemented than when we first reviewed it in 2005, it is opportune to consider recent developments in offender management research and to see how far the NOMM appears consistent with or adaptable to more recent evidence and concerns. First, it is interesting to note a revival of research into the effectiveness of one-to-one supervision in reducing re-offending, and an accompanying revival of interest in the specification, measurement and potentially the development of supervision skills. This has been a focus of interest for some time in Canada, where the original formulation of 'effective correctional practices' by Andrews and Kiessling (1980) led in due course to a meta-analysis by Dowden and Andrews (2004) of the contribution of 'Core Correctional Practices' (CCP) to reductions in re-offending in a large number of reported studies. They looked particularly at a bundle of skills that can be summarised as effective use of authority; appropriate modelling and reinforcement; teaching problem-solving approaches; effective use of community resources; and the development of relationships characterised by openness, warmth, empathy, enthusiasm, appropriate directiveness and structure. Mean positive effect sizes of programmes were greater when these were present, and the article suggests that insufficient attention had been paid to the role of practitioner skills in the research literature on the effectiveness of rehabilitation.

Similar issues are raised by McGuire's interest in building a working alliance between offenders and supervisors (McGuire 2003), by Trotter's well-established research on the effectiveness of pro-social modelling (Trotter 1993, 2001), and by the development of motivational interviewing based on the work of Miller and Rollnick (1992) with substance misusers. The latter relies on building motivation to change by the use of skilled interviewing to explore, for example, discrepancies between people's goals or aspirations and their current behaviour. Such approaches now form a core component of motivational case management models (Porporino and Fabiano 2007). The positive and facilitative role of relationships with supervisors is also highlighted by the recent growth of interest in 'good lives' principles (Ward and Maruna 2007), which are aimed at developing a more encouraging and motivating style of supervision by focusing on offenders' strengths and positive life goals, rather than simply on their criminality and 'deficits'. Similar goals are reflected in McNeill's (2006, 2009) blueprint of a 'desistance paradigm' for offender management, which places strong emphasis on developing and supporting strengths, helping to build social capital, and 'co-designing' interventions through genuinely collaborative relationships (see also Burnett and McNeill 2005).

Empirical evidence of the effectiveness of the 'good lives' approach will take time to emerge, but empirical support for the impact of supervisors' skills is substantial, and is currently the focus of an international network of researchers (CREDOS, the Collaboration of Researchers for the Effective Development of Offender Supervision) who are carrying out further studies in several countries (McNeill *et al.* forthcoming). Such work calls strongly into question the idea that the supervision of offenders can be divided neatly into 'interventions', which change thinking and behaviour and reduce recidivism, and 'offender management', which is mainly about assessment and allocation rather than change. Such a distinction, however convenient for contestability, is no longer supported by research, if it ever was. However, it is also clear that the emerging skills agenda does not simply support those who argue against evidence-based practice, and programmes in particular, on the basis that they disregarded the traditional skills of social-work-trained staff. Traditional social work often emphasised relationship skills but neglected the structuring skills that recent research suggests are equally important. In addition, it appears likely that skills are quite variable and unevenly distributed among both trained and untrained staff, and are certainly not a monopoly of (or guaranteed to be possessed by) any particular group of staff.

One consequence of this focus on skills and practice throughout the offender management process has been to focus attention on a more *holistic* understanding of the work undertaken with individual offenders: for example, well-designed interventions work better when supported by good skills, and skills have more impact when deployed as part of a well-planned process of help and intervention. In addition, research in some countries has looked still more broadly at the organisational context of delivery: for example, the Correctional Programmes Assessment Inventory (Gendreau and Andrews 2001) moves well beyond the familiar territory of programme design to look not only at staff skills but at other areas such as risk assessment, staff training, resourcing, and the culture and management practices of organisations. This holistic assessment, which has been convincingly linked to effectiveness in reducing re-offending (Lowenkamp *et al.* 2006), offers an evidence-based approach to the effectiveness of organisations which has yet to take root in Britain, where traditional pragmatic approaches to inspection and audit remain dominant. One can only speculate how NOMS might stand up to a CPAI assessment of its organisational culture.

A broader approach: partnership, mentors and the rise of the 'third sector'

A further set of developments that may have wide-reaching implications for the future of offender management – and especially for the part played by the probation service – concern the increasing involvement of other statutory, voluntary and private agencies in initiatives aimed at reducing re-offending. Of course, other agencies have always been involved in such work to some extent, particularly through *ad hoc* referrals from probation officers or, more recently, through the commissioned delivery of major elements of court orders, such as Drug Rehabilitation Requirements (formerly Drug Treatment and Testing Orders). Again, many voluntary agencies have a long tradition in assisting short-term prisoners with resettlement, often without any direct involvement with the probation service, which has devoted relatively few resources to those serving under twelve months who are not subject to statutory supervision after release (NACRO 2000; Maguire *et al.* 2000; Clancy *et al.* 2006; Maguire 2007; Hucklesby and Hagley-Dickinson 2007). However, in recent years there has been a step change in the way that many non-criminal justice agencies view their aims and responsibilities in relation to offenders.

Partnerships and pathways

Perhaps the most important influence in this respect has been the Social Exclusion Unit's (2002) report *Reducing Re-offending by Ex-Prisoners*, which argued that the social and personal problems faced by many prisoners were central to their high risk of re-offending, but were so deep-rooted that they were unlikely to be solved by piecemeal measures or by criminal justice agencies acting alone. Rather, a concerted, 'joined-up' strategy was required, led by central government and involving commitment from all the key departments responsible for housing, education, employment, health, and so on. This would identify the resettlement of ex-prisoners as a priority activity, which would be reflected in their performance targets. This led to the creation of a Reducing Re-Offending National Action Plan (Home Office 2004) and the establishment of regional Reducing Re-Offending Partnerships and their associated Pathway groups. The latter (Accommodation; Education, Training and Employment; Mental and Physical Health; Drugs and Alcohol; Finance, Benefit and Debt; Children and Families of Offenders; and Attitudes, Thinking and Behaviour) are made up of senior representatives from relevant agencies, who jointly devise plans and seek and pool resources with a view to improving offenders' access to services to meet their needs. In doing so, they aim to contribute to the reduction of re-offending across the board, not just by offenders currently under probation supervision. 'Offender management' in this context might be provided on a voluntary basis by, for example, drug workers or 'floating support' workers employed by supported housing agencies (see, for example, Maguire and Nolan 2007).

This system is a radical departure from previous practice, in that senior managers from agencies outside the criminal justice system are engaged in jointly planning and commissioning services specifically for offenders – indeed, to some extent agreeing to prioritise offenders over other groups who may have equally pressing needs for scarce resources such as social housing or drug treatment. There is clearly still a long way to go in terms of changing attitudes, particularly in relation to perceptions of 'deserving' and 'undeserving' clients, and the partnerships tend to be handicapped by shortages of funding, but the basic principle has been established that responsibility for aiding rehabilitation is shared by a range of agencies.

The third sector and mentoring

In addition to the growth of partnership working under the Pathway structures, there has been a surge of government interest in ways of involving the 'third sector' – that is, both voluntary and private agencies – in the delivery of services to offenders. This appears to be driven partly by the search for cost-cutting strategies, but also by the broader aim of engaging local communities more fully in efforts to improve their quality of life. Strategies include the provision of funding for 'national third sector infrastructure', the rationalisation of commissioning practices, and toolkits to encourage voluntary agencies to adopt more evidence-based practices (NOMS 2008). Another important aspect is the encouragement of more mentoring schemes, particularly for young offenders, but also for adults (Newburn and Shiner 2005; St James-Roberts *et al.* 2005; NOMS 2007). The voluntary organisation Clinks has been given a grant to set up a Reducing Re-offending Volunteering and Mentoring Network to help raise standards and promote collaboration between small groups. Again, while some mentoring schemes work in partnership with probation services, many receive referrals from a variety of sources and have little or no contact with the latter.

Evidence on the effectiveness of mentoring in terms of reducing re-offending is both limited and mixed, but it can generally be described as 'promising' (Jolliffe and Farrington 2007, 2008). There is also some good evidence from a Campbell review (Tolan *et al.* 2008) that its impact on young people is strongest when emotional support forms a key element of the process. This is consistent with findings from an evaluation conducted by Maguire *et al.* (forthcoming) of the Transitional Support Scheme, an all-Wales project offering mentoring to short-term adult prisoners 'through the gate', as well as with those of the Probation Resettlement Pathfinders (Clancy *et al.* 2006); in both cases, it was the warmth of the relationship (the 'feeling that someone cares', as was said more than once) that was most valued by offenders. The latter study, indeed, found a statistically significant difference between the reconviction rates of prisoners who had substantial contact with a mentor post-release and those who did not.[1]

Finally, mention should be made of developments in the provision of services for women, which have received a strong boost as a result of the Corston Report (Home Office 2007). This called for a 'radical new approach' to dealing with the many vulnerable women found in the criminal justice system, based on treating them 'both holistically and individually – a woman-centred approach' (a phrase with echoes of the the NOMM's aspirations to be 'offender focused'). It has led to the setting up of a number of partnership-based 'one-stop shop' schemes, such as the Together Women project in West Yorkshire, the Women's Turnaround project in South Wales, and the Eden House project in Bristol (Ministry of Justice 2008a). These receive referrals from numerous sources, including prison and probation, as well as self-referrals, and generally offer rapid access to a variety of support services, as well as advocacy and mentoring. Early evaluations have been very positive.

Can the NOMM deliver?

The developments reviewed above provide illustrations of how rehabilitative work with offenders is moving beyond the narrow confines of the criminal justice system and is increasingly being undertaken through partnership arrangements involving a variety of statutory, voluntary and private agencies, as well as the provision of mentors or support workers who act as pro-social role models and develop relationships of trust with offenders. They thus offer glimpses of promising new approaches to 'offender management' from which NOMS and probation services might draw some profitable lessons – holistic and responsive approaches that recognise the multi-causal nature of recidivism and draw on a wide range of resources. Several of them also point to the importance of engagement with localities: for many offenders, rehabilitation is best understood as a relational process building social capital by developing or restoring engagement with reciprocal relationships within communities (Robinson and Raynor 2006). A similar emphasis on community links can be found in recent work by Bottoms and Wilson (2004) and in the Justice Reinvestment movement which has emerged in the USA and has been the subject of increasing interest in Britain (Clear 2004). This advocates investment in disadvantaged communities to create economic development and employment opportunities, making a non-criminal lifestyle more attainable and attractive.

How far is the NOMM geared to delivering this kind of broad and locally engaged strategy for helping people who want to stop offending? In attempting an answer to this question, we have to recognise two sets of constraints that tend to open up a gap between what the model might achieve in theory and what happens in reality. First, constraints on resources have limited the extent to which the original aspirations of the model can be translated into practice. Second, policies and strategies have not always been coherent, and pursuit of some objectives has obstructed others that may in the long run be equally or more valuable. These will be discussed in turn.

Resource issues

Resource constraints and coming budget cuts are a recurrent theme of recent discussions about NOMS and probation. An early modification of the NOMM reframed the principle of continuity so that this no longer meant continuing contact with the same person (relational continuity): the practice of using less-qualified and cheaper staff (mainly probation service officers, or PSOs) to supervise the lower-tier offenders necessarily interrupts continuity from the pre-sentence report stage of involvement with the offender, since the reports can only be produced by qualified probation officers.[2] While there is no clear evidence as yet that such discontinuity is damaging, it conflicts with the clear preference of offenders and practitioners for greater continuity. Offenders in particular do not like having to describe their problems repeatedly to new people simply because their case has been reallocated (Partridge 2004): this is pass-the-parcel supervision (Robinson 2005) and tends to undermine the traditional idea of probation as a contract underpinned by a continuing relationship with a supervisor (Raynor 1985). Offenders may be more likely to keep promises made to somebody they know, and with whom they remain in regular contact. Neglect of the relational dimension of supervision dilutes the impact of practitioners' skills (though, of course, it is also possible that offenders will benefit from a change of supervision if the change is from a less effective supervisor to a more effective one).

A more basic resource issue seems to have emerged in some probation areas: for example, the recent serious incident in London that revealed that a recently trained officer was carrying 127 cases (Scott 2009). This may have been unusual, but our recent discussions with trainee probation officers suggest that pressure on caseloads has led in some areas to a proportion of lower-tier offenders being supervised by administrative staff through a routine checking-in process. More generally, offender managers report spending far more time at the computer completing assessments and case records, or dealing with a variety of accountability procedures, than they are able to spend with offenders. (This is partly a consequence of the adoption of a particularly cumbersome and complex risk/need assessment system, OASys, rather than available simpler alternatives: see Mair et al. 2006; Raynor 2007.[3]) While it is readily acknowledged that informal conversations with officers do not constitute formal research, the sense of overload, and of a system set up to provide information to managers rather than services to offenders, is too widespread to be attributed to normal grumbling or exceptional local circumstances. This is an important issue, given that the evidence reviewed above suggests that it is unwise to reduce the priority and time given to individual contact with offenders: the process of rehabilitation cannot be left solely to 'interventions' such as accredited programmes.

Policy questions

The separation of work with offenders into 'offender management' and 'interventions' may facilitate commissioning, but it risks undermining the integration of individual supervision with other programmes and services, which is necessary, for example, to support attendance at programmes and reduce drop-out. When offenders express the very positive views about mentors that are reported above, this may reflect their greater availability and their more unconditionally helpful approach, which are both currently difficult for probation services to provide. As we have seen, there are well-evidenced concerns about fragmentation in offender management and supervision, but the continued pursuit of contestability as the government's preferred path to improvement, whatever else it achieves, is unlikely to promote greater integration and a more holistic approach. The latest announcement that 15 per cent of unpaid work projects will shortly be 'competed' shows that the market approach remains a high priority (Ministry of Justice 2009).

Other aspects of the contemporary organisation of probation services that may undermine positive aspects of the NOMM stem largely from managerialist and populist efforts to make probation more uniform and 'tougher'. Reputable research reviews (such as Andrews *et al.* 1990 and McGuire 2004) consistently show that the provision of human services for offenders that address their criminogenic needs has a much more positive effect on future offending rates than sanctions that primarily aim to punish or to achieve individual deterrence. These often emerge as having a slight negative effect: they make people worse. Of course, there may be good retributive reasons for using punishment, but those reasons do not include rehabilitation, and so lie outside the scope of this chapter. What does seem odd is to take an organisation that has spent a hundred years specialising in rehabilitation, and to try to turn it into an instrument for the delivery of punishment. It is unlikely to do this well, and there is a risk of undermining and destabilising what it traditionally did do quite well, at least by the standards of the time.

For another example of possible contradiction between policy and effectiveness, we can note that stricter enforcement of community penalties has been a consistent theme of government's 'reforms' of probation since the mid-1990s. There seems little doubt that a more consistent approach was needed: however, stricter enforcement of community penalties was used by politicians as an opportunity for a display of toughness, for example when enforcement requirements in the 2000 National Standards (Home Office 2000) were rewritten through direct political intervention. Probation areas were set targets for increasing breaches, and they did so, helping to increase both prison populations and attrition rates in accredited programmes, and leading practitioners to bend the rules in an attempt to preserve a degree of discretion about when to make allowances for offenders' difficult circumstances (Ugwudike 2008). More recently, there has been some official recognition of how counter-productive an overemphasis on enforcement can be, and the response has been to set targets for compliance, requiring probation areas to increase the proportion of orders that are successfully completed, and restoring some discretion to case managers to determine when offenders have given acceptable reasons for lapses in compliance (Ministry of Justice 2007). This overdue display of common sense has not been widely advertised by politicians.

Some other aspects of offender management under a court order are always likely to be tricky to negotiate. For example, we have argued in relation to resettlement (Maguire and Raynor 2006) that help to support desistance from offending is most effective when it is offered at the right time in relation to offenders' own fluctuating and variable commitment to desist. As noted earlier, other commentators, particularly McNeill (2006, 2009) have advocated a desistance-based paradigm of work with offenders, in which the development of individual and social capital is seen as a necessary underpinning for developing and maintaining desistance. Court orders, on the other hand, often require offenders to engage with programmes quickly and do not usually offer scope for waiting until the most opportune time. Motivational case management (Porporino and Fabiano 2007) offers one approach to trying to improve the 'fit' between the availability of opportunities for change and the offender's readiness to make use of them, but again too much rigidity or coercion can make this difficult. Traditionally probation orders required the offender's consent, and it was the role of probation officers to negotiate an informed and realistic commitment to the resulting contract between the court and the offender, but in 1997 the requirement of consent was abolished because it was (bizarrely) believed to be 'a derogation from the authority of the court' (Home Office 1995: 43), and abolition helped to undermine the contractual and negotiated element in community penalties. Interestingly, something like this approach has been revived in the 'therapeutic jurisprudence' of some drug courts where the continuing dialogue between court and offender helps to pilot a route through the obstacle-strewn course of desistance from substance misuse (McIvor *et al.* 2006), but for most offenders in most courts community sentences are imposed like punishments. Helping offenders to see and make use of opportunities for help and change in this situation will often require substantial personal contact, not simply a process of case administration through routine assessment and referral to an 'intervention' chosen in a mechanical fashion.

Our combined 50 or more years' experience in or around offender management has taught us to be very cautious indeed about predicting the future. The early promise of 'what works' and evidence-based probation may have been blurred and weakened by gesture politics and the frantic reorganisations that accompany New Labour's public sector 'reforms', but some recent figures on the outcomes of accredited programmes in England and Wales are more encouraging than earlier studies. Although presented as management information rather than a full evaluation, and couched in carefully tentative language, a reconviction study of offenders who undertook community-based programmes in 2004 showed interesting results. Although there were the familiar problems of incomplete data and substantial drop-out rates from programmes, comparisons between expected and actual reconviction rates were consistent with a significant positive programme effect: analysis of results for all offenders required to do programmes showed them reconvicting at 10.3 per cent less than the expected rate. For programme completers, this increased to 25.8 per cent. By way of comparison, the corresponding figures for all community orders and for short prison sentences were 6.7 per cent and 0.2 per cent respectively. In addition, international research reviews continue to show that offenders can be helped to change (for example, Sherman *et al.* 1998; Gaes *et al.* 1999; Allen *et al.* 2001; Aos *et al.* 2001; Lipton *et al.* 2002; McGuire 2002; Wilson *et al.* 2005; Davis *et al.* 2008), particularly when the right kinds of programmes are supported by appropriately skilled supervision and the right organisational values and culture (Lowenkamp *et al.* 2006). In the absence of these, even theoretically appropriate programme content can fail to produce results (Project Greenlight provides an example: see Wilson and Davis 2006).

Recent British initiatives show politicians still wavering between possible effectiveness and apparent toughness. Early in 2008 the Ministry of Justice (2008b) announced the allocation of money to a number of Intensive Alternative to Custody schemes intended to divert offenders from short prison sentences. In one way, this represented something of a breakthrough: the language of 'alternatives to custody' had been all but banned in official circles since the 1991 Criminal Justice Act, which made probation and community service sentences in their own right rather than 'alternatives' to anything. In addition, government ministers tended to avoid speaking too openly against the growth of prison numbers for fear of being attacked as 'soft on crime' by the tabloid media. The 2008 announcement could have marked a significant change in attitude and the beginnings of a sustained effort to reduce the prison population in favour of effective community sentences. However, there is a danger that anxiety to make the sentence look as tough as possible (the suggested titles for projects were 'Intensive Control Sentence' and 'Intensive Punishment Sentence') will have unintended effects, with non-completions leading to high levels of imprisonment for breach. For example, one scheme has been promising an unrealistic 100 hours of intervention per week. There is, in fact, no evidence that more intensive delivery in itself improves the effectiveness of correctional programmes (see, for example, McIvor 1992; Merrington 2006; Moore *et al.* 2006) and it can be counter-productive by making it very difficult for offenders to comply.

In conclusion, the rehabilitation of offenders has a long history and, in the light of some of the new approaches and encouraging research results referred to in this chapter, it has potentially a promising future (see also Raynor and Robinson 2009). However, whether the same can be said of probation is, in the last analysis, a matter of political will. Recently we have seen yet another reorganisation, with NOMS recreated as an 'agency' and very few senior management positions held by people with backgrounds in probation. A general election is coming in 2010, and this is usually an invitation to a toughness contest in which the major political parties compete to appear the most punitive. In addition, significant cuts in public spending are in prospect whichever party wins, making it likely that staffing resources will reduce at the same time as a recession-hit economy fuels increases in crime. Probation in England and Wales has had high political visibility since the mid-1990s, and particularly since 2001 when it was made a national service with its roots in a central government department, rather than a local service accountable to local magistrates. In these circumstances it may continue to be difficult to develop the best aspects of the National Offender Management Model. An overloaded and over-managed probation service, among whose front-line staff morale already appears to be quite low (Robinson and Burnett 2007), may find that it has to rely increasingly on other organisations (charities, voluntary organisations, mentoring schemes, even private companies) to provide the time-consuming and intensive levels of personal engagement and community linkage that effective offender supervision requires.

Notes

1 This finding is not conclusive, owing to possible selection effects, but is nevertheless highly encouraging.
2 Of course, there is also inevitably some break in relational continuity when an offender is sent to prison. As noted earlier, while formally the case remains in the hands of an offender manager (and in some cases the latter may visit the offender in prison), in reality most of the one-to-one work is undertaken by an 'offender supervisor', normally a prison officer, for the duration of the custodial period.
3 This problem has now been recognised by NOMS, who at the time of writing are preparing to launch a new version of OASys which is intended to take considerably less time to complete for most types of case.

References

Allen, L., MacKenzie, D. and Hickman, L. (2001) 'The Effectiveness of Cognitive Behavioural Treatment for Adult Offenders: A Methodological Quality-based Review', *International Journal of Offender Therapy and Comparative Criminology*, 45 (4): 498–514.

Andrews, D. A. and Kiessling, J. J. (1980) 'Program Structure and Effective Correctional Practices: A Summary of the CaVIC Research', in R. R. Ross and P. Gendreau (eds) *Effective Correctional Treatment*. Toronto: Butterworth.

Andrews, D. A., Zinger, I., Hoge, R. D., Bonta, J., Gendreau, P. and Cullen, F. T. (1990) 'Does Correctional Treatment Work? A Clinically Relevant and Psycho-logically Informed Meta-Analysis', *Criminology* 28: 369–404.

Aos, S., Miller, M. and Drake, E. (2006) *Evidence-based Adult Corrections Programs: What Works and What Does Not*. Olympia: Washington State Institute for Public Policy.

Bottoms, A. and Wilson, A. (2004) 'Attitudes to Crime in Two High-Crime Communities', in A. Bottoms, S. Rex and G. Robinson (eds) *Alternatives to Prison*. Cullompton: Willan Publishing.

Burnett, R. and McNeill, F. (2005) 'The Place of the Officer–Offender Relationship in Assisting Offenders to Desist from Crime', *Probation Journal*, 52 (3): 221–42.

Carter, P. (2003) *Managing Offenders, Reducing Crime: A New Approach*, Correctional Services Review. London: Home Office.

Clancy, A., Hudson, K., Maguire, M., Peake, R., Raynor, P., Vanstone, M. and Kynch, J. (2006) *Getting Out and Staying Out: Results of the Prisoner Resettlement Pathfinders*. Bristol: Policy Press.

Clear, T. (2004) 'Making Justice Reinvestment Work', *Safer Society*, 23: 15–17.

Davis, R., Rubin, J., Rabinovich, L., Kilmer, B. and Heaton, P. (2008) *A Synthesis of Literature on the Effectiveness of Community Orders*. Cambridge: RAND Europe, RAND Corporation.

Dowden, C. and Andrews, D. (2004) 'The Importance of Staff Practice in Delivering Effective Correctional Treatment: A Meta-analysis', *International Journal of Offender Therapy and Comparative Criminology*, 48: 203–14.

Gaes, G., Flanagan, T., Motiuk, L. and Stewart, L. (1999) 'Adult Correctional Treatment', in M. Tonry and J. Petersilia (eds) *Crime and Justice: A Review of Research*. Chicago: University of Chicago Press.

Gendreau, P. and Andrews, D. (2001) *The Correctional Program Assessment Inventory (CPAI) 2000*. Saint John: University of New Brunswick.

Home Office (1995) *Strengthening Punishment in the Community*, Cm 2780. London: HMSO.

Home Office (2000) *The National Standards for the Supervision of Offenders in the Community*. London: Home Office.

Home Office (2004) *Reducing Re-Offending: National Action Plan*. London: Home Office. www.homeoffice.gov.uk/docs3/5505reoffending.pdf

Home Office (2007) *The Corston Report: A Review of Women with Particular Vulnerabilities in the Criminal Justice System*. London: Home Office. www.homeoffice.gov.uk/documents/corston-report/

Hucklesby, A. and Hagley-Dickinson, L. (2007) *Prisoner Resettlement: Policy and Practice*. Cullompton: Willan Publishing.

Jolliffe, D. and Farrington, D. P. (2007) *A Rapid Evidence Assessment of the Impact of Mentoring on Re-offending: A Summary*, Home Office Online Report 11/07. London: Home Office.

Jolliffe, D. and Farrington, D. P. (2008) *The Influence of Mentoring on Re-offending*. Swedish National Council for Crime Prevention.

Knott, C. (2008) 'Implementing the National Offender Management Model in England and Wales', *VISTA*, 11 (3): 228–35.

Lipton, D., Pearson, F., Cleland, C. amd Yee, D. (2002) 'The Effectiveness of Cognitive-Behavioural Treatment Methods on Offender Recidivism', in J. McGuire (ed.) *Offender Rehabilitation and Treatment*. Chichester: John Wiley.

Lowenkamp, C., Latessa, E. and Smith, P. (2006) 'Does Correctional Program Quality Really Matter? The Impact of Adhering to the Principles of Effective Intervention', *Criminology and Public Policy*, 5 (3): 575–94.

Maguire, M. (2007) 'The Resettlement of Ex-Prisoners', in L. Gelsthorpe and R. Morgan (eds) *Handbook of Probation*. Cullompton: Willan Publishing.

Maguire, M. and Nolan, J. (2007) 'Accommodation and Related Services for Ex-prisoners', in A. Hucklesby and L. Hagley-Dickinson (eds) *Prisoner Resettlement: Policy and Practice*. Cullompton: Willan Publishing.

Maguire, M. and Raynor, P. (2006) 'How the Resettlement of Prisoners Promotes Desistance from Crime: Or Does It?', *Criminology and Criminal Justice*, 6 (1): 19–38.

Maguire, M., Holloway, K., Liddle, M., Gordon, F., Gray, P., Smith, A. and Wright, S. (forthcoming) *Evaluation of the Transitional Support Scheme*, Report to Welsh Assembly Government.

Maguire, M., Raynor, P., Vanstone, M. and Kynch, J. (2000) 'Voluntary After-Care and the Probation Service: A Case of Diminishing Responsibility', *Howard Journal of Criminal Justice*, 39: 234–48.

Mair, G., Burke, L. and Taylor, S. (2006) '"The Worst Tax Form You've Ever Seen?" Probation Officers' Views about OASys', *Probation Journal* 53 (1): 7–23.

McGuire, J. (2002) 'Integrating Findings from Research Reviews', in J. McGuire (ed.) *Offender Rehabilitation and Treatment*. Chichester: John Wiley.

McGuire, J. (2003) 'Maintaining Change: Converging Legal and Psychological Initiatives in a Therapeutic Jurisprudence Framework', *Western Criminology Review*, 4: 108–23. www.wcr.sonoma.edu

McGuire, J. (2004) *Understanding Psychology and Crime*. Maidenhead: Open University Press.

McIvor, G. (1992) 'Intensive Probation Supervision: Does More Mean Better?', *Probation Journal*, 39 (1): 2–6.

McIvor, G., Barnsdale, L., Eley, S., Malloch, M., Yates, R. and Brown, A. (2006) *The Operation and Effectiveness of the Scottish Drug Court Pilots*. Edinburgh: Scottish Executive.

McNeill, F. (2006) 'A Desistance Paradigm for Offender Management', *Criminology and Criminal Justice*, 6 (1): 39–62.

McNeill, F. (2009) *Towards Effective Practice in Offender Supervision*, Report 01/09. Glasgow: Scottish Centre for Crime and Justice Research.

McNeill, F., Raynor, P. and Trotter, C. (forthcoming) *Offender Supervision: New Directions in Theory, Research and Practice*. Cullompton: Willan Publishing.

Merrington, S. (2006) 'Is More Better? The Value and Potential of Intensive Community Supervision', *Probation Journal*, 53 (4): 347–60.

Miller, W. R. and Rollnick, S. (eds) (1992) *Motivational Interviewing: Preparing People to Change Addictive Behavior*. New York: Guilford Press.

Ministry of Justice (2007) *National Standards for the Management of Offenders: Standards and Implementation Guidance 2007*. London: Ministry of Justice.

Ministry of Justice (2008a) *Delivering the Government Response to the Corston Report*. London: Ministry of Justice. www.justice.gov.uk/publications/docs/delivering-the-government-response-to-the-corston-report-web.pdf

Ministry of Justice (2008b) *Prison Policy Update Briefing*, January 2008. London: Ministry of Justice.

Ministry of Justice (2009) *Capacity and Competition Policy for Prisons and Probation*. London: Ministry of Justice.

Moore, R., Gray, E., Roberts, C., Taylor, E. and Merrington, S. (2006) *Managing Persistent and Serious Offenders in the Community*. Cullompton: Willan Publishing.

NACRO (2000) *The Forgotten Majority: The Resettlement of Short-Term Prisoners*. London: NACRO.

Newburn, T. and Shiner, M. (2005) *Dealing with Disaffection*. Cullompton: Willan Publishing.

NOMS (2006) *The NOMS Offender Management Model*. London: Ministry of Justice. www.noms.homeoffice.gov.uk/managing-offenders/

NOMS (2007) *Towards a Volunteering Strategy to Reduce Re-Offending*. London: Ministry of Justice.

NOMS (2008) *Working With the Third Sector to Reduce Re-Offending*. London: Ministry of Justice.

Partridge, S. (2004) *Examining Case Management Models for Community Sentences*, Home Office Online Report 17/04. London: Home Office.

Porporino, F. and Fabiano, E. (2007) 'Case Managing Offenders Within a Motivational Framework', in G. McIvor and P. Raynor (eds) *Developments in Social Work with Offenders*. London: Jessica Kingsley.

Raynor, P. (1985) *Social Work, Justice and Control*. Oxford: Blackwell.

Raynor, P. (2006) 'Probation in England and Wales: Modernised or Dehumanised', *Criminal Justice Matters* 65: 26–7.

Raynor, P. (2007) 'Risk and Need Assessment in British Probation: The Contribution of LSI-R', *Psychology, Crime and Law*, 13 (2): 125–38.

Raynor, P. and Maguire, M. (2006) 'End-to-end or End in Tears? Prospects for the Effectiveness of the National Offender Management Model', in M. Hough, R. Allen and U. Padel (eds) *Reshaping Probation and Prisons*. Bristol: Policy Press.

Raynor, P. and Robinson, G. (2009) *Rehabilitation, Crime and Justice*, 2nd edn. Basingstoke: Palgrave Macmillan.

Robinson, G. (2005) 'What Works in Offender Management?', *Howard Journal*, 38 (4): 421–33.

Robinson, G. and Burnett, R. (2007) 'Experiencing Modernization: Frontline Probation Perspectives on the Transition to a National Offender Management Service', *Probation Journal*, 54 (4): 318–37.

Robinson, G. and Raynor, P. (2006) 'The Future of Rehabilitation: What Role for the Probation Service?', *Probation Journal*, 53 (4): 335–47.

St James-Roberts, I., Greenlaw, G., Simon, A. and Hurry, J. (2005) *National Evaluation of Youth Justice Board Mentoring Schemes 2001 to 2004*. London: Youth Justice Board.

Scott, D. (2009) 'Arrested Development', *Society Guardian*, 10 June: 1–2.

Sherman, L., Gottfredson, D., MacKenzie, D., Eck, J., Reuter, P. and Bushway, S. (1998) *Preventing Crime: What Works, What Doesn't, What's Promising*. Washington: National Institute of Justice.

Social Exclusion Unit (2002) *Reducing Re-offending by Ex-prisoners*. London: Office of the Deputy Prime Minister.

Tolan, P., Henry, D., Schoeny, M. and Bass, A. (2008) *Mentoring Interventions to Affect Juvenile Delinquency and Associated Problems*. The Campbell Collaboration Systematic Review.

Trotter, C. (1993) *The Supervision of Offenders – What Works? A Study Undertaken in Community Based Corrections, Victoria*. Melbourne: Social Work Department, Monash University and Victoria Department of Justice.

Trotter, C. (2001) *Focus on People: Effect Change*. Dinas Powys: Cognitive Centre Foundation.

Ugwudike, P. (2008) 'Developing an Effective Mechanism for Encouraging Compliance with Community Sentences', PhD thesis, Swansea University.

Ward, T. and Maruna, S. (2007) *Rehabilitation*. London: Routledge.

Wilson, D. B., Bouffard, L. A. and Mackenzie, D. L. (2005) 'A Quantitative Review of Structured, Group Oriented, Cognitive-behavioral Programs for Offenders', *Criminal Justice and Behavior*, 32 (2): 172–204.

Wilson, J. and Davis, R. (2006) 'Good Intentions Meet Hard Realities: An Evaluation of the Project Greenlight Re-entry Program', *Criminology and Public Policy*, 5 (2): 303–38.

Chapter 13

What else works – back to the future?

Jo Brayford, Francis Cowe and John Deering

This conclusion will not repeat the arguments already made by individual authors but rather pull out and highlight some common features and themes, acknowledging tensions and problems where they exist, before summarising some of the key elements that might inform a creative and effective practice.

The arguments presented in the preceding chapters have come from a broad range of practice, research and management experience in work with offenders and other socially excluded people. Almost all of the authors have and/or continue to work within criminal justice policy, practice and research. The arguments made are often from those who have been at the heart of theory, policy and practice over the past 30 years in the UK and in some instances globally. This work has not set out as an attempt to create grand theory or offer any false one-size-fits-all alternative to the current What Works agenda. It aims to promote deliberate and rational exploration of what else might work alongside a balanced overview of where policy and practice have been and are currently, pointing forwards to what we might be able to achieve. It also suggests that the notion of 'creative practice' is both helpful and essential to a change-focused practice and arguably any effective probation or offender manager service.

It is important to pull out and highlight some problems that now appear to face both the probation service and NOMS as well as the growing implications of these for wider society and its citizens.

As Cowe *et al.* note (2007), some of the methodological and practical problems of creating evidence-based practice are linked to a What Works top-down approach to research and practice evaluation that appear more premised on implementing a set of programmes (albeit for good intentions) without critically considering the extent to which the practice that develops out of these (both content and process) and the range of theoretical perspectives considered is based on genuine critical enquiry, is applicable to all offenders or is just policy. They argue that What Works needs to rediscover its initial questioning stance and remain open to the idea of current policy approaches not being effective. This openness requires a real commitment to evidence-based practice. The emergence of a rational, ethical and effective policy is dependent on probation practice and its underpinning values being fully informed by research (both theoretical and empirical) and the realities of practice.

These realities include engaging with the lives of offenders and other socially excluded people and the communities they inhabit as well as the wider social structures and various enabling and disabling mechanisms that mitigate for or against an offence-free lifestyle.

Citing Polgar (2005: 8), Cowe *et al.* (2007: 45) outline the key ingredients of an enquiring approach that needs to sit alongside a real engagement with individuals:

firstly, scepticism (all ideas and practices can be open to doubt and analysis); second, determinism (casual relationships, which can be uncovered, behave in a way which if known can lead to an understanding of rules and laws); and finally, empiricism (observation and verification of the world can lead to enhanced understanding of that world).

That is, practice development and practice evaluation require a context and ethos of scepticism that is not cynical in its application; an openness to a range of theories and practices; a critical reflexive approach; and collaboration between practitioners, service users and academics in exploring what works for whom in what circumstances.

The past decades of What Works practice has demonstrated that some things do work for some people in some circumstances. Policy-makers, practitioners and researchers should not as a result of critiques of the current What Works policy throw their hands up in the air as some did in response to Martinson's (1974) 'nothing works' message. Stanley (2009: 161) has recently argued that 'it is clear that accredited programmes are effective for some offenders under some circumstances', suggesting that the RDS would now be 'better employed in studying how these different interventions achieve the effects they do'. The authors' argument in this work is for a creative practice that neither pretends that all things can be applied to all people in any setting nor one that ignores the local context of crime and the local and personal nature of the harms crimes can cause and the potential impact and import of local solutions. A programmes approach is unlikely to engage with the holistic nature of such interventions but may make an important contribution to the overall intervention and relationship-building with the offender. The interaction between the content, context, meanings and direction of practice within which probation interventions take place shapes the practice, values and discourse around social inclusion and exclusion. The relational nature of practice at a personal, interpersonal and local level appear to impact on the efficacy of practice to enable change and desistance. A purely or even mostly programmes-based approach is unlikely to allow for meaningful engagement in all three of these domains.

A local context for rehabilitation has the potential to create local social capital for both offenders and the wider community. Offenders need communities and relationships to which they have responsibilities and within which they can (re)learn to add value to wider society as well as become active social agents determining their own lives. Workers need 'real' communities within which to resettle offenders and enable them to lead constructive lives.

The clear and particular arguments and findings that have emerged from the past decades of What Works (from managers, practitioners, policy-makers, researchers and offenders) should now critically inform policy, practice and research in the field of community and residential interventions. It is suggested that there are lessons to be learned from shifting evaluation and research too far away from front-line practice as this may be undermining of the creativity and open and enquiring approach that is core to both effective risk assessment and change-focused practice. It has also been suggested that proximity to and engagement with offenders' lives is core to enabling change. A top-down (programmes) approach implemented in isolation and ignorance of this is unlikely to be effective.

What policy-makers and practitioners may find disappointing, though, is that there are no simple answers from research that can be applied, like the recipe for a cake, that give the same result each time it is applied to any offender (indeed the use of the word 'offender' may be problematic in encouraging policy-makers, practitioners and researchers to assume a commonality that is inappropriate and an identity that is static). However, this work does suggest key ingredients and methods that are essential to a palatable outcome. The context of practice, the individual communities, victims and offenders are all different and the relational dynamic created by these differences shapes what is possible and what might work. Probation has worked with the notion of risk being dynamic and context-bound for some time. This work argues that change-focused practice needs to recognise and engage with the dynamic and context-bound nature of rehabilitative work, too, be this in relation to neighbourhood, age, gender, race, ethnicity, employment and educational status or individual social capital.

A community or service that sees offenders as essentially 'other' and offering no social capital or potential is unlikely to succeed at enabling a creative and constructive practice that offers non-offending identities and non-offending outcomes. Practice, it seems, is becoming removed from sites of engagement and interventions appear to insufficiently engage offenders in constructive pro-social opportunities. This work offers counter-examples to this. Early work by Ross and Fabiano (1985) that influenced and shaped the current What Works cognitive behavioural fetish in the UK was built upon work that used offenders as active agents in enabling change for other offenders. Fabiano's early work in Canadian prisons with women who self-harm and the current 'buddy' or 'mentor' systems in the UK were premised on the recognition that offenders can be powerful agents of change for both themselves and others. Indeed, creating systems where offenders have the opportunity to focus on helping others or producing something constructive for themselves appears particularly useful as a way of engaging offenders in creating new non-offending identities for themselves. The current programmes approach tends to treat offenders as passive or at best as co-learners in a classroom-type setting. They may also unnecessarily reinforce an 'offender' paradigm on what should be a change-focused interaction looking towards both desistance and pro-social and proactive citizenship; that is, they ignore the potential impact of the language and culture of 'offender' and 'offender management' and may miss the opportunity to offer offenders new and revised 'scripts' and identities (Gorman *et al.* 2006).

There appears to be very little evidence of offenders or other socially excluded people being utilised as active change agents in current policy. This work suggests that 'offenders' who are treated as active agents in their own change, and where appropriate in others', may have as important a role to play as the 'professional' or 'volunteer' in the overall efficacy of the intervention. As Roberts noted in Chapter 5, it is important that we explore the relationship between policy and research and recognise explicitly that policy does not flow logically from research findings. Indeed what gets researched, publically funded and then implemented may already be driven by policy and value perspectives that are *a priori* closed to particular forms of enquiry or intervention.

The predominance of one theoretical or methodological perspective has been shown to be both unhelpful and potentially oppressive to minority groups and to those groups in society whose socialisation, educational attainment and familial structures sit uneasily with the socially constructed view of the coherent and cohesive family unit that makes few direct pulls on the state benefit system. Workers or volunteers who are unable to appreciate, or whose work context discourages them from understanding, the social circumstances of offenders' lives, values and life chances will be less open to an important range of risk, need and change indicators that make up the whole of the person's life they are tasked with 'managing'.

Mainstream approaches to What Works not only risk ignoring the needs of minority groups but in some cases risk by design excluding such groups from high-quality services, leaving mainstream programmes and interventions for the mostly white male majority. Processes that, with good intentions, were designed to identify and promote effective practice can end up swallowing resources and squashing the opportunity for innovative and creative approaches to practice with those groups who may in fact already need this most due to their social membership and identity in wider society. As Durrance *et al*. note (Chapter 7), citing McCullough and McNeill (2007), the tools of probation have had more faith placed in them than in the skill of the practitioner. As Cowe and Cherry note (Chapter 6), this appears to be changing how some practitioners see the scope of their interactions with offenders and may now be shaping a more 'instrumental' and less change-focused practice! Relations that were initially change-focused and seeking to include offenders in wider society now risk excluding them by essentialist approaches that see offenders as risks to be managed.

Probation has historically been relatively more successful than other criminal justice agencies in engaging with and challenging issues of discrimination and oppression for both its employees and service users. The rigours of getting a programme accredited and the shift towards a more segmented approach to practice arguably removes practitioners from sites of oppression and the lived realities of offenders' lives. A What Works approach that demands critical mass in research to justify its validity will by definition exclude those studies and approaches focused on relatively small groups where 'critical mass' is offered as a dictum for blocking research proposals under the accredited programme banner. As a colleague sarcastically questioned, perhaps when we match America in its levels of imprisonment of ethnic minorities will we then be allowed to get on with such research?

Vanstone usefully reminded us in Chapter 2, but not through any rose-tinted spectacles, that historically probation officers sought to be creative and imaginative in their work with offenders and communities. However, key to this creativity and imagination was a policy and organisational context that allowed staff at the front line to be innovative in their approaches and that arguably forced them to hold the very real tensions between the courts, community and individual offender. Regrettably much early creative practice was never evaluated or written up. This book hopes to begin to add weight to a movement that encourages practitioners, theorists and policy-makers to share and open to scrutiny approaches that sit to the side of current orthodoxy. It also encourages a refocusing on the role and function of practitioners and the values that inform these. However, Cherry and Cowe note that it appears that changes in policy and organisational context now risk pulling probation staff away from being active in a tensed relationship between offenders, the courts and communities and may now be pushing practitioner roles towards being monitors or controllers operating within a wider administrative approach. An overly risk-dominated understanding of what the practitioner role is has the potential to undermine the capacity of workers to openly and deliberately be seen to be working to bring about reintegration and resettlement of those the system now casts as essentially 'other'. Cowe (2008a) and others (Annison *et al.* 2008, Deering 2008; Matthews 2009) note that some practitioners appear to have held on to their commitment to a more flexible practice despite the pressures of organisational change; however, it is questionable to what extent individuals can maintain an approach that appears at odds with the mainstream of a risk-driven policy ethos and a punitive practice context.

Were NOMS to develop into a corrections service that ignored the community and relational nature of practitioner roles, it may by design end up discouraging its staff from engaging in approaches with offenders that are likely to enable the rehabilitation and reintegration of those it supervises due to a misguided notion that a purely risk-focused service forms a useful community function. Drakeford and Gregory argue in Chapter 8 for a new 'localism' in the way that we respond to young offenders, noting that increases in the prison population should be seen as evidence of failure, not success.

Criminal justice services that are overly centralised and politically driven risk becoming part of an expensive 'correctional service' that demonstrates its public protection credentials and value by being seen to be effective at locking up ever more adults and young people at an increasing cost.

A risk-focused service that becomes removed from the local contexts of offenders lives and their social, educational and employment opportunities is unlikely to be effective at either risk management or offender reintegration.[1] Moreover, a national service without reference to local contexts and opportunities is less likely to be positioned to enable any real social democracy, social inclusion or society's wider ownership of its/our problems. As Gorman has argued elsewhere (Gorman *et al.* 2006), unless we are able to see that 'offenders are us' or at least part of our community, families and social structures, we may make both change and the context for change less likely to be achieved by design. To avoid this requires the practitioner role to be redefined and restated in relation to wider social contexts with a bridge-building role that holds the very real tensions between 'offenders', 'communities' and 'victims'.

A creative and change-focused service would actively seek to reduce a one-way dynamic that problematises individuals and pulls critical attention away from issues of structure, policy and values in society. It may, both now and in the future, be politically and publically more palatable to be seen to work as an 'offender manager' who is 'victim centred', 'public protection oriented', 'aware of courts' demands', and 'on the side of the community' rather than a practitioner trying to rehabilitate and resettle offenders in the community, balancing risks and needs while seeking to find What Works for this offender in these circumstances. This is no magic bullet and change is and always has been dependent on the nature and quality of the relationship between offender and practitioner and the offenders desire, motivation and context for change.

Offender management that is removed from local contexts and ignores the need to get offenders on board can more easily lead to an offender practice where the offender becomes 'other' or the focus of 'risk management' with no reference to their common humanity, social agency and our shared responsibility for the society we have created. We appear to be at risk of asking one thing of offenders (empathy, a social perspective and a less egocentric and more accountable approach) at the same time that we risk becoming policy, practice or research cadres, enforcing rigid rules assuming that a magic bullet or one-size fits-all approach to recidivism is what offenders should respond to.

It has arguably been politically convenient to develop a consensus against crime and criminals. McCulloch and Kelly (2007: 10) argue that changes to the legislative context for practice, such as the Crime and Disorder Act (1998) and the Management of Offenders and Sentencing Bill (2005) exemplify real shifts providing for extended sentences, increased surveillance, electronic monitoring and polygraph tests: 'These introductions mark a clear shift in emphasis from treatment towards "surveillance through contact", with any notion of therapeutic intervention being lost in the rush to produce defensive risk assessments and ever-new controls.'

However, 30 years of progressive managerialism, a fragmentation of practice skills, such as the removal of those who supervise offenders from the courts and communities, and a retreat to an office-based practice, has seen both the financial cost of 'community' interventions and the prison population increase. Researchers are not without fault either as it can be more profitable and more career-enhancing to be associated with and uncritical of the mainstream programmes, practices and policies of those in power than to be perceived as irrelevant, critical, off-message or not engaged in where things are at.

It is perhaps easier for government and policy-makers to show achievement of performance targets that seek to convince the public that the criminal justice system is 'working', particularly if the ideological bent of government is more towards efficiency and punishment than rehabilitation and social inclusion. It is arguable that attention is now more focused on second-order goals such as programme completion rates, programme throughputs, number of appointments kept and numbers of breaches for non-compliance, rather than on first-order goals such as decreases in offending, improved access to housing and employment of offenders, reductions in the use of custody and the efficacy of community interventions in enabling transition to non-offending lifestyles. It is of note that recent research on social exclusion among those who are homeless (Bonner et al. 2009) reinforces 'the need to support those in transition' and highlights the relationship between early childhood experiences, relation-ship breakdown, substance misuse, financial issues and risk of homeless-ness. Practitioners and researchers may also recognise these as 'criminogenic needs'.

This process has also arguably shifted attention and research monies away from structural issues towards less contentious but politically comfortable projects that seek to make things better or more efficient at the micro level. The 'better services reviews'[2] and restructures that have taken place within the CJS appear to have had little positive impact in relation to the size of the prison population. There may be many reasons for this, but one side-effect appears to be a lack of debate about the amount of public money that now goes to a fairly small number of private sector providers operating in a global corrections market.

Many of the 'new' second-order goals have nothing wrong with them *per se*, indeed in a joined-up system they would link to and support first-order goals. However, a cynic could argue that probation's mana-gerialism appears more interested in justifying its own existence and growth than enabling a changed-focused practice out there in the real world!

A dispassionate look at What Works suggests that a practice and research system that operates in a 'justice' context with little reference to social justice and individual needs has stifled innovative and flexible approaches to supporting individual offenders' resettlement into the community. As well as the growing financial costs of such a *justice* approach, it is arguable that it is unhealthy in a democracy for the wider population to be able to disown crime and criminals as problems for government to solve and to be generally ignorant of the relative costs of a growing custodial estate.

So what might the future hold?

A creative practice is possible that includes a return to some of the values and perspective of the past, not to recreate some mythical halcyon past but to allow a healthy perspective-taking on the present and open up to practitioners and policy-makers a vision of a range of approaches that are possible. Apart from a shift in the values away from ownership of offenders as 'one of us', one of the greatest losses of the past 20 years appears to be a diminishing expectation that individual workers should be both critical and creative. Practice and practice approaches are increasingly prescribed from the centre with little reference to or knowl-edge of local contexts.

One prerequisite of a practice that is creative and constructive is a re-evaluation of the primacy of a top-down approach to What Works and a return to a more questioning What Works?, focused on *this* offender, in *these* circumstances and with *these* victims. The relational nature of practice is key to a change-focused practice. Developing a critical understanding of an offender's identity, risks, needs and potential for law-abiding active social citizenship are a *sine qua non* of understanding what might enable change and desistance. The emergence of desistance theories demands that any assessment of needs or risks includes ideas of individuals developing social and personal capital and an open exploration of how best 'supervision' or 'interventions' might support this.

Practitioners need a practice context that is change-focused as well as risk-focused. An accountable practice is important but this is not the same as a defensive practice or a risk-driven practice. An essential building block for a creative practice appears to be a proper, professional, consistent and empathic relationship between 'supervisor' and 'supervisee'. That is, practice that loses sight of the value, power and relevance of the interpersonal dynamic is losing sight of a powerful mechanism for change and desistance.

A focus on the personal, social and environmental aspects of an individual's life is required alongside and as an enhancement to minimising their risk and risk of harm. Indeed, the more that risk reduction strategies are less dependent for their success on one worker or agency and the more an offender 'owns' their risks and can communicate these as part of a changing identity, the more likely, it is argued, that change will be achieved (Maruna 2000). Developing a collaborative approach to risk assessment can be seen as an important element of the supervisor–supervisee relationship, both in enabling change and in encouraging an openness to be explicit about personal, risks, needs and motivations. It is argued that for this to be meaningful and honest, good risk assessment needs to sit within the wider context of an empathic (but not collusive) relationship.

A strengths-based approach (Maruna and LeBel 2003) that empowers and encourages ownership of risks and a forward-facing orientation towards a non-offending identity is less likely to label and entrench individuals in an offender identity. This needs to be realistic and based on a culture of healthy challenge and respect. It needs to engage with complex issues of identity, values, beliefs and challenge anti-social behaviours.

If practitioners understood more about what offenders want and if offenders understood more about the range of alternative futures they could create for themselves, then the maintaining of an 'offender' or 'excluded' identity might become a less attractive 'choice'. A range of alternative identities that offenders and other socially excluded people can construct for themselves needs to be enabled by long-term support in engaging in training, employment, education and life skills as well as challenging pro-criminal and anti-social attitudes and behaviours. The current structures and pressures of manager–offender interactions appears to leave little time for such work. Engagement of peers or significant others as change agents is now conspicuous by its absence in the content and structure of 'supervision' or 'interventions'. Taking the risk of giving choices, alongside accepting the consequences of and responsibility for the choices one makes can be undermined by an enforcement and compliance approach that is constructed as passive.

Within a probation setting it is likely that the basis of all 'supervision' will remain an order of the court or licence period. It is important that this is used as a backbone to practice, not as its fundamental purpose or function in practice. A purely law enforcement approach risks creating what Bottoms (2001) has called 'instrumental compliance', rather than 'normative compliance' which occurs due to genuine changes in the attitudes, beliefs and outlook of the individual.

It may be that further work is also needed to 'rediscover' the role and potential value of volunteers in a range of probation/criminal justice work. The exploration of the Good Lives Model and Circles of Support by Carich *et al.* (Chapter 10) offers a theoretical framework of support, monitoring and maintenance, the authors note that: 'It is only through a relationship that defines itself within a context of humanity and care that the core member is likely to accept the relationship of being held accountable . . .' (page 202).

Volunteers located within an offenders' community and with local knowledge appear to be an under-utilised resource in current mainstream practice. It is of note that within the Circles model volunteers too are supported, accountable and maintained in what they do to enable them to act as representatives of the community and part of the Circle of Support for the offender too. Volunteers have the potential to provide social capital that enhances and enables change-focused practice to have efficacy beyond the length of any order of sentence. This potential has been recognised within the European context of probation practice; guidelines published by the United Nations state that: 'Volunteers should encourage offenders and their families to develop meaningful ties with the community and a broader sphere of contact by providing counselling and other appropriate forms of assistance according to their capacity and the offenders' needs' (Klaus 1998).

Current policy and practice now occupy a space that has the potential to see a further shift away from core rehabilitative practices and become more focused on short-term risk management. As much as 'homicidal mania' legitimised the power of psychiatry and acclimatised its discourses of protective detention within mental health spheres (Foucault 2000: 185), risk and public protection now appear to be developing new controlling techniques for 'managing' offenders, potentially pulling attention away from knowing offenders, their lives and their communities. The cultural schemes and codes (Barthes in Cuff *et al.* 1998: 224) of risk, public protection and containment appear poised to usurp the rehabilitative and welfare-oriented content of probation's earlier practice and purposes. It would be a considerable 'achievement' if NOMS, under a banner of end-to-end offender management, created a context where staff no longer saw it as their job to develop meaningful relationships with offenders and were discouraged from making links and relationships at a local level that would help them resettle offenders in the community.

This work suggests that there is the potential for a more creative and hopeful future for both offenders and communities.[3] A return to a relational-focused practice, it has been argued, is both helpful to good risk assessment and more likely to motivate offenders to communicate with staff about both their needs and their risks. Change-focused practice requires a space and context that allows worker and offender to create a revised narrative about their lives and offending. As Cowe (2008b: 590) argues:

> Creative practice should recognise offenders' real and potential risks, alongside and interrelated with possible social exclusion and needs. Divorcing one from the other undermines effective risk focussed practice as much as it undermines effective change focussed practice. As probation moves into the 21st century it may need to re-negotiate its change, advisory, helping and employment focussed credentials . . .

If we continue to focus exclusively on issues of risk and control in our intervention with offenders we may well be undermining the various bases for good risk assessment and a change-focused practice. Offenders need to be seen as core to the change process. Programmes and interventions are only possible tools that may be used to assist or facilitate a change-focused relational process, not a substitution for it. Long-term desistance requires the shift towards a non-offending identity and the behaviours and lifestyle that support this (Farrall and Maruna 2004). It appears unlikely that NOMS or any other service can achieve this in isolation from the communities offenders reside within, or without a commitment to enabling meaningful social bonds for offenders that are supportive of such change.

The shift towards seeing offenders primarily in relation to their real or projected risks appears to support a wider ethos that separates offender and practitioner and offender and wider community in essentialist ways. It may be encouraging to some to see offenders' exclusion and a rising prison population (with its accompanying human and economic costs to society) as a form of safety worth paying for. Reintegration can easily decline or disappear if offenders are 'managed' in the community on the basis of their projected status as 'moral dirt' (Hughes 1974; Ferguson 2007). That is, reintegration is less likely to be seen as a useful goal for those constructed as a potential source of contamination to an otherwise 'healthy' community. A constructive and creative practice starts from a basis that 'offenders are us' (Gorman *et al.* 2006). It defines people as having the potential for active citizenship and moves away from seeing the socially excluded as essentially problems or problematic. A creative practice is realistic about the balance between risks and needs and places communities as key to the solutions of crime and community safety. It also affords professional discretion alongside professional accountability to practitioners and managers. Some of the examples presented in this work also suggest that there may be much to be gained from engaging appropriately trained and supported volunteers in this endeavour.

By drawing attention to the risks of swinging away from desistance-based rehabilitative and reintegrative practices, this work hopes to draw the attention of policy-makers and practitioners to 'what else works' and 'what else' might be possible, opening up debate about what could be and suggesting constructive ways (rooted both in real practice experience and critical theorising) of engaging with offenders and other socially excluded people. The various chapters in this work argue that an alterative approach to a risk-driven practice is possible. A practice that retains some key elements and values inherent in a longer rehabilitative and reinteg-rative past would not exclude probation's or other agencies' potential to engage with public protection and risk reduction roles. Indeed, they may prove to be theoretically and practically of mutual benefit. The probation world is changing, and not all of these changes have been for the worse; however, there is a choice as to what role and function the probation/community corrections agencies of the future will play. These choices may say as much about the kind of society 'we' are today as about how we shape the content and context for responding to those at the margins of society in the future. If the wrong choices are made, opportunities for creative and constructive practice may be lost in the statutory domain.

The probation service has had a history of being innovative, creative and flexible in engaging with and delivering community justice. The concept of 'core correctional practices' is not new (Andrews and Kiessling 1980). However, it may be that the language as well as the content of these practices has to be unabashed in being rehabilitative and change-focused in the twenty-first century.

As Durrance et al. note in Chapter 7, the context for twenty-first century probation practice demands recognition of various intersecting identities, drawing on ethnic, religious, national and cultural reference points. Integral to innovative practice, therefore, is consideration of the impact of layers of discrimination, disadvantage and, conversely, advantages con-ferred by membership of different identity groups in our contemporary society. Practitioners, managers, researchers and policy-makers need to keep a critical eye on the personal and political lenses through which practice is created and explored.

Some of the key ingredients of creative practice include a practitioner commitment to a change focus and a dual responsibility for enabling transition for an individual offender in their context(s) and the specific or potential victims. At the heart of this focus is a real and tense engagement with the complex realities of moral and social justice. A knowledge-driven service needs to critically differentiate between 'what works' as a policy assertion and 'what works?' as a genuine commitment to reducing offender recidivism, protecting the public and enabling transition and resettlement for offenders in the real world. Practice needs to move beyond the relatively safe confines of the office, group room or hostel and reconnect offenders with communities. Such an endeavour is unlikely to be either popular or populist. However, the authors argue that not only is it possible, but such an approach is key to reducing re-offending and integrating socially excluded people into society.

As Porporino notes (Chapter 4), there is now a 'counter-movement' to the current orthodoxy of 'what works'. This work argues that such a counter-movement is not rooted in ideological cynicism but rather in the research and practice-informed experiences of practitioners, offenders, policy-makers and researchers. Creative practice is empirical by its nature and evaluation of practice needs to pay attention to the context, mechanisms and outcomes that take place in the real world (Kazi 2003). Creative practice aligns a critically informed scientific realism (Pawson and Tilley 1997) with a value base that has roots in both the traditional reform and humanistic traditions alongside an explicit recognition of the needs and risks that offenders present. It may seek to make use of a myriad settings and activities around which to construct a relational-focused practice, while engaging with improving the social and economic life chances of the individual.

The context for creative practice is therefore as equally concerned with social justice and social inclusion as it is with the accountability and reform of the individual offender. It affords responsibility and social agency to offenders and other socially excluded people, offering them real opportunities to change while holding them personally accountable for the impact they have on others. By design the relationships developed with offenders or other socially excluded people need to have a view as to what happens post-sentence, or after an order or 'intervention' has ended, and offer a tangible opportunity to lose the 'offender', 'other' or 'excluded' identity. Creative and constructive practice is concerned to challenge the 'otherness' and 'exclusion' of those who may be both in need and presenting potential risks. How this is done requires a local, relational and dynamic context that supports an inclusive, accountable (but not risk-averse or risk-driven) and reflexive practice context.

Notes

1   It is important for policy-makers and practitioners to explore the dual role that a more community and individual-focused practice can have on improving the quality of risk assessment as well as facilitating more hopeful and change-

oriented relationships between practitioners and others. Assessment and intervention that become removed from real life contexts are, it is argued, of dubious value. An over-reliance on actuarial versus clinical decision-making may also detract from practitioner skill and ability to develop a solution and change-focused dynamic.

2   Better Services Review – to understand the context of these, readers may wish to look at 17 December 1998 HM Treasury website, noting that 'A revolution in the Government's approach to public services was signalled today by the Chief Secretary, Stephen Byers, with the publication of a White Paper on Public Service Agreements (PSAs): *Public Services for the Future: Modernisation, Reform, Accountability*' (Cm 4181), HMSO.

3   There is reason to believe that practitioners continue to join and work within the service to develop meaningful relationships and assist in the process of positive change, e.g. Annison *et al.* 2008, Deering 2008 and Matthews 2009.

References

Andrews, D. A. and Kiessling, J. J. (1980) 'Program Structure and Effective Correctional Practices: A Summary of the CaVIC Research', in R. Ross and P. Gendereau (eds) *Effective Correctional Treatment*. Toronto: Butterwoth.

Annison, J., Eadie, T. and Knight, C. (2008) 'People First: Probation Officer Perspectives on Probation Work', *Probation Journal*, 55 (3): 259–72.

Bonner, A., Luscombe, R., Van Den Bree, M. and Taylor, P. (2009) *The Seeds of Exclusion 2009*, Salvation Army with the University of Kent and Cardiff University. www.salvationarmy.org.uk/seeds

Bottoms, A. (2001) 'Compliance and Community Penalties', in A. Bottoms, L. Gelsthorpe, and S. Rex (eds) *Community Penalties: Changes and Challenges*. Cullompton: Willan Publishing.

Cowe, F. (2008a) 'Greenhouses or Warehouses? An Ethnographic and Theoretical Study of the Origins, Development and Purposes of Approved Premises', PhD thesis, Cardiff University.

Cowe, F. (2008b) 'Creative Work with Offenders and the Relevance of Contemporary Probation Practice', *Justice of the Peace* 172 (36): 588–91.

Cowe, F., Deering, J. and Vanstone, M. (2007) 'From Eclecticism to Orthodoxy in Practice: Can Theory and Practice Merge in Probation', in S. Smith (ed.) *Applying Theory to Policy and Practice: Issues for Critical Reflection*. Hampshire: Ashgate.

Cuff, E. C., Sharrock, W. W. and Francis, D. W. (1998) 'Perspectives in Sociology'. London: Routledge.

Deering, J. (2008) 'Attitudes, Values, Beliefs and Practices in Probation: Continuity or Change? PhD thesis, Cardiff University.

Farrall, S. and Maruna, S. (2004) 'Desistance-focused Criminal Justice Policy Research', *Howard Journal of Criminal Justice*, 43: 358–67.

Ferguson, H. (2007) 'Abused and Looked After Children as "Moral Dirt"; Child Abuse and Institutional Care', *Historical Perspective in Journal of Social Policy*, 36 (1): 123–39, Cambridge: CUP.

Foucault, M. (2000 edn) *Power: The Essential Works of Michel Foucault 1954–1984*, Volume 3, ed. J. D. Fabion. London: Allen Lane.

Gorman, K., Gregory, M., Hayles, M. and Parton, N. (2006) *Constructive Work with Offenders*. London: Jessica Kingsley.

Hughes, E. C. (1974) 'Good People and Dirty Work', in L. Rainwater (ed.) *Social Problems and Public Policy, Deviance and Liberty*. Chicago: Aldine.

Kazi, M. (2003) 'Realist Evaluation for Practice', *British Journal of Social Work*, 33 (6): 803–08.

Klaus, J. F. (1998) *Handbook on Probation Services: Guidelines for Probation Practitioners and Managers*, Publication No. 60. Rome: United Nations Interregional Crime and Justice Research Institute and the Commonwealth Secretariat.

Martinson, R. (1974) 'What Works? Questions and Answers About Prison Reform', *The Public Interest*, 35: 22–54.

Maruna, S. (2000) *Making Good: How Ex-Convicts Reform and Rebuild their Lives*. Washington, DC: American Society of Criminology.

Maruna, S. and Lebel, T. P. (2003) 'Welcome Home? Examining the "Re-entry Court" Concept from a Strengths-based Perspective', *Western Criminology Review*, 4 (2): 91–107.

Matthews, J. (2009) 'People First: Probation Officer Perspectives on Probation Work – A Practitioner's Response', *Probation Journal*, 56 (1): 61–7.

McCulloch, T. and Kelly, L. (2007) 'Working with Sex Offenders in Context: Which Way Forward?', *Probation Journal*, 54 (1): 7–21.

McCulloch, T. and McNeill, F. (2007) 'Consumer Society, Commodification and Offender Management', *Criminology and Criminal Justice*, 7 (3): 223–47.

Pawson, R. and Tilley, N. (1997) *Realistic Evaluation*. Thousand Oaks, CA: Sage.

Ross, R. and Fabiano, E. (1985) *Time to Think: A Cognitive Model of Delinquency Prevention and Offender Rehabilitation*. Johnson City, TN: Institute of Social Sciences and Arts.

Ross, R. and Fabiano, E. (1985) *The Time to Think: A Cognitive Model of Delinquency Prevention and Offender Rehabilitaiton*. Johnson City, TN: Institute of Social Sciences and Arts.

Smith, S. (ed.) (2007) *Applying Theory to Policy and Practice: Issues for Critical Reflection*. Hampshire: Ashgate.

Stanley, S. (2009) 'What Works in 2009: Progress or Stagnation', *Probation Journal*, 56 (2): 153–74.

Index

Note: the letter 'f' after a page number refers to a figure; the letter 't' refers to a table.